Archetypal Cosmology and Depth Psychology

Archetypal Cosmology and Depth Psychology

Selected Essays

KEIRON LE GRICE

ITAS Publications

I T A S
2016

First published in 2021 by ITAS Publications, Ojai, California.

Chart images created using AstroGold software.

Cover image: detail from *Ojai Totem III* © 2018 by Kathryn Le Grice.

ISBN: 978-1-7355436-0-4

Depth Psychology – Astrology – Cosmology – Myth – Religion

CONTENTS

TABLE OF FIGURES

For Tisse

ACKNOWLEDGMENTS

The collection of essays in this book would not have come into being without the effort, enterprise, and support of many people over the last two decades. I give thanks to my former colleagues at the *Archai* journal, especially to my fellow co-editors involved in first four issues: Rod O'Neal, Bill Streett, Grant Maxwell, and Richard Tarnas. At least three of these essays, in their original form, benefitted from their editorial corrections and suggestions.

I am grateful to Frank Clifford, Steve Buser, and Armand Diaz for permission to republish articles from material previously published by Flare Books, Chiron Publications, and the journal of the National Council for Geocosmic Research, respectively. My thanks also to Safron Rossi with whom I co-edited *Jung on Astrology*. Excerpts of my contributions to that book comprise two of the chapters to follow.

For support in my early years of writing, I am indebted to my father-in-law and mother-in-law, David Davies and Margaret Davies, and to scholarships from the California Institute of Integral Studies in San Francisco and Pacifica Graduate Institute in Santa Barbara.

My recent writings in astrology and depth psychology have been shaped by my teaching over several years, both at Pacifica and the Institute of Transpersonal and Archetypal Studies (ITAS), which I co-founded in 2016 with Jay Dufrechou and Tim Read. The gatherings for ITAS workshops in New York City have been especially inspiring and enjoyable. My appreciation to Jay for helping me organize and host those events, and to the great group of participants.

Above all, I am, as always, deeply indebted to my wife, Kathryn Le Grice, for her loving support, her expert help with the editing, and for the beautiful artwork on the front cover. And, finally, thanks to my son, Lukas, whose love for and knowledge of the natural world are a constant inspiration.

KLG, December 2020

PREFACE

Since the formal establishment of the academic discipline of archetypal cosmology in 2008, I have published a number of essays in journals and multi-authored books that, as a whole, might offer a fairly thorough introduction to the field. These essays are gathered together in this book.

Archetypal cosmology is a multi-disciplinary subject, concerned with the recognition of an underlying order in the universe, manifest in its physical structure and in the expression of patterns of archetypal meaning in human experience. This order is revealed through the changing positions and interrelationships of the planets in the solar system, which are studied and interpreted through the practice of archetypal astrology.

The field of archetypal cosmology considers and develops theories and paradigms that enable us to understand, more deeply and in a new light, the relationship between inner and outer, subject and object, psyche and cosmos. To this end, it draws on a range of different areas of thought—mythological studies (especially the Greco-Roman tradition of Homeric myths), ancient Greek philosophical speculation (notably Pythagoras, Plato, and Aristotle), German idealism and the philosophy of the unconscious, comparative religion, the new sciences, evolutionary cosmology, and above all depth psychology—especially the Jungian, archetypal, and Grofian traditions. Much of my work over the last fifteen years or so has sought to articulate and advance connections between these areas in the hope of presenting a view of reality—a new world view—in which astrological correlations might be better understood. I have been concerned too with the potential role of archetypal astrology for addressing the modern individual's need for meaning and life orientation in our secular age.

In its application, archetypal cosmology introduces a methodology, based on astrology, for analyzing and interpreting the archetypal patterns of individual and collective experience. It can be employed to discern the powers at work in our individual personalities and personal biographies, and thus to help us to become more conscious of our motivations and the energies that move through us, much as the ancients imagined their world as populated and animated by gods and goddesses. It is also employed to analyze the contours, cycles, and major transitions of cultural history, including developments in the arts, events on the world stage, and even changes in religious consciousness. This endeavor can, I believe, help us to identify a complex evolutionary trajectory and self-organizing pattern, unconsciously manifesting through the variegated dramas of human experience, and perhaps then to participate more skillfully in its continued unfolding.

The theoretical and applied components of archetypal cosmology are reflected in the organization of this book. Part I, "Archetypal Cosmology and the Foundations of an Astrological World View," contains essays addressing and challenging astrology's critical reception in modern thought, offering a reappraisal of its truth claims, and considering especially its value as a psychological tool that might help us to come to terms with the unconscious—that dimension of experience that is the primary concern of depth psychology. C. G. Jung's interest in and use of astrology for this very purpose was especially significant in astrology's modern reemergence and reformulation. His views on the subject are considered in this section in excerpts taken from my editorial introductions to the 2017 publication *Jung on Astrology*.

The essays to follow in chapters 3 and 4 describe in outline the development of modern psychologically oriented astrology over the course of the twentieth century and then into the twenty-first with the emergence of archetypal cosmology. "The Birth of a New Discipline," written for the premier issue of *Archai: The Journal of Archetypal Cosmology*, announced and described the formal beginnings of the field, in the wake of the publication of Richard Tarnas's seminal *Cosmos and Psyche* in 2006. Part I also takes up debates about archetypal astrological research, addressed in my article written in 2007 for the journal of the Scientific and Medical Network in the UK in response to participatory theorist John Heron's critique of *Cosmos and Psyche*. The final chapter of the first section then plunges into the complexity of theories put forward by Jung to attempt to explain astrological correlations, with the republication of my introduction to Part IV of *Jung on Astrology*. Many of these theories are related to ideas covered in my first book, *The Archetypal Cosmos*, and show the relevance of Jung's speculations on the nature of archetypes, time, and synchronicity to a coherent astrological world view.

Part II, "Archetypal Astrology, Myth, and Transformation," turns to the application of archetypal astrology. I have included here two essays that explore the nature and qualities of specific archetypes associated with the Sun and Neptune, alongside other essays that demonstrate how an astrological understanding of archetypal principles can be used to illuminate the themes of individuation and the collective evolution of mythic and religious consciousness. The articles show how archetypal astrology might be used in relation to depth psychology, offering us an external frame of reference to map our experience and a form of mythic orientation for life.

As will become apparent, the chapters overlap to a degree in their content. Although edited slightly for context in this book, I chose to stay close to the original form of each of the essays.

PART I

Archetypal Cosmology and the Foundations of an Astrological World View

I

Astrology and the Modern Western World View

It says much about the status of astrology in the modern Western world that before one can enter into a serious consideration of the subject one must first address the question of why so many people refuse to accept that there might be any truth or value in astrology whatsoever.[1] Such is its discredited standing today that many intelligent people are unwilling to even begin to entertain the possibility that astrology might have any legitimate claims to validity. This chapter explores the origins of this extreme skepticism. By examining some of the core philosophical suppositions and scientific paradigms that form the basis of the dominant Western world view, I will consider the reasons why astrology has fallen into disrepute. It will then be possible to make the case for a reassessment of astrology in light of the new understanding of the nature of reality that has emerged over the course of the last century.

Conflicting Opinions

It is a curious, not to say perplexing, fact that although many of the greatest figures in the history of Western thought have been proponents or practitioners of astrology, in the modern era astrology has been roundly castigated and treated with disdain by the scientific and academic establishment. The definitive proclamation of the modern rebuttal of astrology was issued in 1975 in the form of a public statement signed by a group of 186 scientists, including eighteen Nobel laureates, wishing to make their position unequivocal and lay to rest once and for all any lingering suspicions that there might indeed be a correspondence between planetary positions and human experience:

We, the undersigned—astronomers, astrophysicists, and scientists in other fields—wish to caution the public against the unquestioning acceptance of the predictions and advice given privately and publicly by astrologers. Those who wish to believe in astrology should realize that there is no scientific foundation for its tenets.[2]

The statement continues:

> One would imagine, in this day of widespread enlightenment and education, that it would be unnecessary to debunk beliefs based on magic and superstition. Yet, acceptance of astrology pervades modern society. We are especially disturbed by the continued uncritical dissemination of astrological charts, forecasts, and horoscopes by the media and by otherwise reputable newspapers, magazines, and book publishers. This can only contribute to the growth of irrationalism and obscurantism. We believe that the time has come to challenge directly, and forcefully, the pretentious claims of astrological charlatans.[3]

Yet as these scientists sought to enlighten and protect the general public, they were, whether or not they intended to, just as assuredly challenging and refuting those earlier thinkers who had found much of value in the astrological perspective. The list of eminent scholars, scientists, philosophers, and writers favorably disposed to this ancient cosmological system, or who laid philosophical foundations for its subsequent development, makes impressive reading: Pythagoras, Plato, Aristotle, Hipparchus, Ptolemy, Plotinus, Proclus, Albertus Magnus, Dante, Aquinas, Ficino, Copernicus, Kepler, Brahe, Galileo, Bruno, Goethe, Emerson, Yeats, and Jung, among others.

Of course, in itself the fact that astrology has been highly valued by prominent figures in the history of ideas tells us nothing definitive of its actual validity, but it does suggest that astrology is worthy of more serious consideration than it usually receives and that we should look more closely at the reasons it is now so widely rejected. Certainly, it is hard to reconcile the fact that these two groups should come to adopt such starkly opposing positions as to the validity of astrology. Until recently the weight of the academic establishment and of consensus opinion has, of course, sided with the group of scientists in their critique and repudiation of the astrological perspective. Modern scientific knowledge is widely understood to be superior to all earlier forms of knowledge such that we have been able to recognize and discard those former errors of understanding about the nature of reality that appeared to support and explain astrological correspondences.

Thus, astrology's truth claims are deemed to be fallacious, based, it is supposed, on an archaic understanding that modern science has demonstrated to be without foundation. If this is in fact so—if the modern scientific verdict on astrology is indeed accurate—then even those illustrious luminaries cited above, for all their brilliance in other respects, and their undoubted wisdom, were, in their judgment about astrology, under a serious misapprehension.

However, more probable, it seems to me, is that the modern scientific West, in the pursuit of rational and scientific certainty, has excluded much from its field of concern, and that the very theoretical paradigm shaping and defining the scientific enterprise invalidates astrological correlations a priori. For certain phenomena—certain fundamental aspects of the nature of reality—lie outside the rather narrow focus of the scientific method and obdurately defy explanation in terms of the rational materialism of the modern era. Indeed, when we look more closely, we find that what is common to those above-named supporters of astrology is that they were all operating outside of the theoretical parameters and tacit philosophical constraints of the modern scientific paradigm. Many, such as the ancient Greek philosophers, pre-dated by centuries the coming of modernity; others, with a Romantic sensibility, excelled in fields outside of the province of science; and others still, Emerson and Jung among them, transcended the paradigmatic boundaries of their time. Even those thinkers who were instrumental in the genesis of the modern world view, such as Copernicus and Galileo, were not themselves enmeshed in this perspective as their scientific followers were to be.

One wonders if—by engaging the very faculties and modes of understanding that have been quite deliberately omitted from modern scientific investigation—these individuals were therefore able to perceive the value and truth of astrology, whereas the modern academic and scientist, constrained by narrow paradigmatic assumptions, are not. For a discerning appreciation of the astrological perspective is dependent not only on rational analysis and empirical investigation but also on imagination, feeling, introspection and intuition, on interior depth and self-knowledge, on the recognition of universals, and on being epistemologically open to other, deeper modes of analysis apart from the quantitative and statistical.

One wonders, also, if the scientists' repudiation applies not to astrology per se, but only to astrology as presented and interpreted, incorrectly, through the modern scientific world picture. For in the modern era, in keeping with the rational materialism of our time, astrological correlations have been interpreted in materialistic and mechanistic terms, construed, that is, in terms of material forces emitted by the planets that causally affect human lives through measurable physical influences—an understanding that, as we will see, appears to be wholly inadequate to the depth and complexity of the astrological perspective. For although astrological "influences" have been posited since ancient times and are part of the traditional astrological imagination, these were usually conceived as subtle forces or energies rather than as measurable physical forces.

In the postmodern era, as scientists and philosophers become increasingly aware of the formerly implicit theoretical assumptions behind modern science and ever more acutely conscious of the limitations these assumptions impose on our understanding, we now have the opportunity to reconsider the validity of astrology. Postmodern reflections on science, and the emergence of the new paradigm approaches within science, afford us another perspective from which to re-evaluate astrological correlations. Placed in a new theoretical context, we might perhaps see that it is not astrology that is in error but our perception of it, blinkered by our models and paradigms through which we, in the modern West, have come to interpret the nature of the universe.

Science and the Mechanistic World View

To understand the prevailing perception of astrology, and astrology's disparity with the dominant collective world view, we must consider the scientific and philosophical developments that have shaped the modern understanding of the nature of reality. For in the modern West, as is well known, the Scientific Revolution that saw the birth of classical physics and instigated the rapid rise of science and the modern rational world picture created an intellectual climate in which astrology struggled to survive. Astrology's plight was also significantly influenced by the direction of modern philosophical thought, which first established the basis for and then reinforced the dominant scientific world view.[4]

Prior to the Scientific Revolution in the sixteenth century, the accepted cosmological model of the universe was geocentric. The Earth was considered to be stationary at the center of the universe and all the planets, together with the Sun and Moon, were thought to orbit the Earth in circles. This model was known as the Ptolemaic cosmology after Claudius Ptolemy, an astrologer-astronomer from Alexandria, Egypt, in the second century CE, whose theory drew extensively on the ideas of Aristotelian science. Ptolemy's geocentric explanation of planetary motion was accepted by the church. Indeed, Christians later came to believe, as a matter of dogmatic faith, that God had placed the Earth at the center of the universe, and that the human being was master of the world, made in the image of God. The Ptolemaic cosmology supports the geocentric perspective assumed by astrology: the astrological chart is calculated to accurately reflect the position of the planetary bodies of the solar system as seen by an observer on Earth. From the vantage point of the individual looking out into the cosmos, all the planets seem to revolve around the Earth, so as long as the geocentric model of the universe was retained in astronomy the astrological perspective appeared to have objective validity.

However, in order to explain observed irregularities in the brightness, direction of movement, and velocity of the planets in their orbits, the later medieval and Arabic revisions of Ptolemy's geocentric cosmology became inordinately complex. The complexity of geocentric theory could be overcome but only by abandoning the seemingly incontrovertible belief that the Earth was the center of the universe and adopting instead the heretical notion that all the planets, including the Earth, orbit the Sun. Copernicus realized this and in 1543 took the bold step of publishing a heliocentric theory that he had originally developed over thirty years earlier. Kepler's work (supported by Galileo's observation of the heavens using a telescope) confirmed the heliocentric hypothesis, and, despite staunch resistance from the church and the academic establishment, the Copernican revolution was born.

For astrology, this development marked a decisive point of divergence from astronomy because the astronomical cosmology and the astrological one were now seemingly different and conflicting. The geocentric perspective now had no basis in science and was objectively untrue. Thereafter, astrology had to struggle for survival in an incongruent intellectual climate on account of its conflict with the science of the time. While there were no immediate consequences, the wider impact of the Copernican revolution, in particular the impetus it gave to the rise of the scientific world view, was eventually to further alienate astrology from serious intellectual thought.

For the Christianized world the implications of the displacement of the Earth from the center of the universe were momentous. The new heliocentric cosmology directly challenged the authority of the church and biblical scripture, ushering in a period in which any established authority became subject to critical examination in the light of the emerging power of human reason. In this intellectual climate, rationality was to take center stage. Reason and logic were weapons against the false claims of any supposed authority and it was believed that reason could by itself provide accurate knowledge of the world. Educated people began to rely more on rationality and less on faith, more on science and less on the unquestioned authority of church doctrine.

The central figure of the emerging rational philosophy was the seventeenth-century French philosopher and mathematician Rene Descartes whose *Discourse on Method* and *Meditations on First Philosophy* laid the foundations for Western philosophy and science for the next three centuries. Assuming a starting position of absolute doubt about the reality of his existence, and seeking a firm foundation upon which to build his philosophy and overcome this doubt, Descartes came to the conclusion that "so long as I continue to think I am something."[5] This insight gave rise to his *cogito ergo sum*: I think, therefore I am.

Descartes situated human identity in the thinking rational mind or soul set against the body and the external world. "I knew I was a substance whose whole essence or nature is solely to think, and which does not require any place, or depend on any material thing, in order to exist."[6] Reasoning thus, Descartes drew a fundamental distinction between consciousness or thinking and the external, physical world. The thinking spiritual-mental substance (*res cogitans*) is, Descartes claims, a completely different kind of substance from the corporeal world of matter (*res extensa*). According to this view, the material world, initially set in motion by God, is machine-like in its operation and can be objectively described and quantified in terms of mathematical laws. The human being consists of a physical body that is influenced by an incorporeal mind, which is causally interactive with matter. Descartes thus advocates a form of interactive substance dualism.[7]

With this distinction Descartes helped to establish as credible the belief that the material world could be explained without reference to mind because it is possible, he argues, to remove mind and with it human subjectivity from explanations of the functioning of world. Cartesian dualism thus gave further impetus to the belief in the objectivity of scientific explanation. In distinguishing between the subject of experience (the thinking ego) and the object (the material world "outside" of mind), Descartes helped shape the future of the Western world by establishing the philosophical ground for the subsequent development of modern science.

No less significant for the rise of the modern scientific world view were several earlier philosophical developments that had set the Western intellectual tradition on a course towards empiricism, concrete realism, skepticism, and nominalism. With respect to these developments, William of Ockham, writing in the fourteenth century, argued that in the pursuit of knowledge the focus of attention should be restricted to concrete individual entities; he rejected the ontological reality of universal principles, arguing that universals exist only as concepts in the mind; and he also postulated that knowledge can only be attained through sense perception, not by reason alone.[8]

Equally important was the contribution of Galileo. In addition to his crucial telescopic discoveries, Galileo proposed that science should focus exclusively on the supposedly objective, measurable qualities of phenomena such as mass, number, and size, ignoring the supposedly subjective attributes such as color or smell. Here, almost two centuries before Kant's critical turn in philosophy, was a fundamental distinction that in time effectively stripped sensible, humanly perceived qualities from the external world. With this "bifurcation of nature," as Alfred North Whitehead describes it, the world of so-called *secondary qualities*, dependent on fallible human perception and interpretation, and the quantifiable reality of the external world of *primary qualities*, which were seen as independent of human perception, were thrust apart.[9] Along with the Cartesian *cogito*, this was a decisive development that served in time to banish qualitative considerations from the realm of science. That Galileo was himself a practicing astrologer indicates, however, that a mechanistic understanding of the motions of the planets in astronomy need not preclude the belief in an astrological meaning to the planetary positions, motions, and relationships.

Today, of course, it is the focus on the quantitative measurement of celestial mechanics, established by the separation of primary and secondary qualities, that utterly dominates our understanding of the planetary bodies and their motions. Astrology's emphasis on the possible qualitative, psychological, meaningful significance of the planetary dynamics of the solar system is generally greeted with contemptuous disregard by many scientists—a logical consequence of the view of reality sustained by the dominant scientific paradigms of our time. Nothing, it is supposed, could be more removed from scientific investigation, nothing so blatantly false.

Meanwhile, as a result of Copernicus's heliocentric cosmology, science faced a new urgent challenge: it needed to explain why falling bodies drop to Earth rather than to some other place. Until then, it had been thought that this occurs because the Earth, owing to its supposedly fixed position at the center of the universe, is the natural place to which objects must fall. Obviously, the advent of the heliocentric cosmology had rendered this view obsolete, and the stage was set for a new theory, and the entrance into the scientific arena of Isaac Newton.

Drawing together Kepler's mathematical laws of planetary motion, Galileo's ideas concerning terrestrial mechanical motion governed by forces, and Descartes's atomistic-mechanistic philosophy, Newton formulated a robust mathematical framework for modern science. Newton's theories, published in his *Philosophiae Naturalis Principia Mathematica* in 1687, were to form the basis of classical physics until the twentieth century. His response to the challenge of the Copernican revolution was to formulate the theory of gravity, which, together with the three laws of motion, allowed him to comprehensively explain the workings of the physical universe. According to Newton's model, the universe consists of solid, indestructible, material particles existing in empty space. These particles were considered to be the basic building blocks of matter: all physical objects were collections of these fundamental particles. Time was believed to exist independently of the physical universe, flowing inexorably on, creating our experience of past, present, and future. Both space and time were unconditionally accepted as a priori conditions of the material world. After Newton, all events came to be understood as the effects of forces acting upon material bodies.

Newton's model is often referred to as *mechanistic* because, following Descartes, the universe is conceptualized as a giant cosmic machine in which all events are triggered as part of a causal chain. Like a machine, the movement of one part causes another part to move, which in turn affects a further part, and so on. This theory of the mechanics of the universe is known as *determinism*, in which every effect is the necessary result of an antecedent cause—i.e., the cause *determines* the effect. (The apple falls from the tree to the ground because of gravity, the billiard ball moves because it is struck by another ball—to give two widely cited examples.) After Newton, the mechanistic paradigm was successfully applied to all areas of science on both a macroscopic and microscopic level and the laws of classical physics were proclaimed as fundamental laws of the universe. Newtonian science thus brought with it a sense of triumphant mastery as a new world view was born in which scientists at the time sincerely believed they had the power to explain anything using these fundamental laws. The theoretical mastery of the Scientific Revolution then gave rise to the practical achievements of the Industrial Revolution, as the new knowledge and power furnished by science was exercised to the full.

Although it was not Descartes's intention, since his vision of reality retained a deistic spiritual basis, it is testimony to the efficacy of Cartesian philosophy to articulate a common human experience of the relationship between mind or soul and the material world that in the late modern era many intelligent people envisage themselves as thinking beings existing in a mechanistic, unconscious, and essentially meaningless physical universe. Newtonian physics, finding philosophical and psychological articulation in the work of John Locke, cemented the Cartesian dichotomy between inner and outer, and subject and object, as it appeared to demonstrate mathematically that all events within the material universe could be explained solely through cause-and-effect mechanics and that there was no need to take human subjective consciousness into account. The human self thereafter appeared radically separate from the functioning of the material world, distinct in essence from the human body, yet mysteriously interacting with it, Descartes believed, through the pineal gland in the brain. The human self existed in an impersonal, mechanistic world that functioned without any kind of involvement from God, without any inherent purpose or meaning. The Cartesian-Newtonian paradigm, as it is now often called, effected a further separation of the human subject from the world and from nature, a further split between the *interior* psyche and the *exterior* cosmos.[10] The subjective meaning of human experience—human aims, purposes, values, feelings, desires, and so forth—now appeared radically distinct from the objective world. As the modern world view gained ascendancy, any sense of human participation in a meaningful, ensouled universe was eliminated. The astrological supposition of a relationship between planetary cycles and human experience now seemed increasingly untenable. In the material and mechanistic terms through which astrology was understood, it seemed in fact that there was nothing more remote and unrelated to human experience than the motions of the distant planetary bodies in outer space. Unsurprisingly, then, after the Scientific Revolution, in a climate in which materialism and mechanistic determinism reigned supreme, there was no place for the explanations of astrology based on the old geocentric Aristotelian and Ptolemaic cosmology or the medieval system of correspondences.

Freedom and Determinism

The success of Newtonian mechanics in physics saw the extension of deterministic, mechanistic, and materialistic explanations across all disciplines. This extension was accompanied by a gradual decline in alternative forms of explanation, particularly those based on transcendent universal principles, such as the Platonic Ideas. As we have seen, these universals, once thought to be the organizing principles behind the material world, were understood, in nominalist terms, to be merely mental and linguistic categories—to exist in name only, to pertain only to categories of the human mind and not to the external world. With the ascendancy of the modern world view, all phenomena were understood to be explicable solely in terms of natural causes. Those theoretical models and philosophies based on metaphysical factors were deemed unnecessary.

Nowhere is this theoretical orientation more conspicuous than in the modern conception of human nature. Reflecting the application of mechanistic determinism to all areas of investigation, influential theories in both psychology and biology have made it possible to describe and explain human nature such that astrological explanations now seem superfluous, antiquated, and incorrect. Scientific explanations, both of the universe and of human existence, seem to have rendered astrology obsolete. In the modern scientific view, it is unnecessary to postulate the existence of extraneous astrological factors, or metaphysical principles or archetypes, when human life can apparently be explained well enough, we have come to believe, in terms of natural causes, whether of our own biological nature or the effects of external influences.

Behaviorism and psychoanalysis, which are the two traditional schools or "forces" in psychology, and genetic biology that has in recent years deciphered the code of DNA, each put forward deterministic explanations of human life, explanations that have shaped and informed the popular understanding of the origins of personality and the composition of the self. From the psychoanalytic perspective, as is well known, childhood trauma and unconscious drives, repressed desires and sublimated sexual impulses, and the raging battle between instinctual gratification and one's internalized moral code, are the determining factors behind human existence. In the Freudian view, the human personality is unconsciously conditioned by instinctual drives grounded in human physiology; and the emotional complexes of adult life, as more than a century of psychotherapy has shown, often originate from traumatic experiences of early life.[11]

Whereas Freudian psychology brought to light the instinctual and unconscious psychological determinants of human life, behaviorism, first developed by experimental psychologist John Watson in 1913 and later expanded by B. F. Skinner, bypassed the human psyche altogether, focusing instead on the conditioning effects on human behavior of external causes in the environment. Behaviorists see human nature as a product of the environment and all behavior as the result of conditioned responses to external stimuli.[12] Such a conception makes possible a methodological rigor and precision that has delivered important insights into both human and animal learning and motivation. However, many have rightly objected to this narrow characterization of human nature in which, by adopting what has come to be known as the black box approach, consciousness is treated as a largely unnecessary postulate. Human psychology is thus reduced to the analysis of observable, external stimuli and resulting changes in patterns of behavior such that the complexity of human will, of feelings, moods, reflection, and inspiration is almost completely disregarded. With the emergence of behaviorism, then, people were effectively seen as indivisible isolated units lacking interiority; the Newtonian atomistic model of the nature of reality had here fully established itself in the field of psychology. Controversially applying his theory to entire cultures, Skinner thought that human salvation and the cure to the world's problems lies in the mass conditioning of human behavior through the controlled manipulation of environmental stimuli.[13] Human nature, he argues, can and should be totally molded by external conditioning factors to achieve a better society.

Despite their inherent shortcomings, given the explanatory power of both psychoanalysis and behaviorism there is little wonder that they have been extremely influential on the modern mind and its attempts at self-understanding. More generally, deterministic explanations of human life, emphasizing either *nature* (prior determining causes in human biology) or *nurture* (the effects of the environment, particularly during early childhood, on shaping the human personality) have emerged across many disciplines both from within psychology and farther afield. Neuroscience, for example, has focused on the neurochemical processes of the brain in order to explain human consciousness and behavior; Marxist philosophy highlights the influence of social and economic factors on the human condition; and genetics finds causes in the DNA coding within chromosomes.[14] Thus, we arrive at the modern materialistic and deterministic view of the human being as a genetically programmed, biologically driven, and environmentally conditioned physical organism. In such a view, in which the basic makeup of the human personality seems comprehensible in terms of concrete, identifiable causes, the astrological perspective, in which human nature is understood in terms of universal principles associated with the planets, seems both superfluous and incorrect. Because there is no mechanistic causal explanation of a correlation between planets and human experience, people find it difficult to understand how astrological correlations might work, and therefore generally reject astrology as untrue.

The belief in the freedom of the willing self (an idea that goes back to the ancient Greeks and Christianity, but which was propounded by existentialist philosophers in the first half of the twentieth century and is still broadly reflected in the mainstream collective world view today) is another highly influential factor that has contributed to the general suspicion and incredulity with which astrology is viewed. To many people the notion that the planets and zodiacal signs have some kind of power of influence over our lives seems like an affront to our prized sense of free will and self-determination. The popular misconception of astrology that one's fate is unalterably "written in the stars," and that one's free will is impotent compared to the power of one's ineluctable destiny, seems to deprive human beings of the power of self-determination and, in so doing, to mark a return to an oppressive fatalism, to a universe of inescapable predestination. Astrology appears to contradict the idea that we are free to forge our lives and shape our identities through acts of conscious will, to choose and fashion the life we please, and it is therefore perceived as a threat to the sovereign power of the human self. For some people, understandably, this in itself is reason enough to reject astrology out of hand.

The dominant modern world view is thus subject to the influence of two pervasive yet inherently contradictory perspectives: mechanistic determinism, which implies that everything is determined by a mechanistic chain of prior causes, and the belief in the freedom of human will. This is not without problematic consequences, as Whitehead points out:

> A scientific realism, based on mechanism, is conjoined with an unwavering belief in the world of men and of the higher animals as being composed of self-determining organisms. This radical inconsistency at the basis of modern thought accounts for much that is half-hearted and wavering in our civilisation.[15]

Astrology, as it is commonly construed, finds itself caught between both these positions: Because both the human personality and the events of our lives can be described and understood in terms of prior determining factors, and since it is apparent that the future is determined by our own wits and will power pitted against chance and the environment, there seems to be no place for astrological explanations of human life based on the supposed influences of the remote planets. If we shape our own futures, how can astrological factors also be responsible for determining the events and experiences of our lives? If we can explain the nature of our personality and the origin of our life events in terms of prior causes, biological or circumstantial, how can the planetary positions and cycles determine human character or influence our biographical experiences? These questions and concerns, and others like them, have persuaded many that there is little value or truth in astrology.

Debunking Astrology

From this brief exploration of the philosophical and scientific background of the modern Western world, we can see that many of the dominant, though sometimes tacit, assumptions within our world view have contributed to the widespread skepticism towards astrology. In light of the many factors that appear to contradict the basic postulates of astrology, it is hardly surprising that to the modern mind entrenched, whether consciously or unconsciously, in these assumptions, the possibility of there being astrological correlations between the planets and human experience seems fanciful and astrology's truth claims appear to be totally without foundation.

In the modern world the dominant understanding of the nature of reality remains rooted in the mechanistic materialist paradigm that has been so influential within science. Coupled with the idea that astrology conflicts with our cherished belief in human freedom, it is, above all, because our world view is derived from an understanding of the universe originating in classical physics that, as a society, we dismiss astrology. Many critiques of astrology rest on an unchallenged acceptance of the Cartesian-Newtonian causal deterministic framework.

These critiques might be classified into two main categories. The first category is concerned with the explanation of astrological "influences" and the absence of a plausible account of how the planets can causally affect human lives on Earth. It includes, as well, the related question of how such planetary influences are translated into human life. Proponents of astrology are challenged to explain the purported relationship between the planets and human lives in terms of the known forces and mechanics of classical physics. This category thus relates to the general issue of causal influence.

The second category relates to empirical scientific evidence: Can

14

astrology be validated by demonstrating scientifically that there are actual correlations between astrological factors and the conditions of human life? In addition to the question of statistical evidence for astrology, however, this category can be extended to include the wider issue of the relationship of astrology to science in general, and the question of whether astrology and science might be able to coexist without outright contradiction.

Other questions relating to the specifics of astrological theory and the historical origins and development of astrology also merit consideration. Why are the planets associated with certain qualities, archetypal meanings, and themes and not others? How were the planets' archetypal associations initially discovered? How were qualitative attributions made to the planets? Such questions are obviously central to any comprehensive treatment of astrology. Within the constraints of this essay, however, we will be primarily concerned with the two categories of critique: we will consider the direct challenge, both explanatory and empirical, posed to astrology by science.

Beyond the Causal Hypothesis

Perhaps the single most important factor in astrology's repudiation and its subsequent exclusion from the consensus Western world view has been the absence of a satisfactory causal explanation of planetary influence. Astrology is deemed untenable because it cannot be explained scientifically, in linear deterministic terms, in that there is no convincing explanation in terms of any known force of how a distant planetary body can influence human existence on Earth. Discussing possible causal explanations of astrological correspondence, astrophysicist Victor Mansfield, who was himself supportive of astrology's truth-claims, states that of the four known forces in nature that might be used to offer explanations of planetary influence, the strong and weak nuclear forces can be discounted as they do not act over long distances. Of the other two forces, he continues, electromagnetism can be ruled out because "movements of free charges easily shield electric forces, and magnetic forces decrease with distance even more rapidly than gravity." This leaves only gravity itself, which, Mansfield explains, has also been rejected as an explanation of planetary influence by scientists because "the gravitational forces of the doctor and nurse [at birth] are much greater than anything from the planets."[16]

On first inspection, then, the argument against astrology looks watertight. But notice that the repudiation of astrology hinges on the universal applicability of the Cartesian-Newtonian paradigm, the cause-

and-effect model of existence. If this conception of the world is shown to be limited, incomplete, or perhaps even in error, then astrology should not be refuted on the grounds that it cannot be explained in terms of this model. In this scenario, it becomes conceivable that the workings of astrology, although inexplicable in terms of classical physics, can be understood through a different scientific paradigm. If so, the rejection of astrology might be premature.

Despite significant challenges from idealist philosophers, Romantics, and others, throughout the eighteenth and nineteenth centuries the mechanistic paradigm of classical physics became increasingly dominant and widely accepted. The efficacy of scientific determinism was powerfully demonstrated by the rampant success of industrialization, and there was no reason to suspect that the fundamental laws of nature on which this paradigm was based would later be called into question.

In the early twentieth century, however, following the formulation of Maxwell's electromagnetic field theory in the late nineteenth century, the advent of modern physics cast serious doubts over the most basic assumptions on which classical physics is founded and caused an acute sense of crisis among physicists at that time. As Fritjof Capra reports:

> The exploration of the atomic and sub-atomic world brought them in contact with a strange and unexpected reality. In their struggle to grasp this new reality, scientists became painfully aware that their basic concepts, their language, and their whole way of thinking were inadequate to describe atomic phenomena.[17]

At the heart of modern physics two new theories—the theory of relativity and quantum theory—have destroyed the absolute truth claims of many of the fundamentals of classical physics.

Einstein's theory of relativity has dramatically transformed our understanding of space and time. Previously, space and time were thought to have absolute, independent existence. Space was construed as a three-dimensional stage of life, as the unchanging background in which physical events occur and in which objects are situated. Time, likewise, was believed to exist separately from space, independently of the material universe; it was thought that there could be a universally applicable measurement of time. According to Einstein's special theory of relativity, however, this commonsense view of space and time is actually inaccurate. Space and time are not absolute but relative; they are not independent of each other, but are inextricably linked and together they form a four-dimensional space-time continuum. The measurement both of space and time, Einstein maintains, is relative to the observer; we cannot know of an objective reality outside of our viewpoint and thus there can be no universal, objective view of the world and no universal measurement of time. The idea of "simple location," to use Alfred North Whitehead's term, the notion that objects actually exist independently in their own definite regions of space and time, had to be abandoned. The universe was now conceived instead as something akin to a mysterious dynamic process.[18]

Inevitably, because it undermined the scientific basis of the Newtonian world picture and called into question the very idea of an objective reality, relativity theory led to a radical reformulation of the entire framework of physics and it also gave rise to Einstein's epochal insight of the equivalency of mass and energy, which he expressed in the famous $E=mc^2$ equation. Out of this insight came an entirely new understanding of the nature of the material world. In this new vision of the world, as Fritjof Capra explains,

> All particles can be transmuted into other particles; they can be created from energy and vanish into energy. In this world, classical concepts like "elementary particles," "material substance" or "isolated object," have lost their meaning.[19]

Because of Einstein's insight into mass-energy equivalence, the notion that the universe is comprised of a fundamental substance, that it is made up of irreducible material particles in the form of atoms, had to be abandoned. This view is reinforced by quantum theory. Exploration of the subatomic world in quantum physics has thus far suggested that the basic constituents of matter are not solid atoms, moving around in a mechanical billiard ball type motion, but quarks, leptons, and gauge bosons (according to the standard model of quantum physics)—minute packets of energy that are complexly interconnected. The phenomenon known as quantum entanglement has suggested that the elementary particles at the quantum level appear to possess a degree of interconnectedness that goes far beyond the classical understanding of connections in space and time. Accordingly, the universe might now be conceived, Fritjof Capra suggests, as an unbroken web of relations composed of patterns of interconnections. It is therefore meaningless, we are told, to consider a subatomic particle in isolation for it can only be understood in terms of its interaction with other systems. In Capra's view:

Quantum theory has demolished the classical concepts of solid objects and of strictly deterministic laws of nature. At the sub-atomic level, the solid material objects of classical physics dissolve into wave-like patterns of probabilities, and these patterns, ultimately, do not represent probabilities of things, but rather probabilities of interconnections.[20]

The implications of modern physics for understanding the nature of reality are obviously profound. According to Capra, we are now faced with a world of "inseparable energy patterns" rather than a world of solid material objects.[21] The idea of a simple causal chain of events linking one separate material body to another has been replaced by the idea that existence is an undivided, interrelated whole. "Quantum theory forces us to see the universe," Capra asserts, "not as a collection of physical objects, but rather as a complicated web of relations between the various parts of a unified whole."[22]

The Newtonian universe comprised of solid indestructible atoms has thus been succeeded by the incomparably more complex picture disclosed by quantum physics and relativity theory. Although modern physics is far from arriving at any settled conception or unified theory of the nature of reality, these new theories have radically deconstructed the old Newtonian world view. Interpreting the significance of these developments, Allan Combs and Mark Holland have gone as far as to suggest that modern physics is in the process of giving birth to "a new mythos, a new topology of reality."[23] "In quantum theory," they continue, "we recover the view of the world as an unbroken fabric in which seemingly separate events do not occur in isolation but, in fact, form pieces interwoven into a single tapestry."[24]

Reformulating Astrological Relationships

With this context in mind, we can now return to the question of planetary influence. Astrologers, it is supposed, are unable to explain how a planet in the solar system can causally affect human life on Earth. In visualizing this problem, we naturally think of two material bodies (the planet and the human being) existing separately in empty space, a vast distance apart. The causal influence we might imagine in its crudest terms as some kind of force passing in a causal chain between the two unconnected physical objects, from the planet to the person. According to the view of reality that emerges from modern physics, however, we must abandon this way of conceptualizing the problem for several reasons.

First, a planet is not an independently existing material object. What appears to us as solid indestructible mass is capable of being converted into energy. Mass and energy are interconvertible. A physical mass, like that of a planet, is better understood as a concentration of energy existing within the total field of energy of the entire universe. As David Bohm, discussing the nature of atomic particles and their relationship to the surrounding energy field, explains:

> The field is continuous and indivisible. Particles are then to be regarded as certain kinds of abstraction from the total field, corresponding to regions of very intense field (called singularities). As the distance from the singularity increases, the field gets weaker, until it merges imperceptibly with the fields of other singularities. But nowhere is there a break or division. Thus, the classical idea of the separability of the world into distinct but interacting parts is no longer valid or relevant. Rather, we have to regard the universe as an undivided and unbroken whole. Division into particles, or into particles and fields, is only a crude abstraction and approximation. Thus we come to an order that is radically different from that of Galileo and Newton—the order of undivided wholeness.[25]

Second, in this "order of undivided wholeness" material bodies are not isolated from the space around them. Planets and people are not absolutely separate; they both belong to the one undivided energy field of the universe. Physical objects do not exist in empty space or in a void; they exist, as Bohm puts it, in "an immense ocean of cosmic energy."[26] What we think of as empty space is actually, he proposed, a continuous, unbroken field of energy.

Third, according to modern field theory, we cannot draw an absolute distinction between the classical concepts of force and matter. Forces between particles of matter are, says Capra, linked to "the properties of other constituents of matter."[27] This means there is no clear demarcation between the particles that make up material objects and the force between interacting particles, because the force is described as, confusingly, itself an interchange of particles. "Both force and matter," Capra notes, "are now seen to have their common origin in the dynamic patterns which we call particles."[28]

To properly understand astrology, then, I believe we must abandon the popular notion that planets causally influence human experience through physical forces and instead base our understanding of astrological correlations on the holistic interconnected picture of the universe disclosed by quantum physics. As I have argued in *The Archetypal Cosmos*, in which I develop an explanation of astrology in terms of quantum nonlocality, holism, and systems theory, the astrological relationship between planet and person should not be imagined as a force passing between two separately existing entities; rather, it might be better conceived as the result of their mutual participation in the patterned energy field and self-organizing dynamics of the cosmos.

As part of a unified whole and a vast "dynamic web of inseparable energy patterns" the scientific observer and the phenomena being observed are themselves inextricably related.[29] The view of the universe that has now emerged, first out of relativity theory, and later in cosmology, is, first, that all measurements of space and time are relative to the observer, and, second, that human beings are centered in their own perspectives with regard to the cosmos. In astrology, the inescapable subjectivity of human experience is acknowledged by the assumption of a geocentric, person-centered viewpoint—an Earth-based perspective centered on individual human beings. Astrological charts are symbolic maps of human experience based on the actual physical vantage points of individual people, or the location of events. However, the validity of astrology does not depend on the geocentric model being objectively true. Indeed, both Kepler and Galileo were practicing astrologers and saw no contradiction between astrology and their commitment to a heliocentric universe. Moreover, although we know the universe is not actually geocentric, phenomenologically speaking the geocentric perspective remains valid in that, as cosmological evidence suggests, we are always inescapably centered in our viewpoints with regard to the universe. Ancient astronomers, as cosmologists Joel Primack and Nancy Abrams explain, "were wrong astronomically that the Earth is the centre of the universe, but they were right psychologically: the universe must be viewed from the inside, from our centre, where we really are, and not from some perspective on the periphery or even outside."[30] This assertion reflects the ontological and cosmological centering of the universe on individual human lives. As Primack and Abrams point out, the universe centers on the human being in a number of remarkable ways: human beings exist at the center of universal expansion; we are at the center of what they call the cosmic spheres of time; we are centered in the scale of magnitude of the universe; and we are each individually the center of our own perspective looking out at the cosmos. Thus understood, the astrological perspective, which uses charts centered on specific individuals or locations on Earth, is actually in broad agreement with the modern cosmological conception of an omnicentric universe—a universe of infinite centers. According to Brian Swimme, modern cosmology has "discovered an omnicentric evolutionary universe, a developing reality which from the beginning is centered upon itself at each place of its existence . . . to be in existence is to be at the cosmic center of the complexifying whole."[31] Centered in our own perspective, then, we live and breathe here on Earth in the context, first and foremost, of our own solar system. For although the immense vistas disclosed by recent telescopic exploration of space now make astrology's focus on the solar system seem decidedly provincial, it remains the case, of course, that the cycles of the planets in our solar system define our immediate cosmological vicinity.

Putting the above reflections together, we can see that in the light of modern physics the account of planetary influence as presented above requires radical revision. The deeper level of reality revealed by subatomic physics does not contain separately existing material bodies situated in empty space, causally linked by forces. Instead, as we have seen, mechanistic cause and effect descriptions of reality must be seen within the context of a new vision of the universe as an unbroken patterned energy field. The cosmic machine built by Descartes, Newton, and their successors has been dismantled by modern physicists, and the strictly deterministic model of the universe is now viewed as a theory with limitations, a theory that is useful in certain circumstances only. The linear-causal arguments against astrology that once appeared so compelling are drawn from an understanding of the universe that has been shown to be limited, or even inaccurate, and the grounds for the repudiation of astrology have therefore fallen away. This is not to say, of course, that astrology must necessarily be accepted as true; only that it is not reasonable to reject astrology because it is inexplicable in terms of the mechanistic paradigm.

We should be clear, as we proceed, that it is not essential to use relativity theory or quantum physics to explain astrology; rather, it is just that the implications of relativity theory and quantum physics undermine critiques of astrology based on linear, deterministic causal models of planetary influence, which generally presuppose the Cartesian-Newtonian model of the universe that informs classical physics. Relativity theory and quantum physics disclose a very different reality to the Cartesian-Newtonian view, and astrology must be seen in the context of this new reality. Even though it cannot be fully explained in terms of the theories of post-Newtonian physics, however, these theories might provide starting points from which one might begin to explore the possible basis of astrological correlations.

In line with recent developments in modern physics, it seems possible that the relationships between the planets and human experience can be understood not in causal mechanistic terms, but rather as a form of non-causal or acausal correlation. Within quantum physics, the investigation of subatomic particles has uncovered forms of relationship that defy causal explanations, as David Bohm notes:

> It is an inference from the quantum theory that events that are separated in space and are without possibility of connection through interaction are correlated, in a way that can be shown to be incapable of a detailed causal explanation.[32]

It might be that the astrological relationship between the planets and human experience is actually *acausal* in that, although the astrological evidence suggests there is some form of relationship, there appears to be no physical force emitted by the planets causally influencing human experiences—no form of linear, efficient causation passing from planets to people. Rather, it seems possible that there is some kind of deeper connection, some kind of underlying pattern inherent in the cosmos, that connects the celestial with the human order, and it is this underlying order that will be our concern here.

Indeed, what we now typically understand by causality, in the modern scientific sense, is but a partial subset of a more comprehensive understanding of causation as originally set forth by Aristotle. Four basic types of cause were originally identified: the *material* cause, which is the substance of which something is composed; the *efficient* cause, which is the external agent that serves to initiate change (as in the case of one billiard ball striking another thereby causing it to move); the *formal* cause, which is the underlying pattern or form that guides the growth of an organism or flow of events; and the *final* cause, which is the *telos*, aim, and purpose of an entity, event, or process. Of these, only the first two are generally recognized in science, and the efficient cause is closest to what we now understand as causation. We should keep in mind, then, what might be categorized as *acausal*, as falling outside the limits of causal explanations, might include the philosophical ideas of both formal and final causation, and both of these are important for understanding astrological correlations. Indeed, as Richard Tarnas points out, although the relationship between the *physical planets* and human experience might be considered acausal, there appears to be a form of complex underlying causation between the *planetary archetypes* and human experience. He explains:

> While the physical planets themselves may bear only a synchronistic connection with a given human experience, that experience is nevertheless being affected or caused—influenced, patterned, impelled, drawn forth—by the relevant planetary archetypes, and in this sense it is quite appropriate to speak, for example, of Saturn (as archetype) 'influencing' one in a specific way, or as 'governing' certain kinds of experience.[33]

Astrology and the Scientific Method

It is not surprising that attempts to explain astrology in causal mechanistic terms have been unsuccessful. The inadequacy of causal explanations of planetary influence meant that, for the most part, belief in astrology was eradicated, particularly among scientists and intellectuals who could see no rational basis for astrology because it seemed impossible that distant planetary bodies could have any influence on human life on Earth. Meanwhile, logical positivism, the philosophical movement based on the ideas of the so-called Vienna Circle in the early twentieth century, had decreed all metaphysical speculation to be meaningless because unverifiable. Instead, the positivists insisted that all inquiry into truth and the nature of reality should be restricted to what can be investigated in accordance with strict scientific method. Consequently, in academic philosophy questions of language and its meaning now take precedence over metaphysical speculation. By the twentieth century, science and rational philosophy attempted to demystify the world by insisting that only those propositions that could be logically deduced from their premises in accordance with the laws of logic, or expressed in the form of a mathematical equation, or empirically proven in accordance with the scientific method could be accepted as true. Astrology, clearly, did not fall into this category.

In response to the challenge of science, and in accord with this positivistic ethos, empirical evidence has been sought to establish statistically significant correlations between certain astrological variables and some of the more overt conditions of human life. Most famously, the Gauquelin studies investigated the correlation between planetary placements in individual birth charts (the planets that were "rising" on the *Ascendant* (the eastern horizon) or "culminating" on the *Midheaven* (the noon point overhead) and various professions). Revising his earlier skepticism towards many aspects of astrology, in the 1990s Gauquelin stated:

> Having collected over 20,000 dates of birth of professional celebrities from various European countries and the United States, I had to draw the unavoidable conclusion that the position of the planets at birth is linked to one's destiny.[34]

However, despite the impressive results from Gauquelin's research and independent corroboration of the validity of the data from figures such as Hans Eysenck, the significance of these data has been downplayed, and, in the main, subsequent research studies of this kind have met with only limited success. Scientific recognition of the validity of astrology is scant. The vast majority of research studies, employing a variety of different design methodologies, have failed to provide enough widely accepted substantial scientific evidence to support astrology. The academic discipline of psychology, therefore, also flatly rejects astrology's truth-claims. Hence, considering the second category of arguments against astrology, relating to empirical scientific evidence, it would seem that there is little to corroborate the assertion that the planetary positions and cycles have any significant correlation with the events and experiences of human life.

Yet what most scientific researchers into astrology have failed to comprehend and appreciate, I believe, is the essential nature of astrological correlations. For astrology, properly understood, is not concerned with prediction of specific events; nor do astrological symbols reveal the specific, concrete details of human life such as one's career or one's material circumstance. Rather, astrology is based, as we have seen, on the relationship between planetary positions and the archetypal meaning of human experience; and it is because of the archetypal, multidimensional nature of astrology that astrological correlations elude the orthodox scientific method of investigation. That is, it is because astrology is concerned with underlying thematic meanings and not with the prediction of specific, concrete events or the description of specific uniform character traits that scientific tests are unsuitable, and that they are unable either to disprove or to validate astrological truth-claims.

On this point, I must stress also that astrology cannot be tested objectively without taking into consideration both the researcher and the subject under investigation because the discernment of astrological patterns of meaning is dependent, to a considerable extent, on a person's capacity to recognize and comprehend such meaning. The depth, accuracy, and subtlety of the perception of astrological-archetypal themes in human experience are contingent on one's own depth of self-knowledge. The recognition and interpretation of astrological patterns as they are expressed in human life is an art form, which, like every art, demands not only a certain natural aptitude but also years of devoted practice. One must cultivate the ability to think symbolically, to discern the underlying archetypal meaning within a great diversity of outward forms of expression. One's depth of astrological-archetypal insight depends on one having a developed inner life and having acquired a feel for the different astrological principles. One can then relate to these principles not just intellectually, as one might learn fixed interpretations from a textbook by rote, but instead one can get to know what each principle feels like, emotionally and somatically, from having recognized these principles in one's own life experience. For this experience there can be no substitute. A prerequisite for a deep understanding of the workings of astrology, then, is that one must first enter into the astrological perspective, immerse oneself in it. If one is to discern archetypal meaning, one must develop a mode of perception that James Hillman calls the *archetypal eye* by which one can perceive universals and archetypal themes within diverse concrete particulars. While it is obviously unnecessary for researchers who are validating astrology to develop a high level of astrological competence themselves, it is essential that at the very least research studies show awareness of the archetypal nature of astrological correlations. Tests involving randomly selected subjects and control groups drawn from the general population obviously fail to meet this criterion. It is for this reason that, to the best of my knowledge, no scientific research has ever been conducted that could either substantiate or disprove an archetypal interpretation of astrology.[35]

Nevertheless, if astrologers do in fact make definite concrete predictions of future events (as many do) then these deserve to be tested empirically, in accordance with the scientific method. If astrologers posit the existence of relationships between astrological factors and specific careers, or particular interests, or the success or otherwise of relationships, or claim to be able to determine unchanging traits of personality, then these claims too should be empirically validated. Astrology, practiced in this way, should stand and fall by the accuracy of its concrete predictions and the validity of its personality descriptions. But, regarding *archetypal* astrology specifically, how is one to measure and quantify archetypal meaning? Clearly, the empirical validation of archetypal astrology requires a far more sophisticated and nuanced method of inquiry than is currently provided by either quantitative or qualitative research studies in psychology. That said, experts in particular fields (such as cultural history, the history of science, and religious studies) should in principle be able to adjudicate over claims made by astrological researchers into the character of particular periods defined by sets of world transits, although the negative image of astrology might deter scholars from even undertaking evaluations of this kind.

There are many factors that make scientific research into astrology problematic, although not impossible: the challenge of isolating single astrological variables from the multitude of factors used in astrology; the sheer intricate, interconnected complexity of the astrological perspective, which encompasses every dimension of human experience; the tendency for many astrologers, themselves subject to the theoretical bias inherent in the modern world view, to misconstrue the nature of astrological correlations and to make ill-founded and unjustifiable claims of a literal or predictive nature. Most significant, however, as Tarnas emphasizes, is the *multivalent* nature of the planetary archetypes—the fact that the planetary archetypes can manifest in such a great diversity of ways while still remaining consistent with a core archetypal meaning. For it is this inherent multivalence that makes it impossible to predict correspondences between astrological factors and the specific details of human life.

To reiterate, the planetary archetypes, and indeed all astrological symbols, have the same general set of thematic meanings for all people, but they manifest differently in the specific details of every human life. This is the cause of considerable misunderstanding of astrology. The case of so-called "time twins"—two people born at exactly the same time in the same location—has given rise to the question as to why two such individuals often appear to be vastly different from each other perhaps, for example, having completely different interests. If astrology is valid, the argument goes, then astrological twins must be very similar on all counts due to the fact that their birth charts will be identical. But, of course, having the same birth charts indicates only that the charts have the same archetypal pattern, which can manifest in a wide diversity of ways while still remaining consistent with the accepted astrological meanings of the planetary relationships within the chart. How each person expresses this pattern cannot be determined from the information in the astrological birth chart by itself. Aside from interpretive errors, this archetypal multivalence also accounts for why different astrologers give different, yet perhaps equally valid, interpretations of the same charts. Astrological charts refer only to general archetypal meanings and not to the specific, personal factors of life. This point cannot be overemphasized. As Tarnas, discussing the meaning of geometric planetary alignments or *aspects* between two planets, puts it:

> That a given natal aspect can express itself in a virtually limitless variety of ways and yet consistently reflect the underlying nature of the relevant archetypes is of course not only characteristic of all astrological correspondence but essential to it. Astrology is not concretely predictive. It is archetypally predictive.[36]

This means the same astrological factor, while consistently conforming to an underlying archetypal meaning, can manifest in radically different or even diametrically opposite ways. The planetary archetypes are multidimensional and multivalent creative principles, which, although thematically consistent, give rise to a potentially limitless range of forms of concrete expression. A Mars-Saturn planetary aspect, for example, could manifest both as a pattern of defensive aggression and retaliation or as an inability to express anger and to assert oneself; it could be present in the chart of the endurance athlete engaged in a punishing regime of physical training, or in the chart of someone for whom physical activity is impossible because of restrictive circumstance; it refers equally to people who have disciplined themselves to fight and be aggressive, and to people who have been conditioned *not* to fight and to refrain from aggressive behavior. Although, on the surface, the difference between these opposing forms of expression could not be more marked, on closer inspection we can see that they all partake in a common archetypal meaning. Here we have the Mars principle pertaining to self-assertion, aggression, striving and struggle, fighting, physical energy, anger, and the warrior archetype, in combination with the Saturn principle relating to restriction, limitation, concentrated pressure, discipline, structure, repression, fear, and a sense of inferiority. The person who trains to fight—who actually accentuates and improves their ability to fight—is imposing discipline and structure (Saturn) on the physical and aggressive energies (Mars). The person who refuses (Saturn) to fight or show aggression and anger (Mars), although ostensibly pursuing a totally opposite course, is similarly applying Saturnian discipline to their aggressive, assertive, energetic impulses. We can see, therefore, that both possibilities are archetypally consistent—that is, they both conform to the underlying meaning of the Mars-Saturn planetary combination, and often many of these seemingly opposing patterns of behavior are interchangeably present, such is the dynamic complexity of an archetypal pairing.

To recognize archetypal meaning in widely varying modes of expression one often has to examine more deeply the underlying motivations behind patterns of behavior. In the case of the above Mars-Saturn example, one might find that defensive retaliation is a sign of fighting to protect one's unacknowledged weakness; physical training and muscular armoring may serve to bolster or conceal a fragile ego; the hard-edged disciplinarian, similarly, might be motivated primarily by fear. On the other hand, weak passivity may indicate the unconscious repression of anger; and pacifism—ruling out anger or violence because it is perceived as morally wrong or socially unacceptable—might cloak a deeper fear of facing and expressing anger. To uncover the underlying archetypal meanings of our actions we have to discern just what our motivations are behind these actions. Astrology, in this way, encourages a greater depth of insight and understanding of one's nature, which, in time, can give rise to a penetrating self-knowledge—the prerequisite for psychospiritual development.

With a proper recognition of the archetypal multivalence underlying astrology, one can see that it is perfectly possible for two astrologers to give different interpretations of the same planetary configuration that are equally valid in that they both coherently reflect the underlying archetypal meanings of the planets involved. Tarnas himself gives many examples of this multivalence at work in *Cosmos and Psyche*, and this is one of the distinctive theoretical contributions of his work. A statistical analysis of astrologers' interpretations that fails to take into account the archetypal nature of the planetary alignments will be inadequate, noticing only surface differences rather than the underlying themes connecting ostensibly dissimilar behavior patterns. As Tarnas stresses, to properly understand and assess astrological correlations one must cultivate "the imaginative intelligence . . . that is capable of recognizing and discriminating the rich multiplicity of archetypal patterns" in both individual biography and world history.[37]

To sum up, then, if mechanistic determinism is not universally applicable, if there are other types of interconnection between phenomena that appear to coexist with linear causality, then it is possible that astrology and scientific determinism are simultaneously valid. Indeed, archetypal correlations seem to coherently coexist with linear causality in a way that calls into question the notion that all things might be explained in terms of prior efficient causes. From an archetypal perspective, astrology does *not* actually contradict deterministic explanations; nor does a belief in astrology impinge on the freedom of the human will. Rather, astrology offers us another perspective that supplements causal-determinism; it provides a larger and deeper frame of reference, a background context of archetypal meaning that helps to illuminate causal factors and scientific explanations, and to inform our acts of will and conscious decisions. Causal determinism and the archetypal astrological perspective are not mutually exclusive or competing theories but complementary—each illuminates and augments the other.

The dominant scientific understanding of human nature represents only one particular way of looking at things. The scientific view is partial and much has been left out of the picture. Like an extremely focused narrow searchlight, science has brilliantly illuminated certain features of reality, but in so doing it has excluded from view vast dimensions of reality lying outside of the illuminated region. The astrological-archetypal perspective provides a compensatory wide-lens view, as it were, an holistic perspective that seeks to understand human life in terms of the interior significance of our place within, and relationship to, the whole solar system. And astrology also provides a deeper view—an x-ray photograph, if you like—of the underlying archetypal factors pervading human experience. Thus, whether we wish to point to acts of will, genetic heredity, circumstance, or childhood experiences as prior determining factors behind human experience, subsuming all these factors is the deeper framework of archetypal meanings revealed by the astrological perspective. With respect to the planetary archetypes in astrology, we are not dealing with one-dimensional causal factors that can be predicted to correlate with certain events, or actions, or forms of behavior; we seem to be faced, rather, with creative living powers, autonomous principles rooted deep in the structure of reality itself. These creative archetypal principles are not mechanically and rigidly deterministic but, as living processes, they manifest uniquely in each life experience, they are expressed differently by different people, they vary according to context and circumstance, and also according to the degree of human self-awareness. We can think of the planetary archetypes as being analogous to the Olympian gods of ancient Greece. And just as we would not expect to be able to predict and control, to isolate and dissect, or to measure and quantify the actions of gods, so the archetypal principles in astrology similarly transcend the narrow methodological framework employed in empirical testing. The potential value and validity of the astrological perspective cannot be revealed to the clinical gaze and austere analysis of positivistic science.

Notes

1 This essay is a slightly modified version of a chapter in my doctoral dissertation, subsequently published in *Beyond a Disenchanted Cosmology*. *Archai: The Journal of Archetypal Cosmology*, volume II.

2 Bok and Jerome, "Objections to Astrology," 4–6. The primary motivating force behind the release of this statement was the skeptical agenda of Paul Kurtz, the editor of *The Humanist*, renowned for his ardent critique of paranormal phenomena. Kurtz, along with astronomer Bok and science writer Jerome, sponsored the 1975 statement, which was also submitted to newspapers across North America. For further context on the controversy surrounding this statement and attempts to debunk Gauquelin's research, see Denis Rawling's account (http://www.psicounsel.com/starbaby.html).

3 Bok and Jerome, "Objections to Astrology," 4–6.

4 For the survey of science and philosophy, I draw especially upon the following works: Richard Tarnas, *The Passion of the Western Mind*, Leslie Stephenson, *Seven Theories of Human Nature*; T. L.S. Sprigge, *Theories of Existence*; Brian Magee, *Story of Philosophy*; Alfred North Whitehead, *Science and the Modern World*.

5 Descartes, "Discourse on Method," 88.

6 Descartes, "Discourse on Method," 36.

7 For a discussion of dualism and monism, see Keiron Le Grice, *The Archetypal Cosmos: Rediscovering the Gods in Myth, Science and Astrology* (Edinburgh: Floris Books, 2010), chapters 5 and 7.

8 See Spade, "William of Ockham."

9 See Whitehead, *Concept of Nature*. Another aspect of this bifurcation, according to Whitehead, is the separation of our awareness of the experience of the world from the world itself, which purportedly causes that experience. Whitehead's process philosophy and existential phenomenology represent two of the most significant attempts to overcome this separation.

10 While Descartes was not the first to advance either a philosophy of mind-matter dualism or theories of the mechanistic functioning of the external world (the roots of these reach as far back as ancient Greek speculation), his philosophy, together with Newtonian mechanics, was to shape the dominant world conception and inform the scientific enterprise through the modern era.

11 See Freud, *New Introductory Lectures on Psychoanalysis*.

12 Skinner, *Beyond Freedom and Dignity*.

13 Skinner, *Beyond Freedom and Dignity*.

14 For example, according to Marx, "It is not the consciousness of men that

determines their being, but, on the contrary, their social being determines their consciousness." Marx, *Selected Writings in Sociology and Social Philosophy*, 67.

[15] Whitehead, *Science and the Modern World*, 76.

[16] Mansfield, "Astrophysicists Sympathetic and Critical View of Astrology." Mansfield is here addressing the view of well-known astronomer Carl Sagan. For a discussion of Sagan's misunderstanding of astrology, see also Grof, "Holotropic Research and Archetypal Astrology," 55–56.

[17] Capra, *Web of Life*, 5.

[18] Whitehead, *Science and the Modern World*, 49.

[19] Capra, *Tao of Physics*, 90.

[20] Capra, *Tao of Physics*, 78.

[21] Capra, *Tao of Physics*, 92.

[22] Capra, *Tao of Physics*, 150.

[23] Combs and Holland, *Synchronicity*, xxx.

[24] Combs and Holland, *Synchronicity*, xxxi.

[25] Bohm, *Wholeness and the Implicate Order*, 124.

[26] Bohm, *Wholeness and the Implicate Order*, 124.

[27] Capra, *Tao of Physics*, 92.

[28] Capra, *Tao of Physics*, 92.

[29] Capra, *Tao of Physics*, 92.

[30] Primack and Abrams, *View From the Center of the Universe*, 133.

[31] Swimme, *Hidden Heart of the Cosmos*, 85–86.

[32] Bohm, *Wholeness and the Implicate Order*, 129.

[33] Tarnas, "Introduction to Archetypal Astrology."

[34] Gauquelin, *Neo-astrology*, 24.

[35] See, for example, "Astrology and Science, Research results," which provides a summary of ninety-one research studies, of various different types, published in four different journals: *Correlations*, *APP*, *AinO*, and *Kosmos*. A review of the abstracts suggests that none of the studies have shown sufficient appreciation of archetypal multivalence and multidimensionality.

[36] Tarnas, *Prometheus the Awakener*, 20.

[37] Tarnas, *Cosmos and Psyche*, 70.

II

The Colloquy of the Gods:
Excerpts from the Introductions to *Jung on Astrology*

The astrological horoscope, Carl Jung observed in a letter of 1954, "corresponds to a definite moment in the colloquy of the gods, that is to say the psychic archetypes."[1] This statement, one of many similar assertions made throughout his life, is illustrative of Jung's belief that astrology can provide symbolic insight into the workings of the human psyche. Astrological charts, cast for specific moments in time, might be construed as something like a symbolic portrayal of the universal principles, or archetypes, once personified by the gods and goddesses of ancient myth. Indeed, astrology, Jung remarked in a letter to Sigmund Freud in 1911, "seems indispensable for a proper understanding of mythology."[2] However, despite Jung's abiding personal interest in astrology, and his serious exploration of it, his views on the subject have received scant attention from scholars in the field of depth psychology. By contrast, Jung's ideas have been readily embraced by many practicing astrologers and authors of astrology books, perhaps in the hope that the association with Jung might lend to astrology a degree of credibility otherwise lacking, given the natural affinity between the two fields. *Jung on Astrology* is a compilation of Jung's writings in this area, relevant not only to readers in depth psychology and astrology but, more broadly, to any of us searching for deeper life meaning and a greater sense of order in life or for a way to explore the mysteries of human experience.

Questions of the human being's place within the cosmos, of the limits of rationality and causal determinism, and of the scope of human free will and the existence of what was once recognized as the workings of fate or destiny remain critically relevant to us today. Now, as in other periods of our recent past, the challenges of our historical moment impress upon us the need to better recognize and work in harmony with the greater forces, both psychological and physical, shaping our lives. "We know nothing of man," Jung proclaimed in an interview near the end of this life, and it is this unconsciousness of human nature, especially our capacity for destruction and evil, that, he believed, poses the greatest threat to our existence—and perhaps today even to the planet's.[3] No less significant is the need to find sources of individual life meaning and orientation for our future direction, given the increasing secularism of the modern world, with the much-discussed absence of myth and decline in religious belief. In giving his attention to the symbolism, practice, and theoretical understanding of astrology, Jung grappled with each of these concerns. The results of his exploration of astrology, recorded in various places in his *Collected Works* and his other less formal writing, are set out in *Jung on Astrology*.

Astrology held Jung's interest throughout most of his life, evident as early as 1911 in correspondence with Freud ("my evenings are taken up very largely with astrology"[4]) to his many letters on this topic from the late 1950s. Jung's writing in this area is of historical import too, revealing Jung's engagement with astrology as one notable element of a burgeoning cultural interest in the irrational and psychological exploration in the late nineteenth and early twentieth centuries, a movement out of which depth psychology itself arose. At a biographical level, Jung's fascination with astrology, and with other aspects of the occult, was a contributory factor in his professional and personal break from Freud in early 1913. Jung's interest in matters astrological was to continue in the decades to follow and is especially evident in seminars given in the late 1920s and 1930s, and then in letters and formal writing from the 1950s, in connection with synchronicity (the phenomenon of "meaningful coincidence"), modern physics, and reflections on the mind-matter relationship. Although not treated in a dedicated volume of the *Collected Works*, astrology occupied Jung's attention for a fifty-year period as he ruminated on its workings and applied it to illuminate both individual psychology and the evolution of mythic symbolism within Western civilization.[5]

Such is the interconnection between astrology and Jungian ideas that the compilation of Jung's writings on this topic also constitutes an excursion into many, if not all, of the central aspects of his psychology, encompassing his theories of archetypes and the collective unconscious, individuation, synchronicity, the self and mandala symbolism, alchemy, myth, the evolution of the God-image, and more. Perhaps this range is not so surprising when we take into account Jung's view that astrology represents "the sum of all the psychological knowledge of antiquity."[6]

For it could be argued that in certain respects Jungian psychology represents a modern articulation of the concerns of symbolic systems and practices omitted from the modern scientific world view—astrology and alchemy chief among them. At root, both astrology and Jungian psychology might be seen as being engaged with the critical task of developing greater self-knowledge, of bringing to awareness the unconscious factors underlying our life experience. In Jung's view, astrology—whatever else it might be—is a symbolic language of archetypes, the formative principles and patterns in the depths of the unconscious mind.

While numerous astrological books have drawn on perspectives and ideas in Jungian psychology, as noted far less is known about Jung's own thoughts on astrology, which are often buried within discussions of other ideas and scattered throughout his many publications. *Jung on Astrology* was put together to address the need for an exposition of his ideas within a single volume, allowing Jung to speak for himself, as it were, and thus perhaps to allow us to extricate Jung's own thoughts on astrology from the ways Jungian ideas have been used by astrological writers. The book allows readers to see for themselves Jung's enduring fascination with the topic and to read firsthand his own reflections on it, so as to be able to evaluate astrology's significance within the larger corpus of his work and assess its potential relevance for our time.

What is Astrology?

Simply stated, astrology is the practice of interpreting the meaning of observed correlations between human experience and the positions, interrelationships, and cycles of the planets (including the sun and the moon) in the solar system. The movements and positions of the planets are plotted against the zodiac, a symbolic frame of reference based on the ecliptic, the line formed by the apparent movement of sun around the Earth over the course of a year—this apparent movement, of course, as astronomers have known since the Copernican Revolution, is a result of the Earth's orbit around the sun. In astrology, the ecliptic forms the center-line of an imaginary band, extending eight to nine degrees above and below it. The zodiacal band, as it is called, is divided into twelve thirty-degree segments, which comprise the well-known signs of the zodiac: Aries, Taurus, Gemini, Cancer, Leo, Virgo, Libra, Scorpio, Sagittarius, Capricorn, Aquarius, and Pisces. The signs belong to one of four elements—Fire, Earth, Air, and Water—and are thought to possess qualities in keeping with the nature of the element. For example, Fire signs (Aries, Leo, and Sagittarius) are deemed to be energetic, warm, enthusiastic, inspirational, and often extraverted, whereas Water signs (Cancer, Scorpio, and Pisces) are associated with emotional sensitivity, compassion, inwardness, and depth of feeling. The qualities of the signs are thought to influence the astrological meanings and principles associated with each of the orbiting planets as they appear to move around the zodiac through each sign in turn. The planets themselves are symbolically associated with certain dynamic principles and powers. Jung likened them to gods and archetypes, whereas the signs might be construed as something like modes of being or archetypal styles manifest in enduring personality traits. Traditional astrology was concerned only with the seven "planets" known to classical—the Sun, the Moon, Mercury, Venus, Mars, Jupiter, and Saturn. Contemporary astrology, in many of its forms, has incorporated into its symbolism and practice the so-called modern planets, discovered since the late eighteenth century: Uranus, Neptune, and Pluto.[7]

As seen from any viewpoint on Earth, each planet in its orbit appears to pass in turn through each sign of the zodiac such that at any given moment a planet will be positioned in one particular sign, forming a configuration of relationships with the other planets, known as aspects. For instance, if two planets appear close to each other in the zodiac, within a range of about ten to twelve degrees (a conjunction), this is deemed significant, indicating that the principles and qualities associated with those planets are in a powerful, dynamic relationship, stimulating and blending with each other. Similarly, two planets approximately opposite each other in the zodiac are also considered to be in a potent, challenging, and often antagonistic relationship (an opposition), as are those planets close to 90 degrees apart (a square). Other geometric relationships, such as those based on 120 degrees (trine) and 60 degrees (sextile), are also considered. All the planets and their interrelationships are depicted in an astrological chart calculated for any given moment in time.

Alongside the annual passage of the sun around the zodiac, astrology utilizes another frame of reference based upon our experience of the sun's apparent daily motion across the sky, generated by the Earth's daily rotation on its axis. The line of the sun's journey over the course of a day forms a circle, which is divided into twelve equal sections known as houses, with each house designating a different field of experience or area of life. For example, the second house is traditionally thought to relate to finances, the sixth house to health, the eight to death, and the ninth house to travel. In casting an astrological chart—a horoscope—the moment of sunrise on the eastern horizon determines the sign of the ascendant (the start of the first house); sunset, the western horizon, correlates with the descendant or start of the seventh house, with the *medium coeli* (the midheaven), the highest point of the chart, and *imum coeli*, the lowest point, symbolically representing noon and midnight, respectively.[8] Although astrology incorporates a vast and complex array of variables, the planets, signs of the zodiac, houses, and aspects are usually considered to be the most significant factors in astrological interpretations, or chart readings, as they are commonly known.[9]

Perhaps the most popular form of astrology practiced today, outside of newspaper horoscope columns, is natal astrology—astrological horoscopes cast for the moment of birth. Based on the relative positions and placements of the planets at birth, the astrologer synthesizes the meaning of the various factors in the chart to give a portrait of the individual's character and biographical experiences. The birth-chart reading is often augmented by the study of the ongoing movements of the planets in relation to each other as they traverse the zodiac, using methods known as transits and progressions. These methods can be used to gain insight into the qualities of particular periods of time—past, present, or future—and to understand the kinds of experiences and events one might encounter at these times. Historically, astrology has often been used for prediction, most famously, of course, by Nostradamus, whose prophecies were considered by Jung in a chapter in *Aion*, which is included in Part III of *Jung on Astrology*.

Astrology in the Western World

Western astrology, with which Jung was concerned almost exclusively, is thought to have originated in Mesopotamia, the "cradle of civilization," around 3400 BCE.[10] From there, it was transmitted to Egypt and to Greece and Rome, assimilating the character of the deities of these traditions in a form of mythic syncretism, with the planets ultimately taking on the names of the well-known Roman gods and goddesses—Mercury, Venus, Mars, Jupiter, and Saturn.[11] After a period of suppression by the Church, when Christianity became established as the official religion of the Roman Empire, astrology underwent a revival during the Middle Ages and flourished again during the Renaissance, with Marsilio Ficino (1433–1499) an influential figure, before its exclusion from serious intellectual thought after the Enlightenment and the rise of science.

The beginnings of modern Western astrology have been traced to the British theosophist Alan Leo (1860–1917), writing at the turn of the twentieth century (indeed, Jung notes the close connection between astrology and theosophy around that time). The theosophical influence on the direction of modern astrology continued with the work of Marc Edmund Jones (1888–1980) and then Dane Rudhyar (1895–1985), whose astrological writings date from the 1930s, following his emigration from France to the U.S.[12] All three figures were influential in the formation of a psychological or spiritual approach to astrology, in distinction to those forms of practice concerned with the literal prediction of events. Today, psychological astrology, which possesses the most explicit connections to Jungian thought, is one of multiple forms of contemporary astrological practice. Astrology is variously characterized by a range of descriptors, designating its distinct approaches and applications, including mundane (the astrology of world events), horary (answering specific questions), electional (finding the best time for a planned event), traditional, predictive, divinatory, psychological, evolutionary, spiritual, and most recently archetypal. For some practitioners, astrology is to be viewed as a divinatory method akin to the *I Ching* and Tarot. For others, it is a way to develop psychological insight and a source of mythic meaning. Some commentators see it primarily of interest historically, for understanding connections to our cultural past; others see certain forms of astrology as critically relevant today, both in preserving the psychological wisdom of previous eras and in offering an alternative to the disenchanted world view of modernity.

Especially in academia and science, the prevailing view today, however, is that astrology is a pseudoscience whose premises are incompatible with the accepted scientific understandings of the nature of reality. Although three of the progenitors of the modern scientific era, Copernicus, Galileo, and Kepler, were themselves involved in astrology (in the period of the sixteenth and early seventeenth centuries in which astronomy and astrology were still a single discipline), the direction of scientific development thereafter pushed astrology outside the margins of the accepted paradigmatic boundaries of intellectual discourse, where it remains.[13] As explored in Chapter I, one central element in the debunking of astrology is the absence of a satisfactory causal explanation, in terms of known forces, as to how planets could influence human beings on Earth. Other critiques concern the apparent lack of empirical evidence to substantiate astrology's truth-claims, a critique Jung himself made and sought to address.

More broadly, with its apparent perpetuation of archaic notions of fate and predestination, astrology is at odds with a number of foundational assumptions of the modern world view, such as the belief in rational self-determination and causality. If we are self-determining agents, with the capacity to shape the future through acts of free will, how can our lives be fated and controlled by the movements of the planets in the solar system? If our lives can be understood through the study of prior causes (such as genetics, early conditioning, and the environment), how can astrology also influence our experience, especially given that there is no significant demonstrable causal connection between the planets and human beings? Moreover, how can the signs of the zodiac, arbitrarily derived from a physically non-existent frame of reference, and no longer in alignment with the constellations of stars after which they were named, have any bearing on events and experiences on Earth? Astrology's apparent assumption of a geocentric rather than a heliocentric cosmology also seemingly places it at odds with the findings of science since the Copernican Revolution, although astrologers stress that adopting a geocentric perspective does not contradict the astronomical reality of a sun-centered solar system but only symbolically reflects the vantage point of individuals on Earth.

Taken together, such objections constitute a formidable barrier to the consideration of astrology, not only in terms of appraising the intellectual argument for its validity, but also because of the emotional investment in assumptions at the core of the consensus understanding of the nature of reality in the modern West, assumptions that astrology appears to flagrantly contradict. Astrology, as Richard Tarnas has noted, is today often seen as the "gold-standard of superstition."[14] For all the seeming irrationality of astrology, though, Jung believed it to be of great value, for he was struck most of all that astrology, however it might ultimately be conceptualized and explained, somehow *works*, in that it discloses, in a symbolic celestial language, information and insights about the psychology, and thus the "fates," of human beings.

Jung's Views of Astrology

Jung situated astrology within the context of the cultural transformation of Western civilization since the late eighteenth century. In passages from his stirring commentary "The Spiritual Problem of Modern Man" (1928–1931) written almost in parallel with Freud's *Civilization and Its Discontents* (1929–1930), Jung draws attention to the ascent of reason and science in the modern West, displacing Christian faith as the primary modes of understanding the world, and on the compensatory resurgence of the seemingly irrational and unscientific fascination with psychic phenomena, evidenced by the widespread interest in Gnosticism, theosophy, anthroposophy, astrology, and more. Jung himself played no small part in this movement, of course, in that his work helped bring back into the light of day subjects excluded from the modern scientific view of the world—not least alchemy, mythology, and mysticism.

We read here too of Jung's insistence that the modern individual yearns for direct experience of the numinous depths of the psyche rather than accepting second-hand truths inherited from the doctrines of religion, to be followed as a matter of faith. "Modern man abhors faith and the religions based upon it," Jung claims, at the risk of overstatement. "He holds them valid only so far as their knowledge-content seems to accord with his own experience of the psychic background. He wants to *know*—to experience for himself."[15] Astrology seems to offer a path to self-knowledge in accordance with one's own experience, perhaps accounting in part for its popularity in our time— and perhaps accounting too for Jung's own abiding interest in it.

For Jung, then, the recovery of ancient symbolic wisdom and occult knowledge might be viewed as a response to the profound spiritual and psychological transformation of our time—the "metamorphosis of the gods," as he termed it, bringing a fundamental reorientation in the primary symbols by which each civilization gives expression to the numinous psychological powers that he called the archetypes of the collective unconscious.[16] Drawing on the power of the instincts, these formative archetypal principles, Jung believed, unconsciously animate and direct the human imagination, giving shape to the myths, religions, and cultural forms that provide a source of individual and collective life meaning.

For many in the West, the transition out of the Christian era has wrought psychological and spiritual confusion, and even psychopathology born of an unshakeable sense of meaninglessness and existential disorientation, as the old symbolic forms pass away. Indeed, Jung noted that the psychological suffering experienced by all of his patients over the age of thirty-five ultimately arose from the loss of a religious outlook on life.[17] In the modern era, he observed, spirit has "fallen" from the fiery empyrean above and has become "water," evoking the sense that the metaphysical realm of the heavenly powers of old and even of the Kingdom of God are now to be found submerged in the oceanic depths of the unconscious.[18] The "stars have fallen from heaven," he proclaimed in a similar vein; they have fallen into the unconscious, for neither celestial powers of astrology nor the mythic pantheon of an Olympian host have a place in the prevailing understanding of reality in the modern world.[19]

For all its seeming irrationality, astrology represents a still-vital perspective, living on in the collective unconscious, that repository of forms and archetypal patterns that is the source of our psychological and instinctual history. As an historical precursor to depth psychology, with roots in the ancient, classical, and medieval worlds, astrology preserves and carries forth other modes of interpreting reality to those pursued in science, offering a counterpoint to mechanistic determinism, atomistic reductionism, and a narrow scientific empiricism that excludes the experience of meaning. It is a perspective, Jung thought, that is based on the recognition of "meaningful coincidences" (synchronicities, as he called them) between external facts and inner experiences, in this case between planetary positions and constellated archetypal themes in human experience. In Jung's view, astrology is an example of "synchronicity on a grand scale," potentially providing an opening to a deeper background order of meaning.[20]

Jung's personal views of astrology included observations on its value for illuminating the workings of the psyche and critical comments on its shortcomings and misconceptions. We see evidence of Jung's willingness to turn to astrology as an aid to analytical work with his patients. For instance, in a letter to astrologer B. V. Raman in 1947, Jung comments: "In cases of difficult psychological diagnosis I usually get a horoscope in order to have a further point of view from an entirely different angle. I must say that I very often found the astrological data elucidated certain points which I otherwise would have been unable to understand."[21] Yet we also see Jung adopting a critical stance towards astrology, targeting especially the lack of statistical studies to provide evidence in support of it; astrologers, he notes, "prefer to swim in intuition"[22] rather than conduct empirical research.[23] Jung also took issue with the prevailing approaches to astrological interpretations at the time, noting that they were "sometimes too literal and not symbolic enough, [and] also too personal" in that astrology is to do with "impersonal, objective facts" and multi-leveled rather than singular meanings.[24]

Jung essentially understands astrology as a symbolic representation of the archetypal dynamics of the unconscious psyche. As such, astrology pertains to universal motifs and general themes and traits rather than the specific concrete particulars of life. Accordingly, he introduced the term *planetary archetype* to describe the universal principles associated with each of the planets in astrology. His "planet simile," extracted from his alchemical writings in *Mysterium Coniunctionis*, strikingly portrays the symbolic relationship between the planets and archetypes, with the conscious ego standing in relation to the archetypes, as the sun does to the orbiting planets. Jung believed that the psychology of archetypes can help to account for the "inner connection between historical events" and the "general laws" underlying individual development, which are two of the primary areas of application of astrology.[25]

Notes

[1] Jung to André Barbault, 26 May 1954, in *Letters II*, 175–177.

[2] Jung to Sigmund Freud, 8 May 1911 (254J), in *Freud/Jung Letters*, 183.

[3] Jung, "Face to Face Interview," with John Freeman, in *C. G. Jung Speaking*, 436.

[4] Jung to Sigmund Freud, 12 June 1911, in *Letters I*, 24.

[5] For a detailed study of the sources from which Jung developed his understanding of astrology, and the figures who influenced his views, see Liz Greene's forthcoming monograph *Jung's Studies in Astrology*. For a companion volume discussing Jung's use of astrological symbolism as a method of hermeneutics in *The Red Book*, see Greene, *The Astrological World of Jung's Liber Novus*.

[6] Jung, "Richard Wilhelm: In Memoriam" (1930) in *Spirit in Man, Art, and Literature* (*CW* 15), 81.

[7] In astronomy, following the discovery of Eris and other planet-like bodies in the outer reaches of the solar system, Pluto was reclassified as a dwarf planet in 2006, although this change of status is not considered to affect its significance in astrology. See Le Grice, *Discovering Eris*.

[8] Jung employs variant spellings of the terms *ascendant* and *descendant* in his writing.

[9] There are references to each of these factors in the chapters of *Jung on Astrology*, although Jung, it should be noted, does not always use the terms accurately.

[10] Jung admits, "I know far too little about Indian and Chinese astrology" (Jung, *Aion*, 93).

[11] For detail on the origins and history of Western astrology, see Campion, *History of Western Astrology*; Tester, *History of Western Astrology*; Whitfield, *Astrology*; Barton, *Ancient Astrology*; and Bobrick, *Fated Sky*.

[12] Rudhyar's *The Astrology of Personality*, synthesizing Jungian ideas, the philosophy of holism, and theosophy, was published in 1936.

[13] For a discussion of the astrological interests of Copernicus, Galileo, and

Kepler, see Campion, *History of Western Astrology*, vol. 2.

[14] Tarnas, cited in Le Grice, "Birth of a New Discipline," 7.

[15] Jung, "Spiritual Problem of Modern Man," in *Civilization in Transition* (*CW* 10), p. 84, par. 171.

[16] Jung, "Undiscovered Self," in *Civilization in Transition* (*CW* 10), p. 304, par. 585.

[17] Jung, "Psychotherapists or the Clergy," in *Psychology and Religion: West and East* (*CW* 11), p. 334, par. 509.

[18] Jung, "Archetypes of the Collective Unconscious," in *Archetypes and the Collective Unconscious* (*CW* 9i), pp. 18–19, par. 40.

[19] Ibid., pp. 23–24, par. 50.

[20] Jung, "Richard Wilhelm: In Memoriam" (1930), in *Spirit in Man, Art, and Literature* (*CW* 15), p. 56, par. 81.

[21] Jung to B. V. Raman, 6 September 1947, in *Letters I*, pp. 475–476.

[22] Jung, *Dream Analysis*, 20 November 1929, pp. 392–393.

[23] Recent studies, such as the extensive survey of astrological correlations with patterns of cultural history undertaken by Richard Tarnas, have sought to put astrology on firmer empirical ground. See Tarnas, *Cosmos and Psyche*. See also the research in *Archai: The Journal of Archetypal Cosmology*.

[24] Jung to André Barbault, 26 May 1954, in *Letters II*, pp. 175–177.

[25] Jung to Karl Schmid, 26 January 1957, in *Letters II*, p. 345.

III

Twentieth Century Astrology:
From Psychological Astrology to Archetypal Cosmology

Despite its incongruence with the mechanistic materialism of the dominant modern world view, astrology has undergone a renewal in popularity over the course of the last century, particularly since the rise of the 1960s counterculture. Initiated by the pioneering work of figures such as Charles Carter and Dane Rudhyar, the progressive reformulation of astrology has ensured a continued interest in the subject. Previously, astrology's language was somewhat antiquated; often fatalistic and moralistic in tone, it gave the sense of a destiny set in stone, with personality descriptions more befitting the Victorian era. With the modernization of astrology, a new breed of psychologically oriented astrologers emerged, inspired by the nascent disciplines of psychoanalysis and humanistic psychology to bring greater depth, sophistication, and insight to astrological interpretations. Over the last fifty years or so, with the publication of many new textbooks, astrology has become far more widely accessible and it has become an important component of the wider "spiritual revolution" of our time.

The Development of Psychological Astrology
A major movement within astrology during the twentieth century, especially since the 1970s, has been "psychological astrology," a term that refers to an eclectic group of approaches, loosely influenced by certain aspects of twentieth-century psychology. The precursors of this new form of astrology can be traced back to the theosophist Alan Leo at the turn of the twentieth century, who, in a marked shift of emphasis, applied astrology to understand the traits and characteristics of the individual personality rather than to predict events. This development was carried forward by figures such as Charles Carter,

John Addey, Margaret Hone, and Charles Harvey in the U.K., and Grant Lewi and Isabel Hickey in the U.S. In the writing of each of these authors, there was evidence of a shift towards a concern with the personal experience of the individual and a new focus on using astrology to increase spiritual awareness of and insight into one's life purpose. Reflecting the emergence of the modern individual self in the modern era, the twentieth century witnessed the development of a form of astrology geared towards understanding the character, innate potentials, and psychological dynamics of the self and of individual experience. A new form of astrology began to emerge, one that served, rather than precluded, the individual's capacity for subjectivity, autonomy, and freedom of will.

In general terms, with reference to astrology itself, the modern reemergence of astrology can be seen as an expression of the wider spiritual transformation associated with the Neptune-Pluto conjunction of the late nineteenth century that witnessed a number of pivotal developments that have shaped the modern understanding of psyche and cosmos: Nietzsche's proclamation of the "death of God," the decline of the traditional religions, the resurgence of previously submerged occult practices, the emergence of depth psychology, the revolution in physics with relativity and then quantum theory (during the Uranus-Neptune opposition of the early twentieth century), and the influx of Eastern ideas into the West. As we have seen, Jung's work was central to this process of spiritual and cultural transformation. His ideas were to have a profound influence on modern astrology, initially through the work of Dane Rudhyar and also directly through Jung's own exploration of astrological thought, discussed in Chapter II.

Writing between the 1930s and the 1980s, Rudhyar initiated a revolution in modern astrology, pioneering modern psychological and spiritually oriented astrology in both its humanistic (or person-centered) and transpersonal forms—indeed, he was among the first to coin the term *transpersonal*. A polymath and prolific author, he drew together ideas from the emerging philosophy of holism, Hindu thought, Taoism, the *I Ching*, theosophy, and Jungian psychology to present his view of astrology as a way of self-realization rather than a means of prediction or character analysis. Rudhyar's focus was on the place of the individual within larger wholes and cycles of time and on using astrology to provide spiritual meaning and purpose. The first definitive statement of his approach to astrology is given in his 1936 publication *The Astrology of Personality*. Here Rudhyar also incorporated Marc Edmund Jones's system of Sabian symbols, which ascribes a specific symbolic meaning to every degree of the zodiac. In the 1960s, Rudhyar then launched humanistic astrology, which was concerned with using astrology to promote the fulfillment of an individual's innate potentials. Later, Rudhyar distinguished this *individual* or person-centered level of application of astrology, as he called it, from a more advanced *transpersonal* level in which astrology could be used to help spiritually aspiring individuals transcend the limitations of the rational ego. The clearest statement of this later approach is given in *The Astrology of Transformation*.

Alongside Rudhyar, Stephen Arroyo and Liz Greene have been particularly influential figures in the rise of psychological astrology. Arroyo was deeply influenced not only by Rudhyar's work, but also by his reading of Jung and American psychic Edgar Cayce. Writing in the 1970s, Arroyo provided some of the most perceptive insights into the nature and phenomenology of the astrological factors, especially in his *Astrology, Karma, and Transformation*. In effect, Arroyo gave Rudhyar's spiritual approach to astrology a more contemporary, psychological voice, combining depth of insight with a more readily accessible style of presentation of his ideas.

Whereas the writings of Rudhyar possess a characteristic esoteric and explicitly spiritual style and focus, Liz Greene is more classically Jungian and psychological in her approach. Greene's work is marked by a keen awareness of the personal and collective unconscious as primary determining factors behind individual experience. Her writing is also informed by a sensitive appreciation of the complexities of human relationships, of the dynamics of the family and early childhood conditioning, and of the deep mysteries underlying character, vocation, and individual destiny. Above all, with Greene, the astrological chart is seen in the context of the process of the development of personality. The birth chart is a developmental blueprint that details, from an archetypal perspective, the unfolding pattern of the individual's intelligible character. Greene also sought to explicitly incorporate Jung's focus on myths and archetypes into the practice of astrology—an approach also pursued by Tony Joseph in the U.S. before his untimely death in the early 1980s—thereby reconnecting astrology to its former roots in the mythic traditions of Greece and elsewhere. Of all modern astrologers, Greene's work has also had the most significant impact on astrological education and training through the establishment of the Centre for Psychological Astrology in London and Zurich. I should also mention here too the work of Alice Howell, who has done much to connect astrology to the field of Jungian psychology in books such as *The Heavens Declare* and *Jungian Symbolism in Astrology*.

Other influential figures in the field of psychological astrology include Howard Sasportas (who often worked in collaboration with Greene) and Robert Hand, whose works include *Horoscope Symbols*, a comprehensive introductory text, and *Planets in Transit*, an equally comprehensive reference work for transit astrology. Hand's approach, certainly in these two books, reflects a broadly humanistic style, with the recognition of the capacity of the individual to shape how the astrological factors could be expressed in the vicissitudes of personal experience in ways that would promote more favorable outcomes.

Technical Developments in Modern Astrology

The major development in astrology in the modern era has, without question, been the assimilation of the outer planets—Uranus, Neptune, and Pluto—into astrological theory. As many authors have noted, the astrological meanings associated with each of these planets were broadly reflected in the historical events and zeitgeist of the periods in which the corresponding planet was discovered: the discovery of Uranus coincided with the French, American, and Industrial revolutions, for example, and the discovery of Pluto with the development of atomic power, the rise of depth psychology, and the rise of fascism. Here again Rudhyar was the central figure, interpreting the discoveries of the outer planets and the corresponding emergence of the archetypal potentials of the associated planetary archetypes as a kind of teleological unfolding, an evolution of human cultural awareness, and a progressive disclosure of the deeper dynamics of the collective unconscious.

Another significant technical development in modern astrology has been in the understanding of the importance of midpoints. According to midpoint theory, planetary archetypes can be in potent relationships when the corresponding planets form midpoints, with one planet positioned halfway between two or more others. Often an analysis of midpoints helps to account for traits of character and themes of biography that an analysis of natal aspects by itself cannot. Major texts focusing on this area include the influential *The Combination of Stellar Influences* by Reinhold Ebertin and *Working with Astrology* by Michael Harding and Charles Harvey. Alongside midpoints, I should also mention here John Addey's theory of harmonics, which emphasizes the importance of Pythagorean number symbolism in astrology (a lineage further developed by Charles Harvey's work) and astrocartography, developed by Jim Lewis.[1]

More generally, modern astrology has seen moves to simplify astrological techniques with the introduction of keyword approaches to interpretation and a focus on common themes underlying the symbolism of planets, signs, and houses. In retrospect, one can see that the modern era has witnessed a great democratization of astrology. Aided by the revolution in computer technology, which makes biographical data and charts instantly available, and aided too by the mass publication of astrological textbooks, astrology has moved from the hands of a few practitioners into the hands of the many.

Philosophical Suppositions of Psychological Astrology

With the work of Rudhyar and Arroyo, in particular, astrology was elevated to the status of a spiritual path and it was liberated, to a large extent, from the literalism and fatalism of earlier forms of astrology, and set apart too from the superficiality of popular astrology. Increasingly, in the 1970s and 1980s astrology became primarily to do with the inner world of the psyche and the spirit, not the outer world of mundane events. The birth chart was construed as a map of the psyche, a blueprint of the course of individual psychological development.

However, like depth psychology, psychological astrology was addressing itself to subjective individual experience within the accepted reality of a radically disenchanted cosmos in which matter, nature, and the universe at large were seen as unconscious, mechanistic, and essentially dead. Psychological astrology came into existence within a cultural world view that radically rejected astrological truth claims and denied outright the possibility that there could be any relationship between the patterns of human experience and the planetary cycles in the solar system.

Against this background, psychological astrology became subject to the same implicit philosophical limitations that initially shaped the depth and transpersonal psychology movements, such as a tacit, residual Cartesianism in which the human psyche was seen as separate from the external world. Although psychological astrology served the emergence and actualization of the modern individual self, like depth and transpersonal psychology it has at times also inadvertently fostered what Jorge Ferrer calls intrapsychic reductionism, reducing astrology to "nothing but" the expression of intrapsychic psychological dynamics. In psychological astrology, the basis of astrological correlations was often explained (if this issue was addressed at all) as a form of unconscious symbolic projection of the inner dynamics of the psyche onto an essentially neutral, or even meaningless cosmic order.

In general, however, despite the greater psychological sophistication of modern astrology, philosophical questions underpinning the working assumptions of astrology have often been overlooked. A notable exception is Richard Tarnas's *Cosmos and Psyche: Intimations of a New World View*, which directly addresses the place of astrology within the evolution of consciousness, culture, and the Western world view. After introducing an expanded theoretical framework for astrology, drawing especially on Jung's later research into synchronicity, Tarnas then presents a detailed body of evidence pointing to a consistent and coherent correlation between the planetary cycles and the archetypal patterns of world history, from the Axial Age in the first millennium BCE to the present day, encompassing every sphere of human endeavor and every dimension of life—social, political, cultural, artistic, philosophical, scientific, and spiritual. Tarnas's research, which is distinguished by the emphasis he places on the cycles of alignments of the outer planets, suggests the events of world history unfold in close accordance with the framework of thematic meanings associated with the planetary alignments formed during those times.[2]

Moving beyond the conceptual limits of conventional astrology, which has tended to be more literal and concretely predictive in its approach, Tarnas has deepened the philosophical and interpretive precision of the astrological perspective by drawing from the depth psychology of Jung, James Hillman, and Stanislav Grof. Tarnas has explicated the fundamental attributes of archetypal principles, which has given him a more comprehensive grasp of astrological correlations and, crucially, of the limitations of what astrology can actually reveal. Perhaps the most important of these attributes discussed by Tarnas is the inherent *multivalence* of expression of the planetary archetypes in human experience and the concomitant realization that astrology is archetypally rather than concretely predictive—an insight that implicitly characterizes and informs much of modern psychological astrology. From this perspective, any given astrological factor, such as a natal aspect, can manifest in a wide range of different ways while still remaining consistent with a central core of meaning. Accordingly, astrology's proper concern is discerning the universal themes and principles evident in human experience; by itself it can reveal nothing of the specific form these universals will take when enacted in the particulars of life.

The Emergence of Archetypal Cosmology

Tarnas's research has helped to establish foundations for the emergence of *archetypal cosmology*, an academic discipline that is concerned both with empirical research into astrological correlations and with articulating a new world view or cosmology that can support and account for these correlations.[3] In many ways, archetypal cosmology represents a continuation of developments that began with psychological astrology—the recognition of the archetypal significance of the outer planets for understanding the deeper dynamics of the unconscious psyche, the recognition of the participatory role of the modern self in shaping the expression of the archetypal patterns studied in astrology, the use of astrology for providing psychospiritual insight and to increase self-knowledge. However, archetypal cosmology also aspires towards a greater empirical and philosophical rigor, drawing on Pythagorean and Platonic philosophy, mythic perspectives, depth psychology (Jung, Hillman, Grof), process philosophy (Alfred North Whitehead), and the new paradigm sciences (including the work of Bohm, Capra, Sheldrake) to seek to better understand and explain astrological correlations.[4] Crucially, archetypal cosmology situates psychological astrology's emphasis on the individual psyche within a larger cosmological and metaphysical context. Like earlier forms of astrology, archetypal cosmology explicitly recognizes the existence of something like an *anima mundi*—the interiority of the universe at large. From this perspective, planetary archetypes are seen not as wholly intrapsychic factors merely reflected in, or projected onto, the planetary order of the solar system, but as cosmological and metaphysical principles shaping and informing both the inner and outer dimensions of reality. Psyche and cosmos are seen as intimately interconnected, as related expressions of a deeper underlying ground. Archetypal cosmology thus directly addresses, and seeks to overcome, the modern dichotomy between inner and outer, between the subjective human self and the objective cosmos. It seeks to make explicit the deeper unity between psyche and cosmos, microcosm and macrocosm, that has been the concern of astrological practitioners through the ages.

Notes

[1] See John Addey, *Harmonic Anthology* (1976; repr., Tempe, AZ: American Federation of Astrologers, 2004); Charles Harvey, *Anima Mundi: The Astrology of the Individual and the Collective* (London: CPA Press, 2002); and Michael Harding and Charles Harvey, *Working With Astrology: The Psychology of Harmonics, Midpoints, and Astro-Cartography* (London: Arkana, 1990).

[2] Rod O'Neal has called this approach to the study of history *archetypal historiography*. See O'Neal, "Archetypal Historiography."

[3] See Le Grice, "The Birth of a New Discipline" for further details on the emergence of archetypal cosmology.

[4] Many of these areas are addressed in my first book, *The Archetypal Cosmos*, which presents a theoretical synthesis of Jungian depth psychology and the new paradigm sciences in an attempt to develop a new world view to account for astrological correlations.

IV

The Birth of a New Discipline:
Archetypal Cosmology in Historical Perspective

At the turn of the twentieth century, when Sigmund Freud first developed the theoretical framework and therapeutic method of psychoanalysis in Vienna, one could scarcely have conceived of a movement less likely to exert a powerful, lasting influence on the modern mind. Controversial, taboo, ridiculed and rejected by many, psychoanalysis, with its theories of repressed libidinal impulses and childhood sexuality, radically contravened and challenged the deeply entrenched values, mores, and attitudes of the Victorian morality of the era. To many people at the time it must have seemed certain that psychoanalysis was destined to be quickly consigned to history, to be written off as a curious oddity, a failed experiment, a perverted and warped conception of human nature. The early reactions to Freud's publications were scornful and scathing. According to Ernest Jones, Freud's biographer and fiercest ally, "*The Interpretation of Dreams* had been hailed as fantastic and ridiculous . . . the *Three Essays* were [deemed] shockingly wicked. Freud was a man with an evil and obscene mind."[1] Psychoanalysis, moreover, was an affront to the nineteenth century's assured belief in progress and rational self-determination. The notion that the modern human being, despite pretensions to rational autonomy, was in fact the unwitting instrument of unconscious impulses and complexes, and that the pious morality of that time concealed a seething cauldron of instincts whose sublimated expression lay behind humanity's most elevated cultural aspirations and achievements was a message both unpalatable and, seemingly, altogether untimely.[2]

Yet within the space of a few decades, psychoanalysis and its many offshoots in the wider field of depth psychology had achieved a cultural influence extending right across the major urban centers of Europe,

North America, and beyond. Today, over a century after the publication of *The Interpretation of Dreams*, despite the repudiation of some of Freud's more exaggerated claims and unsubstantiated theories, the prevalence and influence of the psychology of the unconscious across many areas of contemporary culture—including psychotherapy, religious studies, comparative mythology, critical theory, and the arts—is as pervasive as ever, and, for all its inherent shortcomings, it has contributed greatly to our understanding of human nature.

That the psychoanalytic movement was a necessary corrective to the values and world view of the nineteenth century is perfectly apparent to us now. Indeed, it seems in retrospect as if the emergence of that movement were in some way a response to the evolutionary imperatives of the time—as if it were just what was required for the modern self to achieve greater self-knowledge and self-awareness, and to outgrow the psychological and moral limitations of that period of history. Of course, it is seldom obvious to those enmeshed in a particular cultural zeitgeist, or those operating within the dominant scientific paradigms of the time, just how these paradigms will change in the future, or what ideas will next seize hold of the human mind and thereafter determine the direction of philosophical speculation and scientific research, or the course of major cultural shifts. In fact, as Thomas Kuhn's work has well described, much psychological energy is usually invested in maintaining the hegemony of dominant paradigms and proclaiming their validity even in the face of mounting anomalies and contradictory evidence.[3] Resistance to radical new ideas and anomalous data is an essential element in the dialectic of change, and this resistance is normally provided by those in the established majority viewpoint.

It therefore remains the fate of the few, often those existing outside the margins of conventional academic disciplines, to serve as emissaries for emerging truths; it is the challenge of a creative minority to nurture and give expression to the nascent ideas impinging on human consciousness. And—as the example of psychoanalysis plainly demonstrates—these few sometimes come from the most unexpected quarters, proclaiming the most unlikely message, and often to a skeptical or even hostile audience.

Basic Postulates of Archetypal Cosmology

Certain parallels might be observed between this precedent and the current emergence of *archetypal cosmology*, an academic discipline developed by a group of scholars and researchers originally based in the

San Francisco Bay Area, California, but now practiced in multiple locations around the world. Archetypal cosmology, which explores the correlation between discernible archetypal patterns in human experience and the structural order within the solar system, draws on the methodology, interpretive principles, and cosmological perspective provided by perhaps *the* most controversial of all subjects: astrology.

Although many people would be quick to reject outright the truth claims of astrology, recent evidence of striking correlations between planetary cycles and the major patterns of world history presented by philosopher and cultural historian Richard Tarnas has given to the discipline a new, unexpected credibility and provided the most compelling evidence yet that this ancient symbolic system, following decades of reformulation through its encounter with depth, humanistic, and transpersonal psychology, is once again worthy of serious consideration.

Archetypal astrology, as this new approach has been called, is based on an observed correspondence between the planets in the solar system and specific themes, qualities, and impulses associated with a set of universal principles and thematic categories known as planetary archetypes. Each of the planetary bodies, as well as the Sun and the Moon, is associated with a distinct archetypal principle. Thus, the planet Mars, for example, is related to a complex array of themes and qualities associated with the warrior archetype and, more generally, to the principle of assertion, action, and aggressive force; whereas Venus, understood in its simplest terms, is related to the principle of eros, romantic love, beauty, and pleasure. Rather like the ancient mythic conception of the gods, and as in the Platonic conception of archetypal Forms, the archetypal principles associated with the planets are recognized to be not only psychological but also cosmological in essence, exerting a dynamic formative ordering influence on both the interior and exterior dimensions of reality.

The central supposition informing archetypal astrology is that one can gain a deep insight into the archetypal dynamics underlying human experience by interpreting the meaning of the positions of the planets in relationship to each other. There are two main components to archetypal astrology: *natal analysis* and *transit analysis*. Natal analysis is based on the premise that the positions of the planets at the moment of a person's birth, relative to the location of birth, can reveal a meaningful archetypal pattern that is expressed both in that individual's personality and in the events and experiences of his or her personal biography. Transit analysis is based on the study of the cycles of the planets over time and the geometric relationships formed between the different planets within these cycles. These changing relationships are understood to be symbolically significant, to reveal corresponding changes in the thematic content and quality of human experience. Two types of transits are studied in archetypal astrology: *world transits* and *personal transits*. World transits relate to the whole world, to the changing patterns of *collective* human experience.[4] Personal transits relate specifically to individuals, and are derived by comparing the positions of the orbiting planets at any given time with the positions of the planets in an individual's birth chart. Here, then, briefly stated, are the essentials of astrological theory. Although traditional astrology is a vast and complex subject with a bewildering array of factors that could potentially be considered, archetypal astrology usually focuses only on these three "forms of correspondence," as Tarnas has called them: the natal chart showing the planetary positions at the time of an individual's birth, the changing planetary positions through time relative to the Earth (world transits), and the relationship between these two (personal transits).[5]

The method employed to analyze and interpret the archetypal dynamics of human experience in terms of the movements of the planets is based on a consideration of the geometric alignment—the specific angle of relationship—formed between the different planets in their respective orbits.[6] The meaning of every planetary alignment or aspect depends both upon the archetypal characteristics associated with the planets involved and the particular angle of relationship between the planets. As in the Pythagorean view, in astrology principles of number and geometry are recognized as fundamental to the deep structure and organization of the cosmos, and these numeric principles are reflected in the geometric relationships between the planets.

It is this method of interpreting world transits that was employed by Tarnas in his 2006 publication *Cosmos and Psyche: Intimations of a New World View*. He found that during the period when two or more planets move into aspect—into significant angular relationship—the world events of that time (revolutions and wars, political and social movements, artistic expressions and scientific discoveries, cultural shifts and spiritual transformations) and the entire zeitgeist (the pervasive mood or spirit of the age) reflect the archetypal meanings associated with that particular planetary combination. For example, Tarnas realized that those periods in history when Uranus and Pluto were in major dynamic alignment (including the years 1787–1798 centered on the French Revolution, the 1845–1856 period of the revolutions across

Europe and the wider world, and the decade of the 1960s) were characterized by a complex of themes associated with the dynamic mutual interaction of the two planetary archetypes: the eruption of powerful revolutionary impulses, the liberation of the instincts (both libidinal and aggressive), the empowerment of mass freedom movements, and a pervasive mood of radical change and turbulence—to give but a few examples. During these periods, in agreement with the established astrological meaning of the planets, the Uranus archetype liberated and awakened the instincts and primordial drives associated with Pluto, as the Pluto archetype simultaneously empowered and intensified the revolutionary, experimental impulses associated with Uranus.[7] In this way, the interaction of the two planetary archetypes shaped the defining themes and character of the entire culture during the periods when the two corresponding planets were in alignment. Tarnas discovered that, potentially, every historical period could be analyzed in this way. The study of the different combinations of these planetary archetypes, he realized, provides us with a powerful method to help understand the shifting dynamics of both cultural history and individual biography.

As with psychoanalysis a century ago, however, it is difficult to imagine a subject more incongruent with the dominant paradigms and established knowledge of the time than astrology. Despite its illustrious past, when it was held in high esteem by many of the world's great civilizations, now, as Tarnas has said, astrology represents "the gold standard of superstition" in that it is seen by many to be the very epitome of the obscure irrationalism and projected mythic thinking that modern science has sought to overcome and dispel.[8] The repudiation of the geocentric model of the solar system after the Copernican Revolution, and the absence of any adequate scientific explanation as to how the distant planets could possibly influence human lives, were believed by many to have deprived astrology of its former claims to validity, and condemned it to cultural and academic obscurity—a position that the inane, superficial forms of contemporary popular astrology have done little to redress. Moreover, the popular misconception of astrology, that human fates are unalterably "written in the stars," seems to deprive human beings of the power of self-determination and to mark a return, therefore, to an oppressive fatalism, to a universe of inescapable predestination. Astrology, as it is commonly understood, appears to contradict the idea that we are free to forge our lives and shape our identities through acts of free will, to choose and fashion the life we please, and it is therefore perceived as a threat to the sovereign power of the human self. For some people, this itself is reason enough to reject astrology out of hand.

I should be clear, then, that the new archetypal understanding of astrology is far removed from the fatalistic predestination long associated with its traditional and popular forms. For astrology, according to Tarnas's helpful definition, is not to be understood as *literally* predictive of future events and therefore indicative of the inescapable workings of a preordained fate, but rather as *archetypally* predictive in that its methods of analysis and interpretation of the planetary positions and movements give insight into the archetypal determinants, the general themes and motifs, evident in our experiences and not to the specific form of manifestation of these archetypes.[9] To understand how an archetypal complex might manifest in the concrete particulars of life one would need to take into consideration many other factors not apparent from the astrology alone: cultural background, economic and social conditions, genetic inheritance, and, crucially, the degree of conscious awareness guiding our actions and decisions. Archetypal astrology is informed by a fundamental insight into the complex participatory nature of human experience. It is based upon the recognition that human experience, although occurring within a framework of cosmically based archetypal meanings, is shaped by the crucial intervention of the individual will. The archetypal principles, moreover, although always thematically constant, are radically indeterminate as to their forms of expression in the concrete particulars of human lives. As Tarnas has pointed out, the astrological archetypes are both multivalent (given to a range of expressions while remaining consistent with a central core of meaning) and multidimensional (manifesting across the various dimensions of human experience).[10]

I should explain also that while astrology is incompatible with the basic tenets of mechanistic science and the materialistic conceptions of the nature of reality that have prevailed in the modern era, it is far more congruent with many of the so-called new paradigm perspectives that have recently emerged in physics, biology, psychology, and elsewhere. The ideas of holism, interconnectedness, interdependence, organicism, self-organization, and non-local causality that have emerged from relativity theory and quantum theory in physics or from the systems approach in biology have presented us with a view of reality sharply divergent from that based on classical physics and the still-dominant Cartesian-Newtonian mechanistic paradigm. It is more congruent, too, with the recent theories of an omnicentric universe emerging out of cosmology and modern physics, which, in recognizing that we are all inescapably centered in our psychological perspectives with regard to the universe, support astrology's assumption of a person-centered (and therefore geocentric) viewpoint. These new models, together with the insights of depth psychology, provide an increasingly coherent and supportive theoretical context within which we can better comprehend the likely basis of astrological correspondences.

Archetypal cosmology thus incorporates not only the study of the correlation between the planetary alignments and archetypally themed phenomena in human experience (archetypal astrology), but also the wider issue of archetypal astrology's relationship to and place within new paradigms of understanding and emerging cultural world views. Drawing on many fields of inquiry, it is concerned with the attempts to understand, in philosophical and scientific terms, the basis of astrological correlations, and the challenge of explicating the implications of archetypal astrology for contemporary global culture.

Origins, Antecedents, and Emergence

The emergence of any new field of research or a new paradigm of inquiry is in some sense always marked by a decisive break with the established body of learning and accepted knowledge of the day—and this is certainly true of archetypal cosmology. Yet invariably, a new field of study, no matter how controversial and radical its premises and implications, is also the result of the confluence of other well-established areas of knowledge, when existing theories, methods, and systems of thinking are brought together in creative and perhaps unexpected ways to give birth to something distinct and original. Psychoanalysis, for instance, came directly out of the late-nineteenth century neurology and hypnotism practiced by Charcot, Janet, Breuer, and Freud. Within a wider context, it brought together major elements of both the Romantic and Enlightenment traditions—confirming, on the one hand, insights into the unconscious basis of human motivations identified by the philosophies of Schopenhauer and Nietzsche, and, on the other, applying to human psychology the rationalism and causal determinism that informed natural science and medicine. Looking back further, psychoanalytic developments such as the recognition of the primary drives of Eros and Thanatos, and the Oedipus and Electra complexes as underlying patterns of human behavior, presented a vision of human nature that, even amidst the scientific materialism of the time, recalled in its language and theoretical formulations the mythic sensibility of ancient Greece—a parallel that was more fully apparent in Jung's later, more explicitly mythic, analytical psychology.

Historically, the roots of much of what now constitutes modern philosophical discourse and scientific inquiry can be traced back to the ancient Greeks, or earlier, when the human mind first grappled with the great questions of origin and purpose, seeking order and meaning behind the apparent flux of the phenomenal world. Atomistic science, for instance, was prefigured in the philosophy of Democritus; systems theory, in its recognition of the role of self-organizing form and pattern, has given emphasis to an idea not unlike Aristotle's concept of formal causation; the heliocentric model of the solar system, with a moving Earth and stationary Sun, was anticipated by the speculations of Aristarchus; and quantum physics, which has disclosed a universe of dynamic change and process rather than one of static material forms, recalls Heraclitus's famous insight that all is flux. In all these cases and more, ancient conceptions of the cosmos, formulated by the Greeks, returned many centuries later to the forefront of intellectual discourse and became pivotal to the dominant conceptions of the nature of reality and the empirically derived models of modern science. As they reach into the future, then, all new movements and new disciplines are, it seems, simultaneously rooted in the past.

It is just this interplay between old and new, ancient and modern, that has given birth to archetypal cosmology. Here too the confluence of many fields of knowledge and culture has contributed to the emergence of this new multi-disciplinary subject—astrology, depth psychology, history, philosophy, cosmology, religious studies, comparative mythology, cultural studies, the arts, and the new sciences. And here too both the philosophical ideas and the earlier mythic sensibility of the ancient Greeks have once again resurfaced, for the astrological perspective, as Tarnas has pointed out, incorporates both the Homeric vision of an Olympian pantheon of gods and goddesses, and the Pythagorean-Platonic conception of the universe as pervasively ordered and dynamically infused with transcendent archetypal forms, both mythic and mathematical in nature.[11]

It is here, of course, that archetypal cosmology sharply diverges from and challenges the fundamental assumptions informing the dominant contemporary Western world view. Under the philosophical influence of rationalism, positivism, and materialism, together with the rise of empirical science and the establishment of monotheistic Christianity as the dominant Western religion, the ancient gods of Greek and Roman mythology were "forgotten"—dismissed first as pagan idols, and then as nothing but fictional creations of the imagination, superstitions of archaic belief systems from a pre-scientific age. After the Scientific Revolution, the idea that the universe is ordered by transcendent principles and that this order is the expression of a universal intelligence—a divine *logos* or *nous*—seemed, to the scientific mind, outmoded, fanciful, and altogether remote from contemporary thought. In the modern era, all explanations of phenomena in terms of transcendent factors, although often fundamental to earlier world views, were repudiated—deemed both unknowable and unnecessary—and replaced by entirely naturalistic accounts. Only the evidence of the senses, subjected to critical reason and the scientific method, could be relied upon in the quest for knowledge. The age of the gods had passed. The age of science and modern industrial society was upon us.

Two critical developments provided essential foundations for the scientific enterprise. Cartesian philosophy established a radical dualism between the inner world of human subjectivity and the external world of matter, between the thinking self or soul (*res cogitans*) and the unthinking extended substance of the world (*res extensa*). Newtonian mechanics then explicated the fundamental laws of nature and provided the mathematical models that enabled scientists to understand the workings of the external world and thus to measure, predict, and control its processes and operations. The external world seemed to be perfectly comprehensible on its own terms without reference to human thoughts, feelings, desires, and so forth. Scientific objectivity was born, and the efficacy of science was powerfully demonstrated by the unprecedented mastery of nature achieved since the Industrial Revolution.

A consequence of Cartesian ontology is that human beings were effectively seen to be inhabiting two separate yet mysteriously connected worlds: one to be accessed by looking out with the senses, the other by looking within introspectively. Increasingly, the sacred and the spiritual dimensions of life were to be approached and accessed only through human interiority, if at all. The material world was viewed as entirely unconscious, devoid of spiritual value or intrinsic meaning, comprised only of inert matter moved mechanistically by external, scientifically measurable forces. Science and spirituality were thrust apart. The sacred was divorced from matter. The cosmos became disenchanted.

In the modern world picture, as Tarnas has described at length, the only source of purpose, value, or reasoning consciousness was taken to be the individual human mind, which was itself seen as a mere epiphenomenon of the brain.[12] The human being came to be conceived as a socially conditioned, biologically driven, genetically coded material organism existing as a peripheral, accidental creature confronted with the unimaginable vastness of a purposeless, soulless, mechanistic universe. Against this desolate vision stood the subjective reality of human self-awareness with its depth of interior experience that belied any reductionist explanations of consciousness. Without a sense of participation in a meaningful universe that a viable guiding myth, narrative, or cosmology could provide, however, the human became subject to all manner of existential distress and anxieties. It was in this context that depth psychology found its place in modern culture, first to try to alleviate the symptoms of psychopathology and then later, with Jung's work in particular, to help modern individuals find their own sense of meaning and spiritual purpose based not on an outmoded religious orthodoxy, nor even on reason, but rather on a living relationship to the dynamisms in the depths of the unconscious psyche.

It is surely more than just coincidence that the unconscious was discovered in precisely the same historical period that brought forth Nietzsche's proclamation that "God is dead."[13] At almost the very moment when the modern self found itself inhabiting an external cosmos in which all trace of the divine had seemingly vanished—a cosmos utterly devoid of spiritual meaning and purpose—human consciousness immediately plunged into the unsuspected interior depths of the unconscious. In this newly discovered inner world, it became apparent that the ancient gods, although long forgotten and unrecognized, lived on. Thus Jung, in a famous passage, remarked:

> We can congratulate ourselves on having already reached such a pinnacle of clarity, imagining that we have left all these phantasmal gods behind. But what we have left behind are only verbal specters, not the psychic facts that were responsible for the birth of the gods. We are still as much possessed by autonomous psychic contents as if they were Olympians. Today they are called phobias, obsessions, and so forth; in a word, neurotic symptoms. The gods have become diseases.[14]

The "gods" had not permanently disappeared, they had just become invisible to the modern mind, with its gaze directed outwards, and its vision blinkered to any other psychological reality save for that of its own conscious awareness and rational volition. Without a vital living mythology, the modern mind did not and could not readily discern the activity of those powerful dynamic forces formerly conceived as gods.

It seemed, in fact, that the only way modern ego-consciousness could be alerted to the existence of autonomous factors outside of its own control was in the form of psychological or physical pathology. And so it was, through depth psychology's exploration of the symptoms and causes of this pathology, that the "gods" were rediscovered, no longer of course as exalted Olympians or celestial powers, but now as wholly intrapsychic factors to be approached through human interiority. "All ages before ours believed in gods in some form or other," Jung explained. "Only an unparalleled impoverishment in symbolism," he added, "could enable us to discover the gods as psychic factors, which is to say, as archetypes of the unconscious."[15]

The discovery and exploration of the unconscious exposed the rationalistic fallacy of the belief in the sovereign power of the conscious ego and of willpower in self-determination. The psychology of the unconscious discredited the psychologically naïve view that we are "masters of our own house," that we have a singular conscious will, centered upon the ego, and that this will is the unassailable determining factor in our lives. Depth psychology demonstrated that we do not have just one will, consciously controlled, but many motivational centers that move us often unconsciously and that may at times work at cross-purposes. The ego, the center of conscious awareness, is just a small part of the total psyche; it is one psychological complex among many, albeit a singularly important one. Depth psychology, in general, demonstrated that much of human life is determined by unconscious factors beyond our control, and Jungian analytical psychology, in particular, articulated the collective, universal, and mythic nature of the multiple archetypal centers in the unconscious—a perspective that was directly comparable to, and subsequently influential on, the archetypal astrological vision.

During the course of his work, Jung had observed that the fantasies and dreams described by his patients could not all be traced back to their own personal histories. Rather, some fantasy images were populated with motifs and symbols that appeared to be drawn from the mythological traditions of our collective past. As Jung examined more closely the content of such dreams and fantasies, he found evidence of a meaningful order within the human psyche, of a previously unrecognized dimension of the psyche that structures and organizes human imagination and cognition. He became convinced that underlying the individual human mind there must be a deeper collective level. Jung postulated that the Freudian model of the unconscious—of a personal unconscious consisting of repressed memories and socially unacceptable impulses, desires, and fears—rests upon an additional, deeper transpersonal "layer," which he later called the collective unconscious or objective psyche.[16] He discovered that human life was not only motivated by instinctual drives rooted in human physiology and psychological material repressed into the personal unconscious, as Freud thought, but that it was also shaped by universal mythological ideas and archetypal patterns in the collective unconscious. This deep foundation and collective stratum of the psyche, in Jung's view, serves as a "storehouse" or "repository" of the instincts and dynamic forms behind human existence, but it is also "the matrix of experience," the pre-existent ground from which the individual personality centered on the ego-complex emerges.[17]

Existing within the collective unconscious are archetypes such as the hero, the shadow, the anima, the animus, the wise old man, the child, the great mother, and the Self. These were conceived by Jung as innate structuring principles and dynamic psychic forms behind human life, principles that are both instinctual and spiritual, both natural and transcendent. Indeed, such is the complex character of the archetypes that Jung felt it necessary to employ a wide variety of terms to describe them: "formative principle[s] of instinctual power," "conditioning factors," "ruling powers," "gods," "universal images," "unconscious dominants," "patterns of behavior," "primordial ideas," "a priori ideational pattern[s]," "transcendentally conditioned dynamisms," "organizing forms"—to give but a few examples.[18] He suggested, furthermore, that the archetypes are "active, living dispositions, ideas in the Platonic sense, that preform and continually influence our thoughts, feelings, and actions."[19] Jung therefore situated his theory of archetypes firmly in the mythic-Platonic tradition. Like the mythological gods and goddesses, the archetypes are the formative principles, supraordinate to human consciousness and will, that structure, order, and animate our life experience.

Despite echoes of the mythic language of the Greeks, Freudian psychology presented a deterministic and reductionist model of the human psyche, one that rejected any kind of spiritual or transcendent value to human experience: Human nature could be understood in terms of unconscious instinctual impulses, rooted in biology, and in causal-historical terms as the consequence of repressed trauma from early biographical experiences. For Jung, however, the complexes of personal biography were ultimately based upon the collective archetypes, which were spiritual factors, possessed of numinous charge and instinctual power, that wrought radical evolution and transformation in human experience, and impelled the psychological developmental process that he called individuation. And it is these archetypes, in their deepest form, that are the primary focus of archetypal cosmology.

If the Greek vision provides the philosophical foundations for archetypal cosmology, its more immediate antecedents and foundations lie here, in depth psychology, particularly in the line running from Jung to James Hillman and Stanislav Grof. In many respects, archetypal cosmology represents a continuation of some of the major contributions of these three theorists, marking a further development in our understanding of the place and significance of archetypes and the unconscious psyche in human experience and in the universe at large.

Jung's research into the phenomenon of synchronicity had alerted him to the possibility that archetypes are not just intrapsychic images apparent in dreams and fantasies since, under certain conditions, archetypes also seem to find expression in external events and circumstances. Synchronicity, according to Jung's most precise definition of the term, is the "meaningful coincidence" of an external event and an interior, subjective experience, occurring simultaneously, in which the external event is clearly related to the individual's psychological state at that moment.[20] Synchronicity is the unexpected, uncanny, and often numinous collision of the inner and outer worlds at a specific moment in time for which there seems to be no linear causal explanation, and which calls into question the radical Cartesian division between mind and matter that has been so influential on the modern world view. In instances of synchronicity, the usual division of mind and matter is transcended, revealing, Jung suggested, the underlying unity of the inner and outer worlds. Psyche and cosmos, he reasoned, appear to be two aspects of a cosmic psyche or *unus mundus*, a single undivided reality.[21] The unconscious, from this perspective, is not to be conceived as a collective layer of the individual human mind, but as something more like a universal field within which we live, one that is inextricably connected to nature and the external world. And the archetypes, at their deepest level, appear to be dynamic ordering factors of this field, the formative principles of a single universal psyche.

The planetary archetypes recognized in astrology seem to relate most especially to Jung's conception of the archetypes *per se*, foundational forms existing behind the archetypal images, whose core meanings can only be intuited, never fully grasped by the intellect.[22] They relate also to Jung's notion of the "psychoid" basis of the archetypes, by which he sought to convey something of their complex essence as principles that are at once both material and psychological, manifest in the materiality of the cosmos yet giving rise to archetypal images and mythic motifs in the psyche.[23] The astrological archetypes associated with the planets are universal principles lying behind the more specific archetypal images identified by Jung. The astrological Moon, for example, which is associated with the emotions, the urge to care and be cared for, and with the receptive, feeling-based dimension of the human personality, includes within its more general, universal meaning at least three Jungian archetypes: the anima, the mother, and the child, which are all connected to the Great Mother archetype, the whole, the matrix of being. These archetypal images, which are overlapping and mutually implicated, are best understood as derivative expressions of the underlying planetary archetypes, as are the gods and goddesses of mythology, which appear to be personified forms and inflections of these deeper universal principles.

Certain aspects of Jung's mythically informed vision were taken up by James Hillman in the late 1960s as he developed his own self-styled "archetypal psychology." Inspired by Renaissance Neoplatonism, Hillman's psychology, which is allied with the work of Henry Corbin, more explicitly articulated and championed the imaginal life of the soul in all its nobility, pathos, beauty, and mythic diversity than even Jung's work had. Although Hillman rejected Jung's Kantian notion of archetypes as unknowable reified entities existing behind archetypal images (seeing such theorizing as just another type of archetypal fantasy, one not to be taken literally), he affirmed and expanded Jung's larger vision of the pluralistic archetypal nature of the psyche. Following Jung, Hillman granted to the imaginal world its own vital reality, honoring the multifarious productions of the psyche—its pathology, its mythic figures and fantasies—in their own right. Contrary to monotheistic conceptions of the divine, and challenging the humanistic idea that the psyche is a function of the singular human self, he believed that the psyche is home to many "persons," and many gods and goddesses, and the ego should therefore give up the illusion of sole occupancy. The realization of the pluralistic or polytheistic nature of the psyche, Hillman suggested, could be achieved by adopting a metaphorical way of experiencing—by cultivating an "archetypal eye" to see through the concrete literalisms of contemporary life to the deeper mythic realities this concealed. This approach, he hoped, could provide a way out of the repressive autocratic control of the modern ego, which he associated with monotheism, and give the soul more authentic expression in modern life.[24] Hillman realized, moreover, that psychological conditions such as depression and neurosis are not simply something to be treated, corrected, and cured, as in the standard medical model of psychotherapy; rather, such symptoms, he argued, are essential expressions of the depths of the soul and the psyche, which, if affirmed and explored, could provide gateways to a richer, more meaningful life.

Finding myths and archetypes in evidence wherever he looked, Hillman also turned his archetypal eye to the wider culture, in the hope that this might restore a more aesthetic and mythic mode of being. Through Hillman's work, according to Murray Stein's summary,

> The doors of analysis were sprung open and depth psychology was taken out of the clinical setting into the world at large. This offered a kind of psychological re-sacralization of the modern world, as myth-making could be taken up by individuals with an eye for archetypal image and structure.[25]

Hillman recognized that gods and goddesses pervade everything— physical symptoms, society, works of art, histories and sciences, psychologies and philosophies. As he once said in his own inimitable way, you can't open your mouth without a god speaking.

Hillman remained steadfastly faithful, in epistemological terms, to his insight into the archetypally conditioned nature of all theorizing and psychologizing. However, in some sense for Hillman everything is imagination; reality is the metaphorical imagining processes of the psyche. What is outside the psyche and its imaginal reality, one cannot really say. Thus, although archetypal psychology transcended the anthropocentrism and, most especially, the egocentrism, of the modern psyche, because of Hillman's outright rejection of metaphysics it has in effect left intact the more fundamental Cartesian dichotomy between self and world, psyche and cosmos, upon which both depth and archetypal psychology were implicitly founded. The psyche is rich with metaphorical resonance, full of soul, the source of all our perceptions of the world, but, lacking an explicit metaphysical framework, it is not exactly clear just how the psyche is actually related to the world.[26] To his credit, Hillman realized that "something further was needed" and that archetypal psychology should not continue to ignore the cosmological context, metaphysical assumptions, and world-relatedness it presupposed.[27] What is needed, Hillman conceded, is a "psychological cosmology" that addresses the relationship of archetypal psychology (and its therapeutic applications) to its deeper cosmological or metaphysical ground.[28]

While he followed Jung in championing the archetypal dimension of the psyche, Hillman adopted a critical stance towards other major elements of Jung's work, such as the concepts of the Self (the center, totality, and integrative capacity of the psyche) and individuation (the process of deep psychological transformation leading to wholeness and the conscious realization of the Self), believing that these concepts supported the monotheistic and linear-developmental perspectives that Hillman was so critical of and eschewed. Both these concepts are, however, extremely significant for archetypal cosmology.

The implications of synchronistic phenomena and astrological correlations suggest that the Self might be construed not only as the center and totality of the individual psyche, but as something like the organizing and integrative principle of a universal unconscious or cosmic psyche. "The Self is not only in me," Jung famously declared, "but in all beings, like Atman, like Tao."[29] Like Atman, the Self is something like an individualized manifestation of the spiritual ground called Brahman in Hinduism; like Tao, the Self is akin to a principle of cosmological order, dynamic harmony, and integration. As a unifying integrating principle of the universal unconscious, it is the Self that appears to underlie and orchestrate the correspondence between the planetary movements and the archetypal dynamics of human experience, impelling the evolution of human consciousness through the medium of the cosmological archetypes much as on a personal level the Self serves as an integrating and transforming teleological principle within the individual psyche. An evolutionary or developmental perspective of this kind is fundamental to archetypal cosmology. For although the orbits of the planets ostensibly describe cyclical patterns of recurrence over time, the archetypal principles associated with the planets also appear to have teleological potentials, possessing an inherent goal-directedness and evolutionary character, moving human consciousness towards wholeness and self-realization. Archetypal cosmology (particularly transit analysis), by enabling one to map the qualitative and thematic changes in human experience, can therefore serve to illuminate the dynamics of both individuation and the evolution of cultural history. "The specificity of detail and cyclical patterning [provided by transit analysis]," as Tarnas concludes in *Cosmos and Psyche*, "radically enhances our understanding of cultural evolution as a vast historical development that is shaped by dynamic archetypal forces, powers that move within a collective psyche that is in turn rooted in and expressive of a cosmic ground."[30]

Meanwhile, at the same time as Hillman was developing archetypal psychology in the 1960s and 1970s, Czech psychiatrist Stanislav Grof was developing transpersonal psychology. Emerging out of the psychoanalytic tradition that included the ideas and therapeutic modalities developed by Freud, Jung, Alfred Adler, Otto Rank, Wilhelm Reich, and others, Grof had pioneered his own experiential psychotherapy based on the powerful healing and heuristic potentials of non-ordinary states of consciousness. These non-ordinary states, which are induced either by psychoactive substances or through accelerated breathing techniques, or which arise spontaneously during psycho-spiritual crises, provide access to progressively deeper dimensions of the unconscious within which what Grof called the perinatal domain (relating to the psychodynamics and unconscious memories of the trauma of birth) seems to be pivotal. Yet the self-exploration of the unconscious is not limited to individual biography or the birth experience. Rather, Grof found that in non-ordinary states of consciousness one can gain access to what appear to be memories of historical, collective, cross-cultural, karmic, phylogenetic, and evolutionary events. Furthermore, these memories seem to be organized archetypally and thematically in such a way that traumatic experiences from one's own biography, for example, are connected to qualitatively and archetypally similar experiences from our collective past. Deep psychological self-exploration in holotropic states, Grof discovered, provides firsthand experience of the reality of a universal, mythic-archetypal unconscious, thereby providing direct support for archetypal cosmology. As a result of his extensive research into holotropic states, Grof now sees ego-consciousness and the human psyche "as expressions and reflections of a cosmic intelligence that permeates the entire universe and all of existence."[31]

Working together at Esalen Institute in California, where they came into contact with astrological practitioners, Grof and Tarnas began to explore whether astrology could be used to help understand the widely varying non-ordinary states of consciousness arising during experiential therapy sessions. Despite their initial skepticism, to their astonishment they found that personal transit analysis was a reliable method of illuminating the archetypal themes, stages, and experiences encountered during these sessions, far surpassing in accuracy and predictive power all other forms of psychological diagnostics. Encouraged by this successful application of astrology, Tarnas then turned his attention to the wider culture, applying methods of astrological analysis and interpretation to the study of biographies and world history. And so began his thirty-year astrological voyage of discovery in which Tarnas conducted a systematic study of thousands of individual charts and the major events and periods of world history, culminating in the publication of his groundbreaking *Cosmos and Psyche*.

Drawing on the understanding of archetypes from depth psychology, Tarnas effectively connected the mythic and archetypal patterns in psychology, history, art, and culture identified by Jung, Hillman, Joseph Campbell, and others to the fundamental universal archetypal principles recognized in astrology, which, Tarnas's research confirmed, are consistently correlated with the movements and alignments of the planets. The astrological research suggested to him that these archetypal principles, which have been described in various ways throughout the history of Western thought, are not, as the modern mind had assumed, wholly nominalistic, intrapsychic factors. They are not just categories of the human psyche unconsciously projected onto a separate external reality as Jung had thought in the early and middle periods of his career; rather, as in Jung's later formulation of the psychoid character of the archetype *per se*, they are creative powers inherent in the nature of reality itself—metaphysical and cosmological principles, as well as ordering factors and archetypal images in the psyche. Archetypal cosmology thus links the insights of depth psychology to the metaphysical and mythological foundations of the ancient Greeks and in so doing provides a cosmological context to depth psychology. By bringing together Jung's reflections on synchronicity and the nature of archetypes, Hillman's archetypal vision and his commitment to archetypal plurality, and Grof's expanded cartography of the psyche—and combining this with the evidence from his own extensive research—Tarnas has presented the astrological perspective in a radically different light, finding in this long-discredited ancient symbolic system something of great value to the postmodern mind, something that could, potentially, radically transform our understanding of the nature of the universe itself.

And so, having been rediscovered first as psychological factors in the human psyche, the archetypes, through this new approach to astrology, are recovering their cosmological status as something like the *archai*—the cosmological archetypal forms—of the Greek philosophical vision. As what appear to be both the ground principles of the psyche and the formative cosmological processes in the universe-at-large, the *archai* represent fundamental mythic-archetypal forms, styles, and dynamisms informing all experience, shaping both the world and human consciousness. And the human unconscious, having been conceived first as a layer within the encapsulated individual psyche, now, on the evidence of astrology and synchronicity, seems to be embedded in something like an *anima mundi* or cosmic psyche—the interiority of the cosmos itself. It is these two concepts—cosmological archetypes and the *anima mundi*—that are the primary focus of archetypal cosmology.

Like the psychoanalytic movement a century ago, archetypal cosmology is certain to provoke disparaging reactions from some quarters and outright dismissal from others. Yet, as with psychoanalysis, perhaps it too is a necessary corrective to the one-sidedness and limitations of the contemporary world view, a response to the evolutionary imperatives of our own time. Perhaps archetypal cosmology and the astrological perspective upon which it is based can now help to heal the damaging dichotomy between the psyche and the cosmos that has defined the modern world view. And perhaps, in time, a deeper understanding of archetypal cosmology can lead us out of the disenchanted cosmology of the modern era and help us to recognize, as the Greeks did, a living universe imbued with archetypal meaning and significance.

Notes

[1] Ernest Jones, *The Life and Work of Sigmund Freud*, ed. Lionel Trilling and Steven Marcus (New York: Basic Books, 1961), 243. As is well known, Freud compared the revolution he launched in psychology to the Copernican revolution in astronomy in that both served to undermine and deflate humanity's self-image. The Copernican revolution is, of course, the paradigmatic example of a scientific-philosophical development that provoked resistance and derisive scorn on its first presentation to the intellectual community.

[2] Freud described the id as "a cauldron full of seething excitations." See Sigmund Freud, *New Introductory Lectures on Psychoanalysis*, Standard Edition, trans. James Strachey (1933; repr., New York: Norton & Company, 1965), 84.

[3] See Thomas Kuhn, *The Structure of Scientific Revolutions*, 3rd edition (Chicago: University of Chicago Press, 1996).

4 The term *world transit* was first coined by Stanislav Grof during his research into astrology with Richard Tarnas at Esalen institute in the 1970s.

[5] Archetypal astrological research as represented by Tarnas's *Cosmos and Psyche* and in the *Archai* journal is not primarily concerned with the other major components of traditional astrological practice, such as the characteristics of the signs of the zodiac, the houses in the horoscope, rulership, and other

related factors. Rather, the focus is predominantly on the planets, their cyclical alignments, and the corresponding archetypal dynamics.

[6] Each planet, as it orbits the Sun, changes its position relative to the Earth. These changing positions are precisely measured by tracking the movement of the planets around the Earth using, as a line of reference, what is known as the ecliptic. Over the course of a year, the Sun appears to move across the constellations of the fixed stars, circumambulating the Earth, and the ecliptic is the circular line based on the Sun's apparent movement. As the planets continue along their orbits, their relative positions on the ecliptic change and they form different geometric alignments with each other. It is this changing pattern of planetary relationships that is studied in astrology in order to understand the changing relationships between the archetypal principles associated with the planets. To know how we are related to the planets at a moment in time gives us insight into how we are related to the different archetypal principles these planets represent.

The major aspects recognized in the astrological tradition are the conjunction (two or more planets approximately 0 degrees apart), the sextile (60 degrees), the square (90 degrees), the trine (120 degrees), and the opposition (180 degrees). Of these, Tarnas found that the quadrature alignments—the conjunction, the opposition, and the square—are usually the most significant in terms of understanding both world events and the major themes of individual biography. In the astrological tradition, these alignments are considered to be dynamic, "hard," or challenging in that they signify relationships between the archetypal principles that generally require some form of adaptation or considerable exertion or struggle to integrate, that tend to promote action to release the inherent energetic tension between the archetypal principles, and that are, therefore, often seen as most problematic or challenging, if ultimately creative and progressive. The trine and sextile, by contrast, are deemed "soft," harmonious, or confluent aspects in that they tend to indicate a relatively well-established, already integrated, mutually supportive, and harmonious relationship between the archetypal principles. At the risk of over-simplification, one can think of the soft aspects as already integrated states of being and the hard aspects as dynamic states of becoming that require integration.

[7] See Richard Tarnas, *Cosmos and Psyche: Intimations of a New World View* (New York: Viking, 2006), 141–205.

[8] Tarnas, personal communication.

[9] Tarnas, *Cosmos and Psyche*, 128.

[10] Tarnas, *Cosmos and Psyche*, 87.

[11] Tarnas, *Cosmos and Psyche*, 73–75 and 86.

[12] Tarnas, *Cosmos and Psyche*, 16–25. See also Richard Tarnas, *The Passion of the Western Mind: Understanding the Ideas That Have Shaped Our World View* (1991; repr., New York: Ballantine, 1993), 416–422; for his discussion of the

ramifications of the Copernican revolution, Cartesian ontology, Kantian epistemology, and Darwinian evolutionary biology for the modern understanding of the human being's place in the cosmos.

[13] See Friedrich Nietzsche, *The Gay Science, With a Prelude in Rhymes and Appendix of Songs* (1887), trans. Walter Kaufmann (New York: Random House, 1974), 181; and Friedrich Nietzsche, *Thus Spoke Zarathustra* (1885), trans. Reginald J. Hollingdale (London: Penguin, 1969), 41.

[14] C. G. Jung, "Commentary on the Secret of the Golden Flower" (1929), in *Alchemical Studies, Collected Works*, vol. 13, trans. R. F. C. Hull (Princeton: Princeton University Press, 1968), 1–56.

[15] C. G. Jung, *The Archetypes and the Collective Unconscious*, trans. R. F. C. Hull (Princeton: Princeton University Press, 1968), 23, par. 50.

[16] C. G. Jung, *Memories, Dreams, Reflections* (1961), trans. Richard and Clara Winston (London: Flamingo, 1983), 420.

[17] Liliane Frey-Rohn, *From Freud to Jung: A Comparative Study of the Psychology of the Unconscious*, trans. Fred Engreen and Evelyn Engreen (New York: Delta, 1974), 96.

[18] These descriptions are taken from various volumes of *The Collected Works of C. G Jung*, Bollingen Series XX, trans. R. F. C. Hull (Princeton: Princeton University Press, 1953–1979).

[19] "Within the limits of psychic experience," Jung proposed, "the collective unconscious takes the place of the Platonic realm of eternal Ideas. Instead of these models giving form to created things, the collective unconscious, through its archetypes, provides the a priori condition for the assignment of meaning." See C. G. Jung, *Mysterium Coniunctionis*, 2nd ed., 1955–1956, trans. R. F. C. Hull (Princeton: Princeton University Press, 1989), 87. What is in question here is exactly what the "limits of psychic experience" are. If the psyche, as Jung suggested elsewhere, rests on a transcendental background and is fundamentally connected to nature and the external world, then Jung's theory of archetypes and the collective unconscious, in its later formulation, is closer to the Platonic position than has generally been assumed. This implication is strongly reinforced by Jung's observations of synchronistic phenomena.

[20] Jung, *Memories, Dreams, Reflections,* 418–419.

[21] Jung, *Mysterium Coniunctionis*, 537–538.

[22] For an exploration of Jung's concept of the archetype *per se* or archetype-as-such, see Frey-Rohn, *From Freud to Jung*, 281–299.

[23] C. G. Jung, *On the Nature of the Psyche* (1954), trans. R. F. C. Hull (London: Routledge, 2004), 101–102 and 110–111.

[24] See James Hillman, *Re-Visioning Psychology* (1975; repr. New York: HarperPerennial, 1992).

[25] Murray Stein, "Spiritual and Religious Aspects of Modern Analysis," in *Analytical Psychology: Contemporary Perspectives in Jungian Analysis (Advancing Theory*

in Therapy), ed. Joseph Cambray and Linda Carter (New York: Brunner-Routledge, 2004), 211.

26 For a discussion of Hillman's antipathy towards metaphysics, see David. R. Griffin, "Archetypal Psychology and Process Philosophy: Complementary Postmodern Movements," in *Archetypal Process: Self and Divine in Whitehead, Jung, and Hillman,* ed. David. R. Griffin (Evanston, IL: Northwestern University Press, 1990), 63–72.

27 See Hillman's essay "Back to Beyond: On Cosmology," in *Archetypal Process,* ed. Griffin (Evanston, IL: Northwestern University Press, 1990), 213–231.

28 Hillman, "Back to Beyond," 220.

29 C. G. Jung, "Good and Evil in Analytical Psychology" (1959), in *Civilization in Transition, Collected Works,* vol. 10, 463.

30 Tarnas, *Cosmos and Psyche,* 204.

31 Stanislav Grof with Hal Z. Bennett, *The Holotropic Mind* (San Francisco: Harper Publications, 1992), 18.

V

Archetypal Astrological Research:
A Response to John Heron's Commentary on
Cosmos and Psyche

In a forceful critique of Richard Tarnas's *Cosmos and Psyche,* published in the Scientific and Medical Network's journal, the *Network Review,* of winter 2007, participatory researcher John Heron calls into question the methodology employed by Tarnas in his study of world transits and thus challenges the validity of the book's central thesis: that there is a correlation between planetary alignments and archetypal patterns of human experience.[1] However, although Heron raises some valuable and stimulating points that invite elaboration and clarification of the methodology and assumptions informing archetypal astrology, I believe his critique is seriously compromised, and ultimately invalidated, by certain crucial misunderstandings and misrepresentations of Tarnas's work. Here I attempt to highlight these and to briefly respond to the various points raised. In the interests of consistency and intelligibility, I have stayed as far as possible within the structure of Heron's commentary, adopting his headings and subheadings to present my responses.

A. World Transit Correlations with Historical Data

A.1 Doubts about World Transit Reliability

From the outset, Heron's critique is built on a misrepresentation of Tarnas's position. Heron interprets Tarnas as saying that personal transits and natal aspects are "statistically unreliable" when in fact Tarnas says nothing of the sort. Tarnas simply makes the point that the study of world transits (as opposed to personal transits) can "more easily lend itself to critical assessments and historical comparisons" because cultural history as compared to individual biography tends to be "more widely known, better documented, and open to more straightforward evaluation."(137)[2] Tarnas chooses to focus on world transits and biographies of culturally prominent individuals because in so doing readers are better able to assess for themselves whether such correlations are indeed valid. It is not that personal transits and aspects in individual birth charts are unreliable, just that world transits, because of their more conspicuous public nature, are better suited for this kind of study.

A Tubful in the Ocean

Heron claims that Tarnas's analysis is too selective and too limited in its scope to establish the validity of world transits: "In order to secure any kind of validity for the world transit theory, you would need to apply the same world transits to a large number of different historical traditions at different periods in different parts of the planet." While any analysis would obviously be more complete by including more data, the period of world history actually covered in *Cosmos and Psyche* is immense, stretching from the beginning of the Axial Age in the sixth century BCE to the present day, and treating in considerable detail many aspects of the cultural histories of Britain, France, Germany, Italy, the U.S., medieval Europe, and ancient Greece and Rome. Although Tarnas readily acknowledges his primary focus is on the recorded history of the West, his analysis, particularly of more recent periods, also encompasses events occurring in many other parts of the world including China, Japan, India, the Middle East, and Latin America. Needless to say, a consensus on world transits arrived at through comparative studies by scholars of different cultures could only strengthen Tarnas's case (indeed he explicitly invites collaboration from historians of other traditions), but by itself the evidence set forth in *Cosmos and Psyche* presents a strong case for the transcultural nature of the archetypal principles and correlations.

While Tarnas's survey of world history is unavoidably selective both geographically and historically, Heron doesn't provide even one example of where he thinks Tarnas's selection might have distorted the analysis. It is true that transit analysis illuminates themes and patterns that might otherwise go unnoticed, but Tarnas is hardly being creative in his marshalling of historical data; his representation of the different historical periods is decidedly not controversial or unorthodox. Indeed, to provide corroboration of his archetypal interpretation of specific periods or events, Tarnas often quotes from primary sources, giving firsthand accounts from individuals central to the cultural events under examination who were, we can safely assume, writing without any awareness of astrological cycles. Of course, one can always call into question the impartiality and completeness of historical records themselves, but many scholars agree that the data Tarnas examines, much of which is relatively recent, is accurately representative of the major occurrences of the different periods of history.

Heron also takes issue with the fact that the body of research in *Cosmos and Psyche* comes, as he puts it, from just "one man, without any quoted agreement from anyone else" to support "innumerable interpretations." Tarnas's study lacks credibility, Heron implies, because it doesn't draw on the work of other astrologers. In response to this, let us be clear, first, that it is simply wrong to suggest that Tarnas was working alone. In fact, he makes a point of stating that *Cosmos and Psyche* is a "collaborative work" (545) that has emerged out of thirty years' research undertaken with many other researchers and scholars, and that benefited from the efforts of over fifty advance readers including several of the world's most distinguished astrologers such as Charles Harvey, long-time president of the British Astrological Association, and Robert Hand, the dean of American astrologers.

Second, although Tarnas doesn't directly quote other astrological texts, each interpretation of the transits is, as he points out, based on the established meanings of the planetary archetypes—meanings that have been independently identified and empirically ratified by countless other astrologers. While astrologers often differ on the specifics of interpretation (for reasons I later address)—just as happens in any other field such as quantum physics, anthropology, or medicine—there is virtually universal consensus among contemporary astrologers as to the basic meanings of the planets, and Tarnas's analysis reflects this.

Finally, and most significant, Tarnas is effectively pioneering a new method and approach to astrology based on an understanding of the archetypal nature of the planetary principles. His is the first major study of its kind, one in which he attempts to lay the foundations for future research that might further develop this new method of *archetypal historiography*, as it has been called.[3] Moving beyond the conceptual limits of conventional astrology, which has tended to be more literal and concretely predictive in its approach, Tarnas has deepened the philosophical and interpretive precision of the astrological archetypal perspective by drawing from the depth and transpersonal psychology of

C. G. Jung, James Hillman, and Stanislav Grof.

One Combination at a Time

A major element of Heron's overall critique is based on what he calls *dissociation*—the idea that an analysis of a single two-planet alignment independently of all other planetary alignments dissociates the analysis from its context in a distorting way. Heron argues that by focusing on two-planet combinations in isolation Tarnas sacrifices the adequacy and accuracy of his analysis in favor of simplicity and clarity. He claims "if all the many concurrent planetary aspects are taken into account then identifying correlations with historical events becomes more obscure and problematic" and that restricting attention to two-planet combinations is likely to lead to "pseudo-correlations."

What Heron doesn't seem to appreciate here, however, is that greater complexity doesn't mean greater obscurity. It doesn't follow that just because the analysis becomes more complex when it includes three or four archetypal principles rather than two that it will therefore be more "obscure and problematic." In fact, the greater complexity of considering multiple archetypal principles actually affords greater, more nuanced archetypal precision. This is evident where Tarnas gives examples in which he does discuss the combination of more than two planetary principles. When, for instance, he examines the three planet alignment of Jupiter, Uranus, and Pluto of the late 1960s, it is possible to discern how during specific months and years the presence of Jupiter (the archetypal principle of expansion, amplification, and successful culmination) gave a distinctive inflection to the longer-term sequences of events characteristic of the Uranus-Pluto combination that were evident throughout the entire decade, such as powerful rebellious and revolutionary impulses, technological empowerment, and mass freedom movements. Thus, in 1968–69, when Jupiter joined Uranus and Pluto in a triple conjunction, there occurred, Tarnas notes, "the peak and full amplitude of the decade's characteristic events" as the Jupiter principle expanded, brought to successful fruition, and gave a breadth of cultural expression to the Uranus-Pluto themes: the protest movement was at its most widespread, a series of unprecedented mass music festivals including Woodstock took place, and, perhaps most notably, the triumphant culmination of the space program with the Apollo moon landing in 1969 brought a sudden, dramatic expansion of horizons on a mass scale. (303–304) We can see here, then, that the introduction of the third archetypal principle, although presenting a more difficult interpretative challenge, actually yields greater archetypal precision and, ultimately, brings greater clarity to the interpretation.

Furthermore, just because an analysis is "*more adequate*" if it includes more archetypal combinations, it doesn't follow that the analysis of two-planet archetypal complexes by itself is therefore *inadequate*. Heron contends that an adequate analysis would have to incorporate not only outer planet aspects, but also aspects of the inner planets (Mercury, Venus, and Mars) and the luminaries (the Sun and the Moon). Failure to include these, he claims, can distort the interpretation of outer planet transits. Obviously if one takes into account all the given aspects occurring at a particular time, one would expect to arrive at a more comprehensive understanding of that period. We must keep in mind, though, that not all transits are of equal weight and significance. The transits of the outer planets, often lasting for periods of several years, are of far greater import than the more fleeting transits of the luminaries and the inner planets whose activated influence is usually restricted to a few days. It is well established in astrology that the major outer-planet cycles are connected with more profound, more enduring changes in human affairs. The shorter transits provide greater definition without radically altering the overall archetypal picture. Thus, in the above example, to know that Uranus and Pluto were in dynamic alignment in the late 1960s is highly illuminating, revealing much about the archetypal energy, feel, and events of that era. Incorporating the shorter Jupiter cycle simply adds greater definition and archetypal clarity to our understanding of the main Uranus-Pluto themes.

Another related point Heron raises in this section concerns the range of meanings associated with the different planetary archetypes. Heron cites a review by astrologer Gary Phillipson who claims that Tarnas stretches the established meaning of the planetary archetypes to "breaking point and beyond." Heron seems only too willing to accept Phillipson's assessment, later describing what he sees as "the astrologically dubious and stretched use of only two planetary principles" in Tarnas's book.

The Phillipson remark is based primarily on a passage in which Tarnas discusses the Uranus-Neptune conjunction of 1985 to 2001 and its connection with heightened religiosity and a shift towards more pluralistic, individualistic forms of spirituality. Although there were many positive consequences of this world transit, more problematically it also gave rise to "many New Age infatuations and eccentric cult movements while simultaneously inspiring and bolstering fundamentalist fanaticisms in many religions throughout the world." (427) One particular and pervasive instance of this was the "widespread evangelical Christian revival in the United States, which," Tarnas notes, "often took the political form of an unreflective reactionary conservatism." (428)

It is to this last phrase that Phillipson objects: "No matter how I put Uranus and Neptune together," he explains, "I don't end up with reactionary conservatism." Quite so, but Tarnas's analysis of the Uranus-Neptune world transit is not intended to account for the evangelical Christian movement's reactionary conservatism (which is typically associated with the Saturn principle), but rather to illustrate that this too is one among many instances of the more radical and pervasive pluralism of the contemporary spiritual environment. Evangelical Christianity relates to the Uranus-Neptune complex in its focus on direct spiritual awakening, revelatory shifts of consciousness, a kind of religious radicalism, its polarized reaction to secular modernity, its idiosyncratic eccentricity, and in that it is one of the multifarious forms of spirituality that became more prominent and charged during that time.

For Heron this confusion on Phillipson's part no doubt provides further confirmation of the research studies he cites suggesting "there is no significant agreement among astrologers about the interpretation of the same astrological configurations." However, beyond such interpretative confusions—of which there have been many, I am sure—there is a deeper reason for the differences in interpretation proffered by different astrologers for the same astrological factors: the failure to adequately recognize and understand the archetypal nature of astrology. Without the fundamental recognition that astrology is, in Tarnas's words, "not concretely predictive but rather archetypally predictive," (128) astrologers have tended to associate planetary alignments, signs, houses, and so forth with specific concrete particulars, or with certain unchanging character traits, or they have used astrology to make definite, literal predictions—an approach that Tarnas rightly eschews.

With a proper recognition of the archetypal multivalence underlying astrology, one can see that it is perfectly possible for two astrologers to give different interpretations of the same planetary configuration that are equally valid in that they both coherently reflect the underlying archetypal meanings of the planets involved. Tarnas himself gives many examples of this multivalence at work, and this is one of the distinctive theoretical contributions of the book. A statistical analysis of astrologers' interpretations that fails to take into account the archetypal nature of the planetary alignments will be inadequate, noticing only surface differences rather than the underlying themes connecting ostensibly dissimilar behavior patterns. As Tarnas stresses, to properly understand and assess astrological correlations one must cultivate what James Hillman called the "archetypal eye," which is "the imaginative intelligence…that is capable of recognizing and discriminating the rich multiplicity of archetypal patterns" (70) in both individual biography and world history.

The final charge Heron levels at Tarnas in this section is that of reductionism, again relating to the analysis involving single pairs of planetary archetypes. He claims: "The integrity of a culture is disrespected when the multifaceted richness of its representative people, products and events is repeatedly reduced to interpretation in terms of only two categories." This would be true if the archetypal categories were fixed and predetermined, and if they reproduced themselves blindly and mechanically in different circumstances and time periods. However, as Tarnas is at pains to stress, the planetary archetypes are multi-dimensional and multivalent creative principles, which, although thematically consistent, give rise to a potentially limitless range of forms of concrete expression. The aim of archetypal analysis is not to squeeze experiences into predefined categories of meaning or to reduce the uniqueness and integrity of cultural history to fixed interpretations, but rather to allow each event and experience to illuminate the archetypal dynamics in potentially unique and novel ways, perhaps, in the process, deepening our understanding of the archetypal categories themselves. There is no forced imposition of meaning here; rather our understanding of the archetypal principles is open to further elaboration by exploring how they manifest in different cultures and in different historical periods. In a hermeneutic circle, the archetypal analysis illuminates the historical data, and the historical data reveals how the archetypal dynamics were expressed in a particular cultural-historical context. Archetypal analysis is intrinsically anti-reductionist.

Eminence as Evidence

Heron insists that Tarnas's focus on culturally eminent individuals as paradigmatic examples of archetypal complexes amounts to a "curious elitist doctrine" in which, from an astrological perspective, the experience of ordinary individuals becomes irrelevant. However, just because more culturally eminent individuals are more "conspicuous embodiments of archetypal tendencies" (136) it doesn't follow from this that, as Heron claims, "the less eminent you are, the weaker the astrological effect." Eminent individuals exhibit archetypal characteristics more conspicuously not because the archetypal influence applies only or more powerfully to them than to less well-known people, but because they have been able to harness and express their archetypal inheritance in a more influential way, usually having a more profound bearing on the historical process.

Far from being elitist, astrology implies that we all partake in the same basic set of archetypal dynamics. To the extent that the archetypal principles can potentially be consciously engaged with by any individual, astrology is in fact inherently democratic. There is no cultural elite to which astrology exclusively applies; it applies to everyone.

A.2 The Problem of Eurocentrism

As we have seen, Heron calls into question Tarnas's claim that planetary archetypes are transcultural—that they are applicable to the entire world and not just to Western civilization. He argues that because the planetary archetypes originated from and are named after Greco-Roman deities, the archetypal categories are rooted in a "Eurocentric mythology" and that they therefore support a "Eurocentric archetypal hegemony."

Heron is laboring here under some basic misconceptions. First, the historical source of the meanings of the planets is actually Mesopotamian, rooted in many centuries of Babylonian and Chaldean observations, and the Greeks subsequently named the planets according to the mythic equivalents in their own tradition. Second, although the planetary archetypes in contemporary Western astrology are associated with certain gods of the Greco-Roman tradition, they are not exclusively identified with them. The planetary archetypes reflect the characteristics of many different deities from many of the world's traditions. They are more general principles of which the mythic gods and goddesses are more specific derivations or inflections. Archetypal characteristics associated with the planets are evident in human lives across all cultures: love, beauty, courage, time, death, growth, limitation, transformation, sacrifice, freedom. The archetypal principles at this more general level transcend their anthropomorphic and theriomorphic inflections as mythic deities in any one cultural tradition. Moreover, as Tarnas emphasizes, the planetary archetypes are at once transcendent (Platonic-Pythagorean), psychological (Jungian), and mythic. (86) They are not to be conceived merely as interior psychological principles that are unconsciously projected onto the planets, but rather as dynamic cosmological principles informing both the inner and outer dimensions of reality, both psyche and cosmos.

The final theoretical issue I will address in this section concerns astrology's apparent dependence on a seemingly outmoded and discredited geocentric model of the solar system. Heron points out that Tarnas draws upon astrological principles "which all originated in the era of geocentric astronomy and its Aristotelio-Ptolemaic worldview." Therefore, because the solar system is not geocentric, it would seem that archetypal astrology must be invalid. This, of course, is one of the central points of repudiation of astrology advanced by many scientists and skeptics in the modern era with the recognition that the solar system is actually heliocentric.

In fact, however, there is nothing in the astrological perspective employed in *Cosmos and Psyche* that contradicts the reality of a heliocentric solar system. Indeed, both Galileo and Kepler were practicing astrologers and saw no contradiction between their heliocentric and astrological convictions. Just because the Earth appears to be a focus of cosmic meaning does not imply it cannot move in an orbit around the Sun.

Moreover, the view of the universe that has now emerged, first out of relativity theory, and later confirmed in cosmology, is that all measurements of space and time are relative to the observer, and that human beings are inextricably bound to their own perspectives. It is impossible, that is, to adopt an objective vantage point outside of one's subjectivity from which to perceive the universe. Therefore, although the geocentric model has been discredited as an objectively valid cosmology, phenomenologically speaking it retains a certain validity in that we are always inescapably centered in our viewpoint with regard to the universe. Ancient astronomers, as cosmologist Joel Primack explains, "were wrong astronomically that the Earth is the centre of the universe, but they were right psychologically: the universe must be viewed from the inside, from our centre, where we really are, and not from some perspective on the periphery or even outside." (133) Thus understood, the astrological perspective, which uses charts centered on specific individuals or locations on Earth, is actually in agreement with the modern cosmological conception of an omnicentric universe. We are all in a sense centers of the universe, and astrology reflects this. Furthermore, despite the immense vistas disclosed by recent telescopic exploration of space, which makes astrology's focus on the solar system seem decidedly provincial, it remains the case, of course, that the cycles of the planets in our solar system define our immediate cosmological vicinity. Centered in our own perspective, we live and breathe here on Earth in the context, first and foremost, of our own solar system.

A.3 The Absence of Rigorous Curiosity

Attachment to the Glasses and Archetypal Intoxication

Turning again to the question of methodology, Heron claims that Tarnas doesn't look for counter-evidence that might falsify his theory, in that he doesn't try to find "events that fit the archetypal qualities of an aspect but fall outside its range of influence." Heron seems to be implying here that if, for example, one were to find events fitting the Uranus-Pluto archetypal complex outside of the period when that transit is supposed to be operative (i.e., in orb) then this would invalidate the transit theory. Now if Tarnas were claiming that the world only experiences Uranus-Pluto type events when the two planets are in aspect then Heron's critique would indeed be to the point. However, this is not what Tarnas is actually saying. The hypothesis advanced by Tarnas is this: World transits correspond with periods of more pronounced and more readily discernible events that reflect the constellated archetypes in which there is a concentrated activation of themes associated with those particular archetypal principles. It is not that transits correspond with sets of discrete events in time that suddenly stop once a transit has passed out of orb. In his research, Tarnas discovered that the "characteristic historical events and cultural trends" associated with specific world transits were not "suddenly turned on and then off, when the transit was over, like bivalent light switches," but that these themes "continued to unfold in diverse ways in subsequent years and decades after the alignment was over." Thus, it is perfectly possible—indeed it is to be expected—that one will observe the continuation of certain trends outside the periods when an alignment is in aspect. In a helpful analogy, Tarnas suggests that transits are better conceived as "fluidly interpenetrating quantum wave patterns" rather than "discrete atomistic Newtonian events." It is fundamental to the understanding of what he calls the *diachronic* patterning of human experience that the past is continually active in shaping the present. World transits show periods of intensification and heightened activation of continuing streams and waves of archetypal energies. Of course, if one found little or no evidence of the relevant activated archetypes in world affairs when the corresponding planets *were* in alignment, then one would be right to call into question the validity of astrological transit theory. But, in fact, what makes Tarnas's research so persuasive is that again and again the planetary alignments he lists do indeed correlate with concentrated clusters of experiences and events that unmistakably fit the meaning of the corresponding planetary archetypes.

Keeping within the Faith and the Temptation of Self-rescue

Heron contends that "the function of anomalous data is simply to alert Tarnas to his deficient astrological know-how" and that Tarnas is therefore unwilling to call into question the overall validity of astrology. Heron argues, moreover, that the inherent complexities of astrology "make it so rich in persuasive forms of self-rescue and self-protection" that one can always find some astrological factor to account for seemingly anomalous data and thus explain away any discrepancies. While this is a legitimate concern, given the plethora of factors regularly employed in the practice of conventional astrology, what is distinctive about Tarnas's approach is that he restricts his attention to the study of the major planetary alignments, ignoring a host of other factors such as signs, houses, angles, elements, and so on, thereby eliminating many potential paths of "self-rescue." As Tarnas says, the events of world history "either obviously fit the postulated archetypal meanings [of the planetary aspects], or they do not." (137) By ignoring much of the often confusing complexity of astrological theory, the strategy of focusing on two- or three-planet combinations thus makes Tarnas's hypothesis more falsifiable. It eliminates many avenues of "escape" by which one might explain away contradictory data.

B. World Transits in the Present and the Future

B.1 The Issue of Upcoming Transits

A Plethora Ahead and the Disappearance of Single Aspect Analysis

Heron suggests that the "veritable plethora" of concurrent transits that have been in aspect during 2007 and 2008 makes it an impossible and ultimately futile task to conduct any kind of meaningful and reliable transit analysis for this period. In particular, he objects to what he sees as a change of tactic by Tarnas: a shift from single-aspect analysis of the past to multiple-aspect analysis of the future.

I must confess that I just cannot see why Heron has a problem with Tarnas's "Observations on Future Planetary Alignments" as, contrary to Heron's claim, Tarnas continues to discuss alignments in exactly the same way as he did throughout the book for world transits in the past. Although Tarnas does indeed note that the overlapping Saturn-Neptune and Uranus-Pluto combinations "could scarcely be more different in character," (479) he actually analyses them quite separately, dealing with Saturn-Neptune on pages 469–478, and Uranus-Pluto on pages 468 and 479–481. There is no "disappearance of single aspect analysis" here. The "complexity theory" Tarnas calls for is simply an acknowledgment that when dealing with future archetypal trends one must be particularly cautious about making any predictions, even of the most general kind, without considering all the major archetypal factors. When analyzing the past, as no prediction is being made, one is obviously on safer ground when pointing out the major correlations with a single specific planetary cycle.

B.2 A Troubling Instability

In his provisional summary, Heron thinks he has identified a "troubling instability" in Tarnas's book. He argues that Tarnas simplifies transit analysis of the past by using two-planet combinations and yet calls for a "complexity theory" of transit analysis of the present and future involving multiple archetypal complexes. However, as we have seen, Heron mistakenly conflates obscurity with complexity; he fails to take into account the different weighting of transits and the actual relationship between outer and inner planet transits; he downplays or ignores the instances where Tarnas does engage in multiple-aspect transit analysis of the past, while he exaggerates Tarnas's use of multiple transit analysis of the future; and he doesn't seem to adequately comprehend the archetypal basis of astrological correlations. In sum, the trouble, it seems to me, lies not with Tarnas's work, but with Heron's interpretation of it.

B.3 The Issue of Indeterminacy and Unpredictability

Perhaps the most interesting theoretical questions raised in Heron's commentary concern the nature of participatory consciousness and its relationship to the archetypal dimension of reality, which he sets forth in the four subdivisions of B.3. I cannot hope to satisfactorily address this complex topic here, but I will comment briefly on what seems to me to be a further misconception of archetypal astrology in Heron's critique.

Tarnas's assertion that "a fundamental recognition of indeterminacy and unpredictability is the bedrock of the entire perspective articulated here" is deemed by Heron to be fallacious. He argues that Tarnas is actually promoting the view that human experience is inherently predictable and predetermined, governed by what Heron calls a "synchronous archetypal mechanism" that operates according to "cosmic clockwork." Heron then poses the following question, which he sees as fundamental to the entire debate:

> Is our primary co-creative access to psychocosmic patterns restricted to the natal aspects and endless multiple transits of the solar system clock? If the answer is affirmative, then this primary access of ours is predetermined and predictable to a very high degree indeed. The only thing that is indeterminate is the concrete outworking of the predetermined psychocosmic synchronicity.

There are several points one might take issue with in this section, but the main thing to keep in mind in this: To recognize the archetypal determinants behind human experience does not mean that human experience is predetermined. To say that human experience is conditioned by a set of archetypal factors that correlate with the planetary movements is in no way a constraint on human freedom because this freedom manifests at the level of enactment, not at the level of archetypal determination.

Human experience can be radically indeterminate and unpredictable at the level of concrete manifestation—the level at which human freedom of will can be exercised—and yet this indeterminacy occurs within an *a priori* thematic framework. The creative tension between this underlying thematic patterning and indeterminacy is the very essence of the relationship between universals and particulars. Human freedom of will is embedded within a background context of foundational but multivalent archetypal meanings. This archetypal context does not limit human freedom of choice, because this freedom is itself an archetypal pre-condition of human experience. That is to say, the impulse to be free, creative, and inventive is itself archetypal. Human freedom is not compromised by the archetypal perspective; it is based upon it.

Heron's choice of words in this section of his critique betrays what seems to me to be an erroneous understanding of the relationship between human conscious experience and the archetypal dimension of reality; it reflects what Jorge Ferrer has called subtle Cartesianism.[4] When Heron describes "human co-creative access to certain patterns of archetypes" this seems to imply that the "co-creative" human is a separate entity that accesses archetypes outside of itself, when in fact the nature of the human subject is itself constituted by these archetypal dynamics. It is not that there is a separate human subject who participates with archetypal factors external to itself; rather, the consciousness of the participating human is already shaped by the archetypal factors with which it participates. Participation goes both ways.

And when Heron writes of being able to "engage your creativity with this, that or the other predetermined configuration of archetypes," this reflects the inherent subtle anthropocentrism of his position: From an archetypal perspective, creativity is not owned by the individual human being ("your creativity"); rather, the human being partakes in the universe's creativity. Creativity is archetypally grounded. Archetypes do not have to be intentionally "accessed"; they are being lived by each of us at every moment of experience, whether consciously or unconsciously. To know about transits is to become more aware of how human subjective consciousness is partaking in the universe's archetypal dynamics.

Full or Partial Co-creativity?

Heron ends his critique by questioning what constitutes full participatory co-creativity. He argues that because human conscious "access" to archetypes is "predefined" in accordance with planetary transits then this imposes a limitation on human intentional freedom. Tarnas, Heron concludes, offers only a partial, restricted, and predetermined form of co-creative participation.

However, Heron's conception of full co-creative participation is limited if it does not recognize that the autonomy of the individual ego is supported and defined by the unconscious archetypal preconditions in which human life is inextricably embedded. Full participation is not the freedom to impose one's own intentional creativity on archetypal factors external to oneself. Rather, it consists in making conscious the set of archetypal dynamics that constitute one's very being, that are shaping one's life experience. The realization of true human freedom and autonomy depends upon making the archetypal dynamics conscious such that one is no longer unconsciously lived by them, but rather consciously participates in their expression. This is fundamental to the process of psycho-spiritual transformation that Jung called individuation. A deep engagement with archetypal astrology can further this transformation process. Knowing how one is related to the planets at a particular time enables one to better understand the archetypal dynamics that are prominent in shaping one's experience at that time.

Notes

[1] John Heron, "A commentary on Richard Tarnas' *Cosmos and Psyche,*" Network Review: Journal of the Scientific and Medical Network, No. 95, Winter 2007, pp 11–16.

[2] Richard Tarnas, *Cosmos and Psyche: Intimations of a New World View* (New York: Viking, 2006). Page numbers for quotations given in parentheses in the text.

[3] See Rod O'Neal, "Archetypal Historiography: A New Historical Approach," in *The Birth of a New Discipline, Archai: The Journal of Archetypal Cosmology,* Issue 1, Summer 2009 (Repr. San Francisco: Archai Press, 2011).

[4] See, Jorge Ferrer, *Revisioning Transpersonal Theory: A Participatory Vision of Human Spirituality* (Albany, NY: State University of New York Press, 2002).

VI

Jung's Explanations of Astrology: Introduction to Part IV of *Jung on Astrology*

Jung entertained multiple explanations of astrology. In the selections in Part IV of *Jung and Astrology*, we witness the shifts in his position as they unfold in response to material he read and to his own reflections and research. To aid comprehension, in that book his various hypotheses regarding astrology are arranged into separate chapters. The commentary that follows here offers some analysis of each hypothesis, drawing out the essential line of argument of the more complex theories. Jung pursues up to seven possible explanations, some overlapping and some contradictory.

1. The Sympathy of All Things. Astrology can be understood in terms of the classical and medieval principles of the "sympathy of all things" and a microcosm-macrocosm correspondence. These ideas, considered in Chapter 11 of *Jung on Astrology*, are extracted primarily from "Synchronicity: An Acausal Connecting Principle," which surveys a range of related ideas that support an astrological conception of the world, including ancient Greek philosophical speculation (Hippocrates, Philo, Theophrastus), Neoplatonism (Plotinus), Renaissance philosophy (Pico della Mirandola), alchemy and medieval natural philosophy (Zosimos, Paracelsus, Agrippa, Aegidius de Vadis), and Kepler's view of "astrological character."

It is an axiom of esoteric thought that the human being is a miniature version or reflection of the entire cosmos. The celestial heavens are deemed to exist within us all ("heaven . . . is infused into man the microcosm").[1] Similarly, classical and medieval thought posits bonds of sympathy linking disparate parts of the universe in a grand system of *correspondentia* connecting the human, worldly, and celestial—an idea captured by the statement "as above, so below." This correspondence ultimately rests in the unity of God or the *anima mundi* or *spiritus mundi* (the world soul and world spirit, respectively).

Jung presents these perspectives as essential background to his theory of synchronicity and to his research into astrology. "Synchronicity," he notes, "is a modern differentiation of the obsolete concept of correspondence, sympathy, and harmony."[2] Especially significant for Jung was the classical and medieval belief, also present in Chinese thought, that there are connections between discrete events and experiences that are not causal, in that there is no apparent causal chain linking them. Rather, such connections or correspondences are deemed by Jung to be acausal, existing in parallel with each other and connected solely by meaning. Regarding astrology, for example, if one were to express anger and assertive force at a time when the planet Mars (associated with the Greco-Roman god of war) is aligned with the sun in one's astrological chart, it would, on this view, not be due to any causal influence of the planet Mars, but on the "meaningful coincidence" of that planetary alignment with a psychological state or a constellation of archetypes in one's psyche.

2. Unconscious Projection. Astrology is a projection of the collective unconscious into the heavens. The practice of astrology might be understood as a symbolic system or perspective in which the planets represent the "gods," that is, the archetypes of the collective unconscious. This second hypothesis, covered in Chapter 12 of *Jung on Astrology*, is perhaps Jung's most consistent and oft-repeated position. Astrology, Jung claims, is a "complete projected theory of human character."[3] To a large extent, Jung is led to the conclusion that astrology is projected psychology by the consideration of the phenomenon of the precession of the equinoxes. Because the signs of the zodiac are no longer aligned with the constellations after which they were originally named, he reasons, there is no physical basis to the alleged influence of the signs on human life. The same line of argument does not necessarily apply to the planets, of course, for these obviously possess substantive physical existence, even though they exert no demonstrable causal influence on human life. Jung's concern here is primarily understanding the alleged influence of zodiacal signs and constellations (which he often refers to as the "stars"), but it is conceivable that the zodiacal signs might be explicable as a form of projected psychology while the astrology of the planets might be explicable in other terms.

Generalizing from his reflection on the signs, Jung concludes that the source of astrological meanings is not from the cosmos but from archetypes in the unconscious psyche, from the microcosm of the individual human being. That is, although astrologers might believe that the planets and signs are the determining factors shaping the human personality, what are taken to be celestial causes are really psychological ones. Just as alchemy is understood by Jung as a projection into the *prima materia* in the alchemical vessel of the psychological transformation process (individuation) occurring within the alchemist's psyche, so astrology is seen as a projection of the qualities and traits of the human personality into the heavens. In both cases, the implication is that the alchemist and astrologer were working under something of a delusion.

Over the centuries, in Jung's view, the increasing differentiation of the ego, the subject of experience, from the world, as object, made it possible to become more conscious of our psychological projections as we progressively left behind the primal condition of *participation mystique*, in which there is no clear distinction between the inner world of thoughts and emotions and external happenings in the environment. To the epistemologically naïve mind, Jung believes, inner and outer blur, or are not adequately distinguished, and psychological reality is mistakenly construed as cosmology or metaphysical reality—a critique Jung levels at theosophy, for instance. Modern science and psychology, Jung maintains, now enable us to recognize these projections for what they are and to withdraw them.

Jung does not address how his view of astrology as projection meshes with his explanations in terms of synchronicity and acausal correspondences. Nor does he attempt to reconcile projection with his numerous assertions that appear to contradict the Cartesian separation of the inner world of the human subject from the outer world—a premise on which the theory of astrology as projection depends. For example, Jung describes the unconscious as a "field of experience of unlimited extent"[4] and likens it to the "atmosphere in which we live."[5] He goes so far as to posit the existence of a *psyche tou kosmou*, a cosmic psyche, and to connect the collective unconscious to the Platonic idea of an *anima mundi*, a world soul.[6] If such speculations are accurate, it might be that the unconscious actually pervades the environment all around us and is not an encapsulated realm located exclusively within the individual, as we tend to assume. This implies, in turn, that archetypal meaning might be inherent to the universe itself, and not restricted to a separate, isolated psyche, projecting its meanings into the external world and into the heavens. Jung's reflections on the psychoid nature of the archetypes, discussed under points 6 and 7, also support this supposition.

3. Astrology as Divinatory Practice. Astrology is a mantic method, a means of divination, in which astrological interpretations and predictions are forms of synchronicity manifesting as meaningful "lucky hits."[7] In considering Jung's view of astrology as divination, Chapter 13 of *Jung on Astrology* sets forth the rationale behind his "astrological experiment" and presents the conclusions he drew from it, despite the experiment's fatal errors in calculation—indeed, because of these errors.

Jung's experiment proposed to investigate whether there are statistically significant correlations between marriage and certain planetary configurations formed between the astrological birth charts of husband and wife in married pairs, compared to unmarried pairs. As noted in the editorial comments within the chapter, although the results of Jung's astrology experiment ultimately concluded that correlations between the astrological factors and marriages were *not* statistically significant, initial errors were made in calculation such that the data appeared at first to lend support to astrology. Jung took this susceptibility to error, distorting the results in favor of corroborating astrology, as itself significant, viewing it as a synchronistic occurrence through which the unconscious conspired to influence the outcome in line with the researcher's "lively interest" and personal investment in astrology.[8] In Jung's view, synchronistic factors had produced something like an experimenter bias.

Addressing this matter in *Jung and Astrology*, Maggie Hyde makes a helpful distinction between two different kinds of synchronicity discussed in Jung's writing, which she terms "Synchronicity I" and "Synchronicity II." She describes the former as "the (meaningful) interdependence of events among themselves,"[9] emphasizing something like an "objective pattern" in the nature of things, with synchronistic acausal correlations between the objective fact of the planetary positions and meanings or events observed in human experience.[10] The latter, Synchronicity II, emphasizes the "subjective participation of the observing psyche," with synchronicity recognized as a significant factor in the subjective act of interpreting astrological meanings, much in the manner that Jung attributed the mathematical errors in calculation in his astrology experiment to synchronicity, with the expectations and emotional state of the researcher unconsciously entangled with the calculation of the results.[11] Hyde emphasizes that the astrologer cannot escape his or her subjectivity when reading the chart and seeking to uncover meaning in the astrological configurations. What emerges as significant during any particular reading is guided by a synchronistic collusion between astrologer, client, and the astrological symbols.

Impressed by what had happened during his experiment, Jung was led to conclude that in the practice of the astrology "a secret, mutual connivance existed between the material and the psychic state of the astrologer."[12] Astrology works, in this view, because of the astrologer's and the client's psychological investment and participation in the horoscope reading, with the emotionally charged context of the reading providing the necessary conditions for synchronicity to occur. Thus, even if the astrologer uses the wrong birth data, and therefore an incorrect astrological chart, the horoscope reading can still be valid since astrology, the reasoning goes, depends not on accessing an objective order in the universe, but on the astrologer using chart symbols, unconsciously guided by synchronicity, as a way to divine the meaning of the moment. Synchronicity II therefore goes hand in hand with the view of astrology as divination. In this respect, casting a horoscope is similar to doing a reading with Tarot cards in which the unconscious seemingly directs the selection of cards in answer to a question posed by the querent. Astrology, in the divinatory view, accesses the inner world of psychological meanings, functioning as a kind of symbolic mirror of the psyche, irrespective of whether there is an objective order to which astrological factors refer.[13] Because all things can be read symbolically, it does not necessarily matter which particular astrological variables are used, for, as Cornelius, Hyde, and Webster note, "every factor conceivable by an astrologer is capable of generating valid symbolism."[14]

Jung later refers to this (Synchronicity II) as "our narrower conception of synchronicity" that "needs expanding" since it is restricted to specific exceptional incidents of the revelation of subjective meaning during astrology readings rather than constituting a general principle of consistent correspondence between human experience and an objective order in the nature of things.[15] He comes to the conclusion that "synchronicity in the narrow sense is only a particular instance of general acausal orderedness"—a topic addressed under point 7.[16]

4. Physical Influence and Causal Explanations. There is a physical mechanism to explain astrology in the form of photon radiation emitted by the sun impacting the Earth's magnetic field. Astrology, therefore, works via efficient and material causation: there is a physical cause producing an effect in human beings. To date, there is no satisfactory causal explanation in terms of the four known forces – the strong and weak nuclear forces, electromagnetism, and gravity – to account for how planets and signs could physically influence human beings.[17] Perhaps for this reason, a survey of literature in the field suggests most astrologers today eschew explanations of astrology in causal terms, with many preferring to construe astrology as symbolic or synchronistic.[18] Jung himself rejected explanations of astrology based on the idea of physical "vibration," a view he attributed to theosophy.

However, even late into his life Jung was reluctant to abandon causal explanations entirely, pivoting back to this line of inquiry as he worked on the astrology chapter in the synchronicity monograph in the 1950s. Having argued in other places that astrology should be viewed as synchronistic, Jung gave serious consideration to the possibility of there being a physical, causal explanation of astrology—influenced especially by the reading of German physicist Max Knoll's theory connecting solar proton radiation and planetary constellations. Indeed, Jung goes as far as to explicitly reject the idea that astrology is a mantic method and also argues that both synchronistic and causal explanations might be simultaneously valid. The causal influence, he conjectures, might be based on the influence of the seasons, manifest through the date of one's birth—an influence transmitted via photon radiation from the sun impacting the Earth's magnetic field. With this kind of explanation, he fancies that there is "some prospect today of a causal explanation in conformity with natural law,"[19] and he is therefore "inclined to rank astrology alongside the natural sciences."[20]

5. The Qualities of Time. Astrology depends upon the qualitative significance of time. Time is not an empty frame of reference, as we commonly assume, for each unique moment possesses a certain quality, which astrological horoscopes symbolize. "Whatever is born or done at this particular moment of time," Jung declared, "has the quality of this moment of time."[21] He devotes considerable energy to articulating this view, especially in his seminars and writing from the late 1920s and 1930s, which comprise many of the extracts included in Chapter 15 of *Jung on Astrology*. Jung argues that the astrological study of the movements of the planets in the heavens is a method of understanding the changing qualities of moments in time. He employs something like the following line of argument:

a. Time is derived from the observation of the flux of things, of change in the universe.

b. Change is generated by the movement of energy, or the transformation of energy from one form to another.

c. Therefore, time is an aspect of energy.

d. Astrology is an indication of the condition of universal energy at particular moments in time, functioning like a cosmic clock or watch, with the positions of the planets like the hands of a clock indicating the state of things at a particular moment.

e. Fate is identical with time. To observe the movements of the planets as an indication of passing time is thus to observe fate as it fulfills itself.

By the 1950s, however, Jung felt impelled to qualify his position, noting in a letter to André Barbault that he chose to replace the notion of the qualitative significance of time with the concept of synchronicity, which he develops more fully in the material presented in Chapter 17 of *Jung on Astrology.*[22]

6. Pythagorean Numerical Archetypes. Astrology rests upon transcendental numerical archetypes, as in the Pythagorean and Platonic understanding of number as an a priori ordering principle. In this view, astrology has its foundation in the qualitative significance of number, "in conjunction," Jung notes, "with the numinous assemblage of gods which the horoscope represents."[23] For Jung, as in astrology, numbers are held not only to be instruments for counting and calculation (the quantitative aspect of number), but they are also thought to possess universal symbolic meaning. The number one, for example, implies unity and beginning; two is associated with duality and the tension of opposites; and three suggests harmony arising from the reconciliation of opposites. This kind of numerical symbolic logic runs throughout astrology. The twelve signs of the zodiac are derived from the qualities of number, generated by the subdivision of the 360 degrees of the zodiac. Similarly, the meanings of specific aspects (the geometric relationships between the planets) are also based on the meanings of the small whole numbers from which they are derived—the conjunction pertains to the number one, the opposition to two, the trine to three, the square to four, and so forth.

Although he was initially concerned with the role of number as a psychological ordering factor in the unconscious (he called number the "archetype of order"[24]), his later reflections on the psychoid dimension of the archetype led him, as we read in his letters, towards a Pythagorean view of number as an ordering principle intrinsic to all of reality, both the inner world of the psyche and the external world, although he did not make this position explicit in his formal writing. Jung introduced the term *psychoid* in the 1950s to designate the tendency of the archetype, at its deepest level, to pass over from instinct into an "organic substrate"[25] and to "fall in with fundamental forms of the physical process in general."[26] "Archetypes," he proposes, "are not found exclusively in the psychic sphere, but can occur just as much in circumstances that are not psychic."[27]

In the selections in Chapter 16 of *Jung on Astrology*, then, Jung poses the question as to the relationship between number and "something as archetypal as astrology."[28] The answer, in terms of Jung's own statements, might be formulated as something like the following argument:

a. Number is an archetypal ordering principle in the unconscious psyche ("the unconscious uses number as an ordering factor"); numbers "have an archetypal foundation."[29]

b. At a deeper level, archetypes in the unconscious have a psychoid dimension, such that they also pertain to physical processes in the material world. Presumably, then, this implies that numbers, as archetypes, also have a psychoid dimension.

c. This supposition accords with Jung's assertion that "number, like meaning, inheres in the nature of all things,"[30] which draws Jung close to a Pythagorean position, as he himself recognizes: "The fact is that the numbers pre-existing in nature are presumably the most fundamental archetypes, being the very matrix of all others. Here Pythagoras was certainly on the right track . . ."[31]

d. It is possible, therefore (and this seems to be the implication of Jung's speculations on number), that astrology is based on a transcendental numerical order, manifest both in the psyche and in the universe at large.

As we will consider below, Jung's reflections on number should be viewed alongside his theory of synchronicity.

7. Synchronicity and Acausal Parallelism. Astrology is a form of synchronicity, reflecting an acausal parallelism or correspondence between planetary positions and experiences in human life, partly explicable in terms of the psychoid nature of archetypes. Focusing on synchronicity in general rather than astrology specifically, the hypothesis presented in Chapter 17 of *Jung on Astrology* is not explicitly applied by Jung to understand astrology, yet it constitutes what is, arguably, his most developed and sophisticated explanation of it. Arising out of and subsuming Jung's view of astrology as archetypal, synchronistic, and rooted in numerical forms is the idea that astrology might be explained in terms of a "general acausal orderedness."[32] Jung understands this as an "underlying principle"[33] of arrangement, an a priori archetypal order in the nature of things, which stands behind specific instances of synchronicity (this is Synchronicity I, in Hyde's scheme).

As an example of "synchronicity on a grand scale,"[34] astrology might conceivably be understood as the expression of this acausal orderedness, which Jung considers to be an "all-pervading factor or principle in the universe."[35] This position emerges from Jung's speculations on the intersection of depth psychology and physics and from his reflections on the mind-matter relationship. Contemplating these questions also led him to posit the existence of a "transcendental psychophysical background"[36] to the empirical world and drew him close to the medieval notion of the *unus mundus*, "where there is no incommensurability between so-called matter and so-called psyche."[37] The psyche and the cosmos are considered to be two related aspects of the unitary reality that is neither psychological nor material.[38] Thus Jung: "The common background of microphysics and depth psychology is as much physical as psychic and therefore neither, but rather a third thing, a neutral nature which can a most be grasped in hints since its essence is transcendental."[39]

Proceeding further, Jung ventures to suggest that the archetypal background can be viewed as a "potential world"[40] and as a "universal factor existing from all eternity," which manifests itself in acts of "continuous creation" in time.[41] It stretches the limits of our comprehension to fully grasp Jung's intended meaning here, but he seems to be proposing that what is eternally present, in the transcendental background of reality, appears to us as a succession—as an ordered unfolding of the ground in a series of temporal moments, supporting specific synchronistic and acausal correlations between the psyche and cosmos, of which astrology is one form. Recalling here Jung's explanation of astrology in terms of the quality of time, we could say that astrology, as an indication of the changing qualities of moments in time, might be used to map the unfolding of eternal archetypal reality of the "potential world" into a temporal sequence.

To summarize briefly, then, this explanation of astrology depends upon the idea that there is a psychoid archetypal order, at a deeper dimension of reality, functioning as a kind of organizing principle of both the psyche and the cosmos—hence Jung's enthusiasm, in a letter of 1957, for the idea of a "transcendental 'arranger'" behind acausal synchronistic correlations.[42] If there is indeed such an organizing principle underlying the psyche and the cosmos, it is conceivable that the physical configurations formed by the planets in the solar system might be organized according to the same transcendent numerical archetypes that also order and inform the collective unconscious— thereby helping to account for the relationship posited in some forms of astrology between planetary configurations and archetypes. Such a view contradicts the idea that astrology might be wholly explained as an unconscious projection of the psyche into the heavens, for the observed correspondences between planetary configurations and activated archetypal themes in human experience could conceivably be better explained as a special kind of constant synchronicity based on the underlying order described earlier.[43]

Although speculative, this hypothesis perhaps constitutes the most coherent and comprehensive position emerging from Jung's engagement with synchronicity and astrology, one that is broadly in accord with certain perspectives in the new-paradigm sciences.[44] This hypothesis also has much in common with the classical and medieval explanations of astrology (discussed under point 1).

Jung does not further develop these reflections in relation to astrology. The material in Chapter 17 and in Chapter 16 of *Jung on Astrology*, on numerical archetypes, represents the terminus of his exploratory thinking on synchronicity and, by inference, astrology. Thus, he concedes, in the same letter of 1957:

It seems to me that for the time being I have exhausted my psychological ammunition. I have got stuck, one the one hand, in the acausality (or "synchronicity") of certain phenomena of unconscious provenance and, on the other hand, in the qualitative statements of numbers, for here I set foot on territories where I cannot advance without the help and understanding of other disciplines.[45]

In concluding this overview, it should be stressed that in most cases the various explanations summarized here are not mutually exclusive. As the basis of astrology, there could, for example, be an objective order of archetypal meaning inherent in the underlying structure of reality and, at the same time, projections of the unconscious into observed patterns in the heavens. Indeed, given the plethora of astrological techniques and variables employed today, with astrologers finding significance in their own preferred approaches, it is almost certain that projection shapes the interpretation of the celestial patterns symbolized in astrology. Equally, there are surely synchronistic elements at play in the subjective act of the interpretation of astrological charts, evident in those instances in which valid meaning is conveyed even when an astrologer inadvertently works with the wrong chart data.

Whatever explanation of astrology one finds most compelling, what is most striking is just how many elements of Jung's theories and understanding of the psyche are pertinent to an astrological view of the world. Taking seriously the claims of astrology, alongside the evidence of synchronicity, led Jung to contemplate the deepest mysteries and fundamental questions of existence, such as the nature of space and time, the relationship between mind and matter, and the possibility of meaning existing outside of human consciousness. That he was not able to provide conclusive explanations of astrology is, in the face of these great mysteries, entirely to be expected, although his speculations present rich possibilities for further theoretical elaboration.

Notes

[1] Jung, "Synchronicity: An Acausal Connecting Principle," in *Structure and Dynamics of the Psyche* (*CW* 8), p. 490, par. 926.

[2] Jung, "On Synchronicity," in *Structure and Dynamics of the Psyche* (*CW* 8), p. 531, par. 995.

[3] Jung, "Religious Ideas in Alchemy" (1937), in *Psychology and Alchemy* (*CW* 12), p. 245, par. 346.

[4] Jung, "Relations between the Ego and the Unconscious" (1928), in *Two Essays on Analytical Psychology* (*CW* 7), p. 184, par. 292.

⁵ Jung to Fritz Künkel, 10 July 1946, in *Letters I*, p. 433.

⁶ Jung to Stephen Abrams, 21 October 1957, in *Letters II*, p. 399.

⁷ Jung to Hans Bender, 10 April 1958, in *Letters II*, p. 428.

⁸ Jung, "Synchronicity: An Acausal Connecting Principle" (1952), in *Structure and Dynamics of the Psyche* (*CW* 8), p. 478, par. 905.

⁹ Hyde, *Jung and Astrology*, p. 128.

¹⁰ Ibid., p. 134.

¹¹ Ibid., pp. 128 and 131. The divinatory approach to astrology is also advanced in Geoffrey Cornelius, *The Moment of Astrology*.

¹² Jung, "Synchronicity: An Acausal Connecting Principle" (1952), in *Structure and Dynamics of the Psyche* (*CW* 8), 478, par. 905.

¹³ As Cornelius, Hyde, and Webster put it: "Astrology-as-divination is a metaphoric mirror. Horoscope factors are treated 'as if' they are metaphors revealing salient features of the subject of the horoscope" (*Astrology for Beginners*, p. 165).

¹⁴ Cornelius, Hyde, and Webster, *Astrology for Beginners*, p. 172.

¹⁵ Jung, "Synchronicity: An Acausal Connecting Principle" (1952), in *Structure and Dynamics of the Psyche* (*CW* 8), p. 516, par. 965.

¹⁶ Ibid.

¹⁷ The term *causal*, as used by Jung, implies physical and efficient causation, which are two of the four types of causation identified by Aristotle. Efficient causation is what we today think of as cause and effect, the billiard-ball model in which A causes B causing C, and so on. Physical causation is the matter of which something is comprised. Although he flirts with explanations in terms of cause and effect, Jung far more often describes astrology as synchronistic and acausal, a form of connection between discrete phenomena in which there is no direct influence or causal chain between them. The Aristotelian categories of formal and final causation, pertaining, respectively, to the organizing pattern and the end or goal of a process or organism, have clearer associations with synchronicity and the functioning of archetypes in human experience. See, for example, Jung's reflections on teleology and finality in Jung, "Synchronicity: An Acausal Connecting Principle" (1952), in *Structure and Dynamics of the Psyche* (*CW* 8), p. 493, par. 931, and his view of the archetype as an organizing form.

¹⁸ For one notable advocate of causal explanations of astrology, see Seymour, *Astrology: The Evidence of Science*.

¹⁹ Jung, "Synchronicity: An Acausal Connecting Principle" (1952), in *Structure and Dynamics of the Psyche* (*CW* 8), p. 528, par. 988.

²⁰ Jung to Hans Bender, 10 April 1958, in *Letters II*, p. 429.

²¹ Jung, "Richard Wilhelm: In Memoriam" (1930), in *Spirit in Man, Art, and Literature* (*CW* 15), pp. 56–57, par. 82.

²² See Jung to André Barbault, 26 May 1954, in *Letters II*, pp. 175–177.

²³ Jung, "An Astrological Experiment" (1958), in *Symbolic Life* (*CW* 18), pp.

497–498, par. 1183.

[24] Jung, "Synchronicity: An Acausal Connecting Principle" (1952), in *Structure and Dynamics of the Psyche* (*CW* 8), p. 456, par. 870.

[25] Jung, "On the Nature of the Psyche," in *Structure and Dynamics of the Psyche* (*CW* 8), p. 177, par. 368.

[26] Jung to H. Rossteutscher, 3 May 1958, in *Letters II*, p. 437.

[27] Jung, "Synchronicity: An Acausal Connecting Principle" (1952), in *Structure and Dynamics of the Psyche* (*CW* 8), p. 515, par. 964.

[28] Jung, "An Astrological Experiment" (1958), in *Symbolic Life* (*CW* 18), pp. 497–498, par. 1183.

[29] Jung, "Synchronicity: An Acausal Connecting Principle" (1952), in *Structure and Dynamics of the Psyche* (*CW* 8), pp. 456–457, par. 870.

[30] Jung to Robert Dietrich, 27 May 1956, in *Letters II*, p. 302.

[31] Jung to Patrick Evans, 1 September 1956, in *Letters II*, p. 327.

[32] Jung, "Synchronicity: An Acausal Connecting Principle" (1952), in *Structure and Dynamics of the Psyche* (*CW* 8), p. 516, par. 965.

[33] Jung, "Synchronicity: An Acausal Connecting Principle" (1952), in *Structure and Dynamics of the Psyche* (*CW* 8), pp. 500–501, par. 938.

[34] Jung, "Richard Wilhelm: In Memoriam" (1930), in *Spirit in Man, Art, and Literature* (*CW* 15), p. 56, par. 81.

[35] Jung to Stephen Abrams, 21 October 1957, in *Letters II*, p. 400.

[36] Jung, *Mysterium Coniunctionis* (*CW* 14), p. 538, par. 769.

[37] Jung to Stephen Abrams, 21 October 1957, in *Letters II*, p. 400.

[38] Jung here advocates a form of neutral or dual-aspect monism with regards to the mind-matter relationship. For a discussion on neutral monism, see Leopold Stubenberg, "Neutral Monism," *The Stanford Encyclopedia of Philosophy* (Winter 2016 Edition). For a discussion on dual-aspect monism, see Harald Atmanspacher, "Quantum Approaches to Consciousness," *The Stanford Encyclopedia of Philosophy* (Summer 2015 Edition).

[39] Jung, *Mysterium Coniunctionis* (*CW* 14), p. 538, par. 768.

[40] Ibid., par. 769.

[41] Jung, "Synchronicity: An Acausal Connecting Principle" (1952), in *Structure and Dynamics of the Psyche* (*CW* 8), p. 519, par. 968.

[42] Jung to Werner Nowacki, 22 March 1957, in *Letters II*, p. 352.

[43] A number of the ideas discussed in this chapter are taken up by Jung's foremost collaborator, Marie-Louise von Franz, in *Psyche and Matter*. See especially, "The Synchronicity Principle of C. G. Jung," pp. 203–228.

[44] For a synthesis of Jungian psychology and the new-paradigm sciences, in support of an astrological world view, see Le Grice, *Archetypal Cosmos*.

[45] Jung to Werner Nowacki, 22 March 1957, in *Letters II*, p. 352.

PART II

Archetypal Astrology, Myth, and Transformation

VII

The Archetypal Dynamics of Individuation

As described by C. G. Jung, individuation is a process of deep psychological transformation leading the individual towards the realization of the Self—the organizing center and the totality of the psyche. Individuation represents an advanced stage of psychological development by which the individual "I," the conscious ego, becomes aware of, and engages in a dialectical encounter with, the unconscious, encompassing both the repressed contents of biographical experience and complexes (the personal unconscious) and the universal stratum of the psyche (the collective unconscious). The individuation process is impelled and informed by archetypes—numinous formative principles and conditioning factors existing *a priori* in the depths of the collective unconscious that give a thematic predisposition and continuity to human experience. Jung saw archetypes—which include the shadow, the hero, the anima and animus, the wise old man, the mother, the father, rebirth, the spirit, the child, and the trickster—as the fundamental motifs behind mythology and religion, the underlying determinants of human experience that are evident in numinous dreams and fantasy images, and that manifest in every typical life situation.[1] At root, although they function autonomously, the archetypes are all aspects of the Self, which initiates and draws forth individuation, imposing a labor of transformation on the individual ego. Individuation, ultimately, leads to the realization of the Self as a greater authority in one's life, sometimes experienced as a higher will beyond that of conscious willpower—a will that is akin, Jung thought, to the will of God, to be uniquely realized within every individual life.[2]

As Jung and Joseph Campbell have demonstrated, the sequence of transformations occurring during certain aspects of individuation is symbolically portrayed by myths of the hero's journey.[3] These myths, Campbell suggests, tend to loosely adhere to a certain pattern or template—the *monomyth*, as he termed it—comprising three fundamental stages: separation or departure, initiation or transformation, and return or incorporation. The monomyth depicts, first, the hero's separation from the ordinary daylight world of consensus reality in response to a "call to adventure," which is followed, second, by a threshold crossing, typically marking an initiatory "descent into the underworld" and sequence of transformative experiences on a "road of trials." Last, the adventure culminates with the attainment of a boon or treasure, and subsequent return journey in which the hero brings back and disseminates the boon to the culture. The treasure, the "pearl of great price," understood psychologically, might be interpreted as a symbolic representation of the precious gift of individual selfhood, and with it the realization of a unique life destiny and calling.

In this chapter, by exploring connections between archetypal themes evident in human experience and particular planetary alignments in both natal charts and transits, I present the case that astrology can be used to help illuminate the archetypal dynamics of the individuation process and the hero's journey.

Planetary Archetypes and Mythic Themes

The universal principles associated with the planets in astrology seem to relate to Jung's conception of archetypes *per se*, universal forms underlying the archetypal images he identified, such as the shadow, hero, and anima.[4] For example, the planetary archetype associated with Pluto—which is related to themes such as instinctual dynamism, the depths of experience, death-rebirth, transformation, evolution, compulsion, and empowerment—is connected to the Jungian archetypes of the shadow (containing the repressed instincts and primitive drives) and rebirth, as well as the compulsive, possessive quality associated with all archetypes (particularly evident in what Jung calls the archetype of the mana personality) and the fated quality often associated with the Self. The astrological Moon is associated with the anima (the feminine principle within the psyche), and the archetypes of the mother and the child. Saturn is associated with the wise old man or senex, the father archetype, and with the inferiority complex and negative emotions contained in the shadow. Uranus has particular connections with the trickster archetype, especially in its association with creative disruption. The Sun, pertaining to themes such as the quest for identity, the heroic task of carrying the light of conscious self-

103

awareness, and with the centralizing principle of the psyche, is naturally connected to Jung's concept of the hero archetype and to the realization of the Self. And Venus and Mars, to give two final examples, are associated with the idealized images of female and male contained in the anima and animus, respectively. In short, each of the principles associated with the planets in astrology seems to be related to one or more Jungian archetypes and particular qualities exhibited by these archetypes.

The planetary archetypes are also connected to gods and goddesses of mythology, and to a number of prominent motifs of the hero's journey. Thus Pluto is associated with Hades, the Devil, Dionysus, Shiva, Mara, Kali, the Uroborus, the alchemical god-man Mercurius, and many other mythic deities. It is also associated with Kundalini power, the mythic underworld, hell, and purgatory, and the motifs of descent into the underworld and transformation. Neptune is associated with the principles of divine love and universal compassion, personified by figures such as Christ and the Buddha. It is also related to the yearning for paradise, and the quest for mystical experience of oneness or transcendence, central to the esoteric branches of all religious traditions. Saturn relates to the patriarchal authority of Yahweh in the Old Testament, to Chronos and Father Time, to the stern hand of fate, and to the spiritual wisdom and authority by the guru or wise old man figure.

Again, as these few examples suggest, each planetary archetype is connected to many different mythic figures from the world's religious and cultural traditions. Each mythic figure represents one or more different aspects or characteristics of the planetary archetypes, which possess universal meanings that cannot be adequately portrayed by any one single deity or concept. The planetary archetypes, as Richard Tarnas has emphasized, are multivalent and multidimensional principles.[5] That is to say, they are indeterminate creative powers that manifest in a wide variety of ways across all dimensions of reality. Although they always reflect an unchanging central core of meaning, these archetypes do not have singular fixed modes of expression that might be exhaustively described using a few simple keywords. Nor can one determine from astrology alone how the archetypes will actually manifest in human experience. Astrology pertains to the universal dimension of human experience—to general themes and motifs—not to particulars.

Understood in this way, astrology provides a cosmological and mythic-archetypal framework that can provide sustaining meaning and orientation for human experience.[6] Such orientation is particularly valuable during individuation when one's very identity undergoes a profound transformation, which naturally throws one into states of chaos, disorientation, and perhaps even trauma. In this context, one can use astrology to gain some objective perspective on and insight into the themes, dynamics, and timing of such experiences. Natal astrology allows one to better understand the major mythic themes and archetypal dynamics expressing themselves through one's life experience as a whole; transit astrology and the study of progressions enable one to gain insight into which particular themes are prominent at particular times of one's life.[7]

The planetary archetypes associated with the outer planets—Uranus, Neptune, and Pluto—are associated with experiences of enduring, consequential, and deep-rooted transformation, and of all the planetary archetypes are therefore the most immediately connected to individuation.[8] The archetypal principles associated with these so-called transpersonal planets are, at once, powers of immense evolutionary, creative potential and of immense, life annihilating destruction. They are instinctual and archaic in essence, and yet also transformative, spiritual, and progressive. They can act to sensitize, inspire, and deepen our conscious experience, but also to obliterate, dissolve, and disrupt.

Uranus: Individualism, Awakening, and Creative Genius

The Uranus archetypal principle is often experienced as the impulse to break free from patterns of conventional existence, to separate oneself from the common crowd. The motive power of this archetype is connected to the desire to go one's own way in life, to seek out one's own unique experience, to bring forth one's creative genius. It is connected with the impulse to become a unique individual, *sui generis*, a goal which is a central to the individuation process, as Jung explained:

> Individuation means becoming an "in-dividual," and, in so far as "individuality" embraces our innermost, last, and incomparable uniqueness, it also implies becoming one's own self. We could therefore translate individuation as "coming to selfhood" or "self-realization."[9]

Especially in those cases in which the urge to authentic individual experience is not consciously willed, we can observe the archetypal Uranus in its characteristic role as trickster, liberator, and awakener, manifesting as the sudden awakening "call to adventure," or the unexpected disruption in one's life that jettisons one onto a new life path. "A blunder—apparently the merest chance—reveals an unsuspected world," as Joseph Campbell observes in *The Hero With a Thousand Faces*, which "may amount to the opening of a destiny."[10] Such is the activating and releasing quality of the archetypal Uranus to prompt or impel one on a path of individual development.

The Uranus principle is expressed through the capacity of the shadow archetype, informed by the deeper *telos* of the Self, to undermine one's conscious intentions, to trip up the ego, as it were, and to break apart the artificial certainties and protective strategies we often depend upon. To individuate, one cannot cling to the established forms and values of the past; one has to commit oneself to one's own emerging truth, as one seeks to emancipate oneself from the often staid and hackneyed patterns of conventional life. A developed expression of the Uranus principle brings a fresh, unique, ever-unfolding, indeterminate quality to experience.

Unsurprisingly, Uranus is prominent in the birth charts of many figures well known for their individualism or figures whose creative brilliance and individual genius sets them apart.[11] For example, the life and work of Friedrich Nietzsche, born in 1844 during a Jupiter-Uranus conjunction, is characterized by a rebellion (Uranus) against moral principles (Jupiter), a championing of the "free spirit," and an impassioned commitment to individual excellence and nobility— themes all connected with the combination of these archetypes. As is evident in Nietzsche's writing, the Jupiter-Uranus combination is associated with the emergence of new philosophies and world views, with the aspiration for a greater ascent of the spirit, and with the activation of ever higher potentials; it correlates with the unexpected opening of expansive new vistas, the exhilaration of creative possibilities, and the euphoric experience of freedom. Central motifs of this archetypal complex, as Richard Tarnas has noted, are well conveyed in the following passage from Nietzsche's *Daybreak*, both through its vision of a future condition of greater strength and possibility, and in its symbolism of soaring birds and open expanses of space stretching into the unknown future:

> We aeronauts of the spirit! All those brave birds which fly out into the distance, the farthest distance—it is certain! Somewhere or other they will be unable to go on and will perch on a mast or bare cliff-face—and they will be even thankful for this miserable accommodation! But who could venture to infer from that, that

there was not a immense open space before them, that they had flown as far as one *could* fly! All our great teachers and predecessors have at last come to a stop . . . . But what does that matter to you and me! Other birds will fly farther! This insight and faith of ours vies with them in flying up and away; it rises above our heads and above our impotence into the heights and from there surveys the distance and sees before it the flocks of birds which, far stronger than we, will strive whither we have striven, and where everything is sea, sea, sea![12]

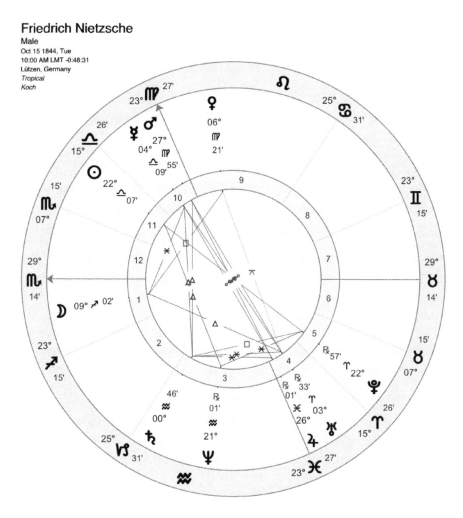

Figure 1: Friedrich Nietzsche's Birth Chart [13]

Elsewhere, in another apt image of the Jupiter-Uranus pairing, Nietzsche describes the *Übermensch* Zarathustra—his vision of a future form of godlike human—as the nimble-footed "cosmic dancer" who defies the Saturnian "spirit of gravity," climbing ever higher, reaching further into the distance, and preaching a gospel of a greater, fuller future for the human being.

Similar themes are also evident in the life and person of Joseph Campbell (with a natal Sun-Mercury-Jupiter conjunction in a T-square with a Uranus-Neptune opposition) who held in high regard the pursuit of one's own individual path through life, an approach well exemplified, he thought, by the Knights of the Round Table who "thought it would be a disgrace to follow the way or path of another" on the quest for the Holy Grail.[14] Campbell also professed his admiration for the pioneering space exploration program of the 1960s, bringing us a dazzling new holistic perspective on our planet, and for the technological brilliance that made possible the epic scale of the Manhattan skyline—both reflecting the Jupiter-Uranus complex's association with ascent, expanded perspectives, and enormity of scale (Jupiter) combined with new innovation, brilliance, and technology (Uranus). Generally, like Nietzsche, Campbell was an enthusiast for higher human possibilities, advocating a life-affirming individualistic philosophy.

Both Nietzsche and Campbell also had Uranus in major aspect to Mars (Nietzsche had a Mars-Uranus conjunction, Campbell a Mars-Uranus trine), which in Campbell's case seems to have been expressed, in the early part of his life, in the field of athletic achievement (pertaining to Mars). As a young man, Campbell went to Columbia University in New York where he excelled in what would today be called the 800 meters. He recounts with pride one particular race in which he was running the final leg of a relay, and, after receiving the baton, was able to make up a thirty-yard deficit to catch the runner in front and power past him. In Abraham Maslow's terminology, Campbell had a peak experience; he was "in the zone," as we might now say. This experience seems to have made a deep impression on Campbell. Even late into this life, he retained an admiration for the nobility of athletic training and achievement, and the camaraderie and aspiration to excellence shared by men and women in this field. The ethos of the athlete appealed to Campbell's developed sense of Apollonian style excellence and elegance in mind, body, and spirit. Such themes—peak experiences, athletic excellence, the championing of individual freedom, the positive exuberance with which he advocated following a life path of one's own—are all directly related to archetypal dynamics associated with Campbell's Jupiter-Uranus square and his Mars-trine-Uranus alignments, which shaped his own particular path of individuation and his world view. For Nietzsche, the same combination of archetypal principles found expression in the high spirits and good humor evident (alongside the polemic) throughout his philosophy, and in his vigorous mountain hikes in the Alps or along the precipitous mountain path of Eze in the Côte d'Azur, where he composed his epic *Thus Spoke Zathathustra*. The same complex was evident, too, in his philosophy of abundant health of body and spirit, even as he was ailing under the pressure of the psychospiritual transformation process in which he was embroiled.

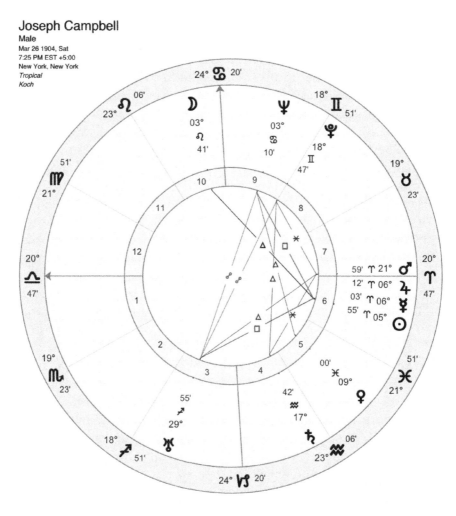

Figure 2: Joseph Campbell's Birth Chart

By themselves, Mars-Uranus alignments are often expressed as a rugged and forceful individualism, as an ardent commitment to authenticity, as assertive rebelliousness, and a restless craving for exciting new experience, traits well exemplified by the Beatnik poets— Kerouac, Ginsburg, Cassidy—each born with Mars and Uranus in hard aspect, and also by Jim Morrison (Mars-Uranus conjunction), lead singer of The Doors, who repeatedly screamed "wake up!" during a number of live performances in the late sixties in an effort to forcibly jolt his audience out of its existential slumber. In archetypal terms, Uranus is connected to the trickster, the rebel, the liberator, and the awakener—dynamic patterns of being emboldened and energized in these figures by the Mars archetype, resulting in a fierce form of individualism and a rejection of the conformist patterns of conventional existence in favor of a life of constant change, experimentation, and new stimulation.

The problematic forms of expression of archetypal complexes involving Uranus, especially as it relates to individuation, include an over-emphasis on individualistic freedom at the expense of the spiritual life and the discipline necessary for psychological transformation, willfulness, restlessness and an impatient recklessness, an inability to accept limitation of any kind, and a precocious brilliance out of balance with other aspects of the psyche. For instance, considering again the Mars-Jupiter-Uranus combination, alongside the more positive qualities of this complex we can see the exaggerated individualism and dissociated intellectual genius in the case of Nietzsche who proclaimed himself "6000 feet above man and time" and who was unable to accept the more ordinary, commonplace aspects of human nature—an attitude that condemned him to a life of wandering and desperate solitude.[15] Nietzsche was totally separated from the dominant values of his culture, forced onto his own path by his philosophy and his world view.

Similar themes are evident in personal transits, with the Uranus archetypal principle often serving a liberating or awakening function that draws forth one's unique creative talents and launches one onto a path of individuation. The archetypal Uranus electrifies, pointedly stimulates, and makes acute themes associated with other planetary archetypal principles. Under the influence of an activated Uranus, dormant complexes and drives in the psyche break into conscious awareness and cannot be ignored. Uranus thus facilitates the process of becoming conscious that is fundamental to individuation.

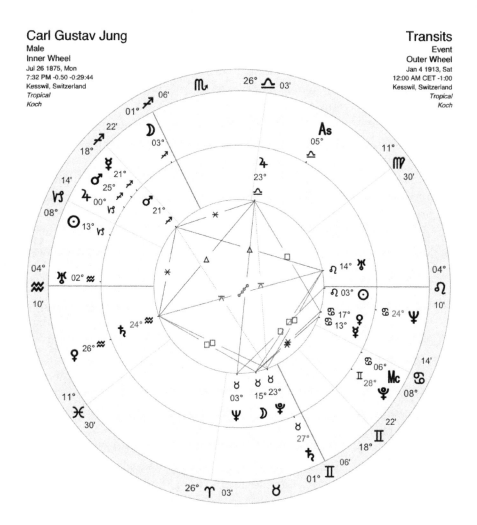

Figure 3: C. G. Jung's Birth Chart,
with Transits for January 4 1913

For example, the period of Carl Jung's "confrontation with the unconscious" beginning in 1912, coincided with a Uranus transit to his natal Sun-square-Neptune alignment.[16] This transit was evident in a number of ways, each consistent with the meaning of the archetypes involved, exemplifying the significance of the archetypal Uranus for individuation.

First, it was at this time (in 1912) that the original version of Jung's *Wandlungen und Symbole der Libido* was published, setting out his own mythological interpretation of incest theory—a bold deviation from the established Freudian position he had previously been aligned with. He

111

subsequently broke away from Freud, resigning his position as President of the Psychoanalytic Association, and thus committed for better or worse to the uncertainty of his own unique life path—a typical occurrence during Uranus hard-aspect transits to the Sun. Figure 3 shows Jung's transits for January 4th, 1913, close to the date Jung received a letter from Freud beseeching him to "take your full freedom" and "spare me your supposed 'tokens of friendships'"—a letter that virtually finalized the rupture between the two men.[17]

Second, the Uranus transit to Jung's natal Sun-square-Neptune also coincided with a series of destabilizing and revelatory experiences during his encounter with the depths of the unconscious. Reflecting Neptune's association with myth, dream, fantasy, altered states of consciousness, and so forth, the Uranus transit to Neptune brought forth a stream of vivid fantasies, throwing Jung into states of profound disorientation and confusion, undermining his capacity to function in the world. He experienced jolting disruptions to his ordinary conscious experience, and encounters with numinous personified spirit figures, such as Philemon, that were to serve as guides to his own psychospiritual development.

Third, it was out of the weltering confusion of this experience that Jung developed his understanding of the individuation process. Reflecting a major theme associated with the Uranus-Neptune archetypal combination, he pioneered a new individual approach to spiritual experience that has since been extremely influential on contemporary forms of spirituality. The individualistic, inventive, and creative qualities of Uranus were here brought to bear on the Neptunian archetypal and spiritual dimensions of experience.

In sum, then, during the Uranus transit to his natal Sun-Neptune alignment, Jung effectively found and forged his own life path, entered the critical period of his own individuation process, and developed his unique individual approach to the unconscious from which all his subsequent creative work emerged.

Neptune: Transcendence, Dissolution, and Synthesis

Turning now to the Neptune archetype, in respect of individuation this principle is associated, as we touched on above, with the realm of the collective unconscious. The Neptunian sensibility—expressed through dreams, fantasies, the imagination, visionary capacities, the religious instinct, the eye for symbol—is the means by which one engages with the collective unconscious during individuation. Neptune is specifically associated with the symbolic reading of one's life experience, the quest to cultivate a mythic perspective on life, and the desire to recover a more enchanted, magical way of being in the world. Through the Neptune archetype, one attunes to spiritual ideals and inspiring visions, or one seeks transcendence through mystical experience, or one mythologizes and perceives the underlying connections and unity between all things. The aspiration to discover the Kingdom of Heaven, the quest for paradise, are Neptunian phenomena.

In Jungian terms, Neptune is connected to the Self and the incarnate "god-image," to the archetype of the spirit, and to an encounter with the numinous dimension of reality. The Neptunian principle is associated with the activity of the transcendent power of the Self that, behind the scenes, orchestrates the spiritual adventure and leads consciousness on the journey towards individuation. In the soul that is inwardly ready, the Neptunian principle manifests in the spiritual realization or enlightenment experience which turns one's gaze away from the external things to the inner world of the spirit. This principle can also manifest as a regressive longing to return to a womb-like state of blissful preconscious unity to escape the painful alienation of ego-consciousness. Indeed, the regression of libido, as Jung called it, when energy is withdrawn from the extraverted activities of life and directed inwards, is essential for individuation, stimulating the fantasy-making activity of the unconscious.

During individuation, when psychospiritual transformation begins in earnest, the Neptune principle is often first observed in the dissolution of the existing form of the ego-structure—the "dissolution of the persona," to use Jung's term.[18] Through this process, the former cohesive unity of the personality disintegrates into separate parts, and there is a return to the undifferentiated psychological state the alchemists called the *massa confusa*. The boundaries separating the ego and the unconscious are partly dissolved, and the clear demarcation of the conscious ego and personal identity is blurred. The problematic sides of this experience include narcissistic self-absorption, delusory states of consciousness, a schizophrenic detachment from reality, and unconsciously identifying with the archetypes—all of which reflect the characteristic Neptunian themes of dissolution, confusion, lack of clarity, delusions, and projections.

By giving in to the regressive longing to return to the paradise of the womb, to a state of pre-conscious unity, one is exposed to all those illusory ideals, images, wishes, and images that lie in the background of the psyche, subtly distorting one's experience. In facing the unconscious, one has to attempt to become conscious of the archetypal images that move consciousness without our realizing. One has to differentiate the ego—the personal "I"—from the multitude of archetypes and instincts.

In mythic terms, this experience is suggested by the "belly of the whale" motif, when the conscious personality is engulfed by the unconscious, pulled down into the depths, which does indeed feel like being pulled underwater—an experience suggested, too, by the motif of the *night-sea journey*, to use Leo Frobenius's term.[19] In the watery depths, one is charged with the onerous task of cleansing the "doors of perception," removing the distorting blemishes from the mirror of self-reflective consciousness such that one can see the world as it really is. The aim of individuation, according to Jung, is to arrive at a realistic view of oneself and the world, which can only be attained after one has liberated oneself from the unconscious compulsion and reality-distorting influence of the archetypes.

The danger, throughout individuation, is that one might give away one's unique conscious selfhood by unwittingly identifying either with an idealized image of oneself—a persona—or with an archetypal image in the unconscious, such that one's consciousness is possessed by the archetype and true individuality is lost: one becomes nothing but a hero, for instance, ever struggling tragically against adversity, seeking adventure and conquest; or one identifies completely with the wise old man (or mana-personality) and solemnly believes oneself to be a being of superior wisdom devoid of less exalted traits; or one falls prey to the manic godlike inflation that comes from identification with the Self. The possessive quality here, it should be pointed out, is more directly related to the Pluto archetype; but Neptune represents the archetypal images themselves, and the illusion, the escapism, the self-loss, the hypnotic allure of the archetypal unconscious.

For all its great dangers, however, the dissolution of the persona and the ensuing absorption in the world of archetypal images is a prerequisite for the reintegration and reorganization of the psyche around the Self—the deeper center and totality of the psyche. "Dissolution," as Jung notes, "is a pre-requisite for redemption."[20] The redemptive quality of the Neptune principle is manifest, during subsequent stages of individuation, in the movement towards the synthesis of the disparate parts of the psyche around the Self. The redemption of the ego occurs by the re-establishment of psychological unity; one's "eye is made single," to put this in the familiar words of the Bible, and the raging conflict between the disparate parts of the psyche is healed. To the redeemed individual, the Neptunian principle might be recognized in the beatitude of Heaven, in the experience of 'paradise regained,' and in the recovery of a magical enchanted sense of participation with the natural world. Myth has many fitting images of this attainment: ambrosia as the elixir of the gods, the fountain of youth, the mystic marriage of the individual and God. In alchemy, the archetypal Neptune is well described by the *aqua permanens*—the "wonderful waters of transformation"—that are contained within the Philosopher's Stone, the endpoint of the alchemical opus.[21]

As one would expect, many of the above themes are evident in a number of people born with major Sun-Neptune aspects. This archetypal complex is found, for instance, in many prominent figures for whom the spiritual dimension is a directly experienced reality: Jung himself (Sun square Neptune), Pierre Teilhard de Chardin (Sun conjunct Neptune), Saint Thérèse of Lisieux (Sun square Neptune), and Saint Teresa of Avila (Sun sextile Neptune). To this list we might add Roberto Assagioli, pioneer of transpersonal psychology and explorer of spiritual experiences (Sun square Neptune); and Sri Aurobindo, pioneer of integral yoga (Sun trine Neptune).

In persons of a mystical inclination, Sun-Neptune complexes can manifest as a Christ-like sacrifice of the individual self to the greater life of the spirit, a form of spiritual heroism in which one's consciousness, or even one's identity, becomes a channel for the divine. The emphasis in such cases is less on self will and more on serving as an emissary for the spirit. Equally, as in Jung's case, there can be a struggle to preserve one's individual self against the potentially overwhelming influx of the archetypal unconscious and as the impulse to harmoniously align oneself with the spirit, with the Tao or the Logos—the principle of cosmic order.

Aspects of Neptune to other planets in the natal chart give an indication as to how such themes will be experienced in the individual's life. The Venus-Neptune complex, for example, is connected with a spiritualized expression of the anima, or the blurring of spirituality and romantic love, taking the form of anything from romantic flights of fancy and unconscious romantic projection to a mystic's love of the divine and a transcendence of personal romantic inclinations. The latter is clearly evident in Teilhard whose love for the divine in the material world and the figure of Jesus Christ assumed a personal, almost romantic quality. The placement of Teilhard's Sun and Venus in Taurus is reflected in the characteristic earthy cast of his mysticism, which focused on the spirit in the heart of matter, and re-conceived Christianity in terms of the evolution of the material universe.[22]

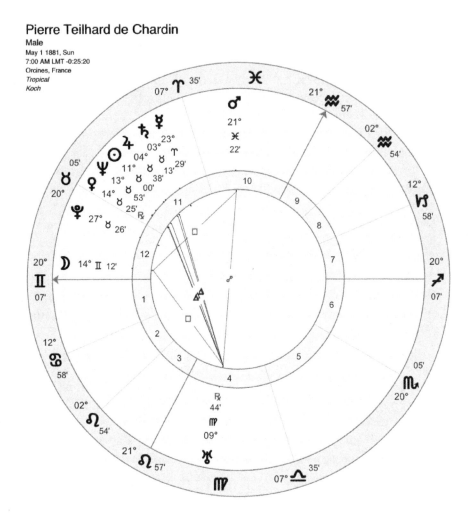

Figure 4: Pierre Teilhard de Chardin's Birth Chart

With Mercury-Neptune aspects, by contrast, Neptunian themes evident during individuation—such as synthesis, mythologizing, a symbolic or metaphorical reading of life experience, access to subtle dimensions of reality—are typically expressed through the intellect. Thus, we can observe the signature of Mercury-Neptune complexes in the grand philosophical synthesis of Hegel, the psychic knowledge and mystic philosophy of Rudolf Steiner, the mythic studies of Joseph Campbell and Mircea Eliade, and the metaphors and mythic imagery in the song lyrics of Bob Dylan and Bruce Springsteen—each born during major Mercury-Neptune alignments.[23]

Similar motifs are evident during major Neptune transits and progressions to Neptune, which typically coincide with openings to the fantasy products of the unconscious, periods of hermetic withdrawal from the world, spiritual experiences, and periods of heightened mythic or artistic sensitivity, often with a prophetic or visionary quality.

Pluto: Instinctual Compulsion, the Underworld, and Rebirth

Whereas the Neptune principle pertains to the spiritual dimension of reality and the imaginal realm of the collective unconscious, the archetypal Pluto pertains to the instincts, seething passions, and irrational drives in the depths of the unconscious—impulses that need to be brought to the surface of consciousness and purged. Pluto symbolizes the dark spiritual power of nature that seeks its own evolutionary transformation in the light of human self-reflective awareness. The Pluto principle is thus associated with perhaps *the* major theme of the individuation process: psychospiritual death-rebirth. This theme is especially connected with the interaction of the Pluto and Saturn archetypes, indicated by natal alignments or by transits between the corresponding planets.

In psychology, the Saturn archetype finds expression in the crystallized forms and rigid structures of the ego-complex. Saturn is connected, too, with the emotion of fear and the instinct for self-preservation that underlie the ego and its mechanisms of defense. Saturn symbolizes the old ruling principle of the psyche; it is associated with the principle of repression, control, and censorship, and it is thus well described by the Freudian notion of the superego. In mythic terms, Saturn is personified both as an old king, symbolizing a negative life-resistant form of the wise old man or senex, and as the 'guardian of the threshold'—the barrier that must be overcome if one is to live out one's own life adventure, realize one's potential, and access the transcendent. In essence, before it is transformed during the work of individuation, Saturn represents the principle of negation and resistance in the psyche that manifests as a "no" response to life—the inability to accept and affirm life in all its suffering and struggle, as well as its joys and pleasures.

The agent of transformation of the crystallized ego is the archetypal Pluto. Pluto symbolizes the elemental force of nature, ever destroying and creating, moving inexorably on, ensuring that life is always dying to the old and being born to the new, like the mythic Uroborus, the tail-eating serpent or dragon, consuming itself in the perpetual cycle of instinctual life. In Jungian terms, Pluto is associated with elemental and instinctual power repressed into the shadow. It is connected, as well, with the Dionysian power of Nietzsche's *Übermensch*—and the daimonic force that empowers the individual to far greater deeds that would be possible by conscious willpower alone.

The transformative impulse associated with Pluto works by a process Stanislav Grof has called *pyrocatharsis*: the burning out and destruction of a psychological complex or pattern of behavior by driving it to its extreme, intensifying it.[24] In the case of Pluto-Saturn combinations—whether in natal alignments or transits—experiences of fear, negation, contraction, resistance, limitation, and repression can all be transformed through extremity of expression. This archetypal combination is thus associated with the experience of eternal damnation, the fiery torments of hell, and the agonies of purgatory. Saturn-Pluto archetypal complexes can be experienced as a 'pressure cooker' of transformation, like an alchemical alembic, in which the ordinary human ego undergoes a death rebirth. Indeed, the entire alchemical transformation process essentially reflects Pluto-Saturn dynamics, incorporating themes such as the transformation by fire (*calcinatio*), the *nigredo* phase of the death (*mortificatio*) and dismemberment of the old ruling king or dominant principle (*Sol*, the old Adam), and the purging of impurities, which symbolizes, Jung believed, the impulse to become free of instinctual compulsion.

As Mircea Eliade has shown, alchemy has its roots in both metallurgy, the mining of ores deep underground and smelting of the ores in fire to create metal; and in shamanism, in which the shaman undergoes a descent and death experience, often involving extremes of suffering and encounters with animal powers.[25] These themes—the underground realm, depth, fire, intense heat, the animal world—are all unmistakably Plutonic. The Pluto archetype is also evident in myth in the motif of the "descent into the underworld," and it is symbolized by encounters with denizens of the depths and the confrontation with fearsome beasts, or as volcanic eruptions of elemental power and consumption by fire, and so forth.

With the Pluto archetype acting on Saturn, as it were, the repressed power of the instincts effects a transformation of the ego structure: the old crystallized forms of the Saturnian structure of the ego are destroyed; the normal limits of the human personality are broken down that a new wholeness might be realized. Conversely, with Saturn acting on Pluto, the instincts themselves are to be contained and controlled—the prerequisite for their transformation. One must bring Saturnian discipline and control to bear on the passions, and one must invoke established moral values as one confronts the primitive uncivilized instincts in the unconscious. For it is only by such an endeavor that blind instinctual compulsion that characterizes much of human existence can be brought to an end. Individuation, mediated by the Saturn and Pluto archetypes, brings the death of the animal man. In Christianity, the primary symbol of this death, and of the overcoming of the unregenerate instinctual state of being, is the Crucifixion.

Unsurprisingly, we can see many of these themes associated with the Pluto-Saturn combination in the lives and works of figures who have explored experiences of psychospiritual transformation in depth, including spiritual philosophers Alan Watts and Sri Aurobindo, as well as Nietzsche and Jung—each born with Saturn and Pluto in major aspect. Aurobindo, for example, with natal Mercury, Saturn, and Pluto in a grand trine, set out, in his voluminous written works, comprehensive in-depth psychological analyses of the experience of evolutionary transformation by which matter could be spiritualized through the medium of human consciousness. He remains one of the most systematic and insightful articulators of the labor of spiritual transformation.

In Nietzsche's case, his exhortation to a life of more intense suffering—a descent "deeper into pain than I have ever descended"—as a prerequisite for further evolution, gives voice to one essential dimension of his Saturn-Pluto archetypal complex, as does his firsthand testimonies of the "heartbreaking last hours" of psychospiritual death-rebirth.[26]

Such themes are also evident in Jung whose description of individuation as an arduous Herculean labor and his testimony of his prolonged struggle with the dark forces of the unconscious are but two of many instances that reflect the Saturn-Pluto dynamics in his own life. Jung's experience of this complex is well conveyed in his account of his "confrontation with the unconscious," described in *Memories, Dreams, Reflections*, and dramatized in the dialogues and fantasies of the *Red Book*.[27] One can recognize in Jung's accounts of this period the Pluto archetype in the "demonic" and "brute" strength that possessed him, enabling him to survive the onslaught of the unconscious. Specifically, one can see Pluto empowering and intensifying the Saturnian capacity for resistance and endurance. At the same time, the Plutonic power of the instincts was destroying the old structure of the ego and its persona, symbolized by the crashing blocks of stone and the elemental power of the thunderstorm.

As I have argued elsewhere, when considering the significance of the Pluto archetypal principle for individuation, one can, I believe, discern an underlying developmental trajectory often apparent in the lives of people who deeply engage the dimension of experience associated with Pluto.[28] This trajectory, to briefly summarize, is defined by several distinct stages: (1) an unconscious instinctual empowerment of the ego, when the drives associated with Pluto compel the emerging individual ego to assert itself in the world, to conquer and plunder, and to exert its power and try to satisfy its instinctually driven cravings; (2) a frustration of instinct by the Saturnian context of human life (the pressures of material existence, the hard facts of one's reality, the inherent limitations of life, the slow pace of change, responsibilities and duties to others, and so forth) with a simultaneous intensification of the unfulfilled drives and desires associated with Pluto; (3) an increasing schism between the ego, attuned to an outer objective reality, and the instincts, hell-bent on gratification—a schism that, if too extreme, can lead to the experience of alienation or estrangement from the instinctual basis of life and with it a loss of vitality, zest, and life power; (4) a "descent into the underworld" of the unconscious in order for the ego to recover lost power and potentials; (5) an ensuing death-rebirth struggle through which the ego and the instincts are both transformed; (6) and finally an ascent, resurrection, and the realization of the greater wholeness of the personality in which the instinctual compulsion associated with the Pluto archetype is overcome.

As these brief examples illustrate, the archetypal principles associated with Uranus, Neptune, and Pluto are the primary agents of individuation, representing themes and motifs that are central concerns of the world's mythic and spiritual traditions. By using archetypal astrology, one can better understand one's unique relationship to these principles and thus discern how these themes are expressing themselves in one's own life experiences. In an age when myths are widely dismissed, leaving the individual shorn of orientation to the powers of the psyche, archetypal astrology enables us to understand our own relationship to the "gods." It provides an archetypal framework to give deeper context to our lives, and to help us navigate even the most challenging of experiences.

Chart Data
(courtesy of Astrodatabank, unless stated otherwise)

RR = "Rodden Rating"—a system of classification used by Astrodatabank to indicate the reliability of the birth data.

Roberto Assagioli, 27 February 1888, 11:10, Venice, Italy (45n27, 12e21). Source: Birth certificate in hand. RR = AA.

Sri Aurobindo, 15 August 1872, 05:00 (Local Mean Time), Calcutta, India (22n32, 88e22). Source: Biography. RR = B.

Joseph Campbell, 26 March 1904, 19:25 EST (+5), New York, NY. USA (40n42, 74w00). Source: Erin Campbell quotes his mother, 1981. RR = A.

Neal Cassidy, 8 February 1926, 02:05 MST (+7), Salt Lake City, UT (40n45, 111w53). Source: From memory/biography. RR = A.

Bob Dylan, 24 May 1941, 21:05 (+6), Duluth, MN, USA (46n47, 92w06). Source: Birth certificate. RR = AA.

Allen Ginsberg, 3 June 1926, 02:00 EDT (+4), Newark, NJ. USA (40n44, 74w10). Source: Quotes letter from his assistant. RR = A.

Robert Graves, 24 July 1895, 04:26 GMT (+0), Wimbledon, England (51n25, 0w13). Source: Biography. RR = B.

G. W. F. Hegel, 27 August 1770, Time unknown, Stuttgart, Germany (48n47, 9e11). Source: Wikipedia. http://en.wikipedia.org/wiki/Georg_Wilhelm_Friedrich_Hegel (accessed 12 December 2011)

Carl Gustav Jung, 26 July 1875, 07:29 UT, Kesswil, Switzerland (47n36, 9e20). Source: Gret-Baumann Jung (C. G. Jung's daughter). RR = A.

Jack Kerouac, 12 March 1922, 17:00 EST (+5), Lowell, MA, USA (42n38, 71w19). Source: Biography. RR = B.

Jim Morrison, 8 December 1943, 11:55 EWT (+4), Melbourne, FL, USA (28n04, 80w36). Source: Birth certificate. RR = AA.

Friedrich Nietzsche, 15 October 1844, 10:00, Rocken, Germany (51n15, 12e08). Source: Biography. RR = B.

Bruce Springsteen, 23 September 1949, 22:50 EDT (+4), Long Branch, NJ (40n16, 74w16). Source: Bruce Springsteen Special Collection.

Rudolf Steiner, 25 February 1861, 23:15 LMT, Kraljevica, Hungary (45n16, 14e34). Source: Birth certificate. RR = AA.

Pierre Teilhard de Chardin, 1 May 1880, 07:00 LMT, Orcines, France (45n47, 3e05). Source: Birth certificate. RR = AA.

Saint Teresa of Avila, 7 April 1515 (Gregorian), 05:00 LMT, Avila, Spain (40n39, 4w42). Source: Biography. RR = B.

Saint Thérèse of Lisieux, 2 January 1873, 23:30 LMT, Alencon, France (48n26,0e05). Source: Birth certificate. RR = AA.

Alan Watts, 6 January 1915, 06:20 GMT, Chislehurst, England (51n25, 0e04). Source: Biography. RR = B

Notes

[1] Many of these archetypes are discussed in Jung's seminal *The Archetypes and the Collective Unconscious*. The individuation process is discussed in his *Two Essays on Analytical Psychology* and is the central focus of all his major works on alchemy, especially *Mysterium Coniunctionis*.

[2] On the Self's association with the will of God, Jung writes: "The Self . . . by virtue of its numinosity, compels man towards wholeness, that is, towards the integration of the unconscious or the subordination of the ego to a holistic 'will,' which is rightly conceived to be 'God's will'"(C. G. Jung, *Letters II*, p. 14). Following the convention in this quote, I am capitalizing the Jungian concept of the *Self* to distinguish it from the usual connotation of the term individual *self*, which is more or less synonymous with Jung's term the *ego*.

[3] See Jung, *Symbols of Transformation*, and Campbell, *Hero with a Thousand Faces*.

[4] For further detail on the relationship of astrology to Jung's theory of archetypes, see Le Grice, *Archetypal Cosmos*, 55–78, 90–94, 152–178.

[5] For a discussion of the archetypal multidimensionality and multivalence inherent in astrology, see Tarnas, *Cosmos and Psyche*, 85–87.

[6] For the connections between archetypal astrology and mythology, see *Archetypal Cosmos*, 34–94, 263–287.

[7] Progressions are a technique of forecasting based on the advancement of the natal planetary positions by one day or one degree for each year of life. The advanced positions are then compared to the natal chart positions, and aspects formed between these two sets of positions are interpreted.

[8] The archetypal principle associated with the dwarf planet Eris—which

appears to be related to themes such as the tension of opposites, evolutionary discord, cosmic justice, counterbalancing reactions, and the violation of nature—might also be extremely significant for individuation. See Le Grice, *Discovering Eris*.

[9] Jung, *Memories, Dreams, Reflections*, 414.

[10] Campbell, *Hero with a Thousand Faces*, 51.

[11] For examples of Uranus's association with individual brilliance and creative genius, see Tarnas, *Prometheus the Awakener*.

[12] Nietzsche, "Daybreak," aphorism 575 in *A Nietzsche Reader*, 205. For Richard Tarnas's analysis of the Nietzsche's Jupiter-Uranus complex, see *Cosmos and Psyche*, 335–348.

[13] Nietzsche was born in the village of Röcken, in Saxony-Anhalt, Germany, which is now incorporated into the town of Lützen.

[14] Campbell, interview with Bill Moyers, *The Power of Myth*.

[15] Nietzsche, "Ecce Homo" in *Basic Writings of Nietzsche*, 751.

[16] See Jung, *Memories, Dreams, Reflections*, chapter IV, 194–225.

[17] Bair, *Jung: A Biography*, 238.

[18] Jung, *Two Essays on Analytical Psychology*, 156–171.

[19] See Campbell, *Hero with a Thousand Faces*, 90–95.

[20] Jung, *Mysterium Coniunctionis*, 283.

[21] Jung, *Mysterium Coniunctionis*, 277.

[22] See Teilhard de Chardin, *Heart of Matter*.

[23] For my analysis of the metaphors and imagery in Bruce Springsteen's song lyrics, see Le Grice, "A Last Chance Power-drive" and "Land of Hope and Dreams."

[24] Grof, *Psychology of the Future*, 48.

[25] See Eliade, *Forge and the Crucible*.

[26] Nietzsche, *Thus Spoke Zarathustra*, 175, 111

[27] See Jung, *Memories, Dreams, Reflections*, 200–201.

[28] I explore the significance of the archetypal Pluto for individual psychological development in Le Grice, "A Last Chance Power-Drive."

VIII

The Solar Myths and Opicinus de Canistris: A Book Review of the Notes on Jung's Seminar at Eranos 1943

The central focus of *The Solar Myths and Opicinus de Canistris*, published by Daimon Verlag in 2016, is an impromptu lecture given by C. G. Jung at an Eranos Conference in Ascona, Switzerland, in 1943 in which he provides psychological commentaries on solar myths and on a series of symbolic illustrations by Italian medieval priest Opicinus de Canistris (1296–c. 1352 CE). For anyone with an abiding interest in Jung's work, this book is a real gem, providing numerous fascinating insights on a range of topics such as the dark side of the divine, Christianity, the tension of opposites, mythic symbolism, and the evolution of human consciousness. For our purposes, this review of that book will highlight the astrological symbolism in the priest's visions and the evolution of solar myths, associated with the archetype of the Sun, in step with Jung's understanding of the development of ego-consciousness over time.

As we learn in the foreword (by Thomas Fischer) and the introduction, the genesis of the book was the fortuitous discovery, in 2012, of some handwritten lecture notes in Jung's former house in Kusnacht. These notes comprised "six untitled, small slips of paper" (p. 4) giving a rough outline of the 1943 talk. As it turns out, the discovery—by the book's editors Riccardo Bernardini, Gian Piero Quaglino, and Augusto Romano—was serendipitously aligned with their endeavor, already underway, to bring to publication a transcript of this very lecture.

Jung's speaking notes, which are reproduced in the original German in the appendices and translated in the main section of the book, provide an intriguing glimpse into Jung the man, preparing to give a lecture, as any of us might, listing keywords that would trigger his amplifications on specific topics, and producing different versions of his planned talk as he revised his thoughts. The notes, which were likely "stimulated by the very papers he had listened to during the conference," (p. 36) supplement more detailed transcripts recorded at Eranos by two of Jung's students: Rivkah Schärf Kluger and Alwine von Keller. Both these accounts, although challenging to follow in places, are mutually consistent and complementary, forming the centerpiece of this publication.

The book is helpfully divided into clear sections presented in logical sequence. A sixty-four-page introduction by the editors provides essential background to the Eranos conferences and their significance for the scholarly development and dissemination of Jung's thought. Jung gave fourteen talks at Eranos between 1933 and 1951, and, as one would expect, was very much the dominant presence at the gatherings, which explored a diverse range of topics and viewpoints, fostered by the atmospheric setting and enriched by the contributions of figures such as Neumann, Corbin, and Kerényi—the latter speaking at the 1943 gathering. Jung, we learn, had not originally intended to present at that year's event, but had acceded to popular demand, giving "an exciting and multifaceted impromptu talk" (p. 28) to "about twenty-seven people," (p. 25) which served as "an astounding epilogue" (p. 28) to the conference outside of the regular program of presentations.[1]

As noted, Jung's talk consisted of two components: the first, an exegesis of solar myths, and the second, on which the editors place greater emphasis in their introduction, a psychological commentary on images from the *Codex Palatinus Latinus 1993*, attributed to Opicinus.

Jung had a deep interest in figures of a mystical or visionary disposition—including Goethe, Nietzsche, Hölderlin, Hildegard von Bingen, Niklaus von Flüe ("Brother Klaus"), Paracelsus, Jakob Böhme, Meister Eckhart, and alchemists such as Gerhard Dorn and Michael Maier—who each came face to face with the numinous power of the unconscious, some succumbing to a tragic fate as a result. Jung's psychological analysis of the illustrations of Opicinus provides a further example of this kind, exploring the fate of an individual within a medieval Christian view of the world, struggling to come to terms with the tension of opposites in his psyche, and failing to successfully face and integrate the shadow. Reading *The Solar Myths*, one gets the sense that Opicinus had a visionary revelation of the kind Jung's describes in "Psychology and Literature." Such a revelation bursts forth

from the hinterland of man's mind, as if it had emerged from the abyss of prehuman ages, or from a superhuman world of contrasting light and darkness. . . . Sublime, pregnant with meaning, yet chilling the blood with its strangeness, it arises from the timeless depths: glamorous, daemonic and grotesque, it bursts asunder our human standards of value and aesthetic form, a terrifying tangle of eternal chaos.[2]

The editors' introduction provides essential details of Opicinus's life, based on the priest's autobiographical testimony—a life which appears to have been largely unremarkable until the onset of an illness in 1334, during which he fell into a coma for ten days.

When he came out of the coma, he had been weakened both physically and psychologically. He could not speak. His right hand was paralyzed. He complained of a serious loss of memory. Along with his illness came apparitions and nightmares that tortured him. He recorded a vision that he had in June, when he saw "a vase in the clouds." In his bizarre annotations, the vase has a remarkable role since, by a play on the double meaning of the word, *canistra* ("vase"), it is linked to his own name, Canistris. He also had recurrent visions of the Virgin Mary with her son in her arms. She appeared sorry and was sitting on the ground, stricken with sorrow because of Opicinus' spiritual perdition. Nevertheless, Opicinus tells us, "the weakening of my right hand was transformed into a strengthening of my spiritual potential." (pp. 42–43)

The visions were recorded by Opicinus as fifty-two drawings in the *Codex Palatinus Latinus 1993* on which he is believed to have worked until his death. The drawings, as the editors note, are "full of annotations and correspondences that are theological, symbolic, astrological, historical, and cartographic." (p. 45) Indeed, Opicinus, who was appointed scribe to Apostolic Penitentiary by Pope John XXII, was an astrologer, and thus "tried to superimpose classical astrological symbolism on such features of the Christian calendar as the feast days of the saints" and "produced an interpretation of his city, Pavia, in the light of 'Christian astrology.'" (p. 45)

A peculiar and striking aspect of his illustrations is his projection of anthropomorphic and theriomorphic symbolism upon the geography of Europe and North Africa. Continents and seas take on human or bestial form, and apparently represent the extreme tension of opposites playing itself out in Opicinus's psyche. The editors explain:

In Opicinus' cartography . . . the Mediterranean Sea is actually represented as a demonic world, a dark "anti-world," in contraposition to the luminous world of dry land. In plate 39 of the *Codex Palatinus Latinus 1993* (figures 43 and 43*bis*) in particular, if Europe is represented symbolically as a figure of male gender and Africa as a woman (in other representations by Opicinus, the genders of the two continents may be inverted), the Mediterranean appears as a demonic figure—Jung notes, from Alwine von Keller's account—"with a goat's beard" and the Atlantic as a monstrous animal, probably a fish, which swallows up Europe from the north-western coast of France. (p. 35)

For Opicinus, the world assumed a sexualized character ("a gigantic and geographical copulation," [p. 47] as Claude Gandelman described it) and is thus consistent with Mircea Eliade's understanding of the sexualized hierophany or sacred cosmology behind the origins of alchemy, which was concerned with reconciling the same pairs of conflicting opposites that appear in Opicinus's cartographical art.[3]

Jung's analysis centers on the conflict between the upper realm of the light of God in the form of *sol*, the sun, and the lower realm of "*aries*—ram, horned ram, goat beard, and . . . the devil," as depicted in the *Codex*. (p. 98) Identifying with the light side, the "lamb of God," Opicinus, in Jung's judgment, was unable to integrate the dark side of the divine and was caught in an irreconcilable tension of opposites between Christ and the devil, good and evil, light and dark. Jung explains, "He wanted to rule this fearsome conflict out and shut himself off inside the *corpus mysticum* of the Church." (p. 98) Unable to face the conflict within himself, Jung adds, "he did not . . . master . . . the splitting-in-two in his *unconscious*, which was the problem of the new era. This is a picture of a schizophrenic." (p. 109)

Jung sees in some of Opicinus's drawings the basic structure of a mandala, incorporating circles and quaternities, no doubt compensating for the psychological turbulence the Italian priest was experiencing. Alongside this, the editors draw our attention to the wealth of symbolic and allegorical content, such as the Christian image of a "new Jerusalem descending from heaven," the alchemical *coniunctio* of *sponsus* and *sponsa*, astrological symbolism, and juxtapositions of opposites such as sun and moon, East and West, spirit and flesh, and the "bright" inner man and the shadow of the outer man. (pp. 48–49) The age, decaying condition, and fine detail within the Opicinus documents make some of the illustrations of the *Codex* difficult to clearly discern, in electronic format at least, so we can be grateful to the editors for their careful commentary.

While the Opicinus material provides a fascinating and unique case study, perhaps the principal theoretical contribution of the 1943 lecture is to be found in Jung's treatment of the emergence of human ego-consciousness, as symbolized by the development of solar myths over time. Jung notes that "the Sun is basically a living symbol for the illumination of consciousness." (p. 83) Solar creation myths thus refer to the process of "becoming conscious" (p. 83); just as the sun rises out of the darkness at dawn, consciousness emerges daily from the dark ocean of sleep and dream, and ego-consciousness, over the millennia, is progressively differentiated from the dim twilight existence that characterizes the primordial condition of *participation mystique*. Like the sun, the individual human ego, carrier of the light of consciousness, rises up out of the dark primordial mists towards a pinnacle of illumination.

This process ultimately leads, Jung suggests, to the Christian revelation, especially the Gospel of John, and is further developed in the theological speculations of the Scholastics. (p. 86)

> By now we have observed how the Sun god runs through a development in older culture and, in fact, takes on . . . a more and more spiritual shape; and, in the end, this light of the Sun becomes the light of John's logos, which shines out in the darkness and undoubtedly means spiritual illumination and the raising of human consciousness. It is the light of the *gnosis theou*. (p. 86)

Although Jung (and others, such as Erich Neumann) has made similar arguments elsewhere, in this lecture Jung more explicitly connects the development of solar symbolism to the emergence of a differentiated ego-consciousness. For Jung, the course of development of solar myths reflects a profound transformation in the human psyche by which the conscious ego emerged as an independent and autonomous self-willing agent, bringing a concomitant progressive strengthening of the human will. The fortification of an independent will enabled human beings to move beyond the *heimarmene* of the ancient world—characterized by fatalism, compulsion, crippling superstitions, and subservience to the will of the gods. As Jung puts it, "The dependency of people of the ancient world on *heimarmene* is [due to] this lack of consciousness that one is in the hands of." (p. 88) In the ancient world, human will, to the extent that it existed at all, was secondary in its power and authority to the will of the gods.

If the emergence of ego and an autonomous human will is a great cultural achievement, as Jung believes, it also brings with it certain attendant dangers, which he proceeds to discuss. With the development of the individual human subject, a subtle but consequential shift takes place which places singular emphasis upon the willing agent—the "I" principle—utterly disregarding divine will.[4] From the Renaissance and the Reformation on, Jung argues, "the individual no longer said: I *know*, I *will*, but the sound-stress shifted and now he said: *I* know, *I* will. As the human being became conscious of his size and freedom, the undermining of godly authority began." (p. 108)

This psychological transition gave birth to a dualism—between subject and object, God and nature, consciousness and unconscious, light and dark—that so defines the modern era, for better and for worse. It is a dualism that finds primary philosophical articulation in the work of Descartes. As Jung describes it:

This freedom of human consciousness, the emancipation of the judgment and will from dependency on what is higher, brought one, I would like to say, one problem into the world—*duality*, a problem that really had never been there before. There had never been the sovereignty of the person in this sense. There had always been higher controlling powers at hand, which put a damper on things. So, this duality brought about a foundation of human consciousness, which had never been there before. (p. 89)

For Jung, of course, the light of human consciousness, supported by a differentiated ego, fulfils a singularly important role in the world. He repeats in this lecture his proclamation of the world-constitutive power of consciousness: "consciousness has a meaning that is entirely extraordinary. . . . Without consciousness, nothing exists. The world had really been nothing at all until somebody said: that is the world; that *is*." (p. 86) Similarly, here, as in *Answer to Job*, Jung stresses the critical role of the human in bringing the unconscious divine (the "Dark Father") to consciousness. (p. 104) As we read in von Keller's transcript: "[God] revealed a functioning independent human consciousness. Now, the human being is instrumental; he was invented for that. God wanted consciousness so that he could be expressed." (p. 104)

It is on this note that the two components of Jung's talk come together. The dualism between the light loving God and the dark power of nature, personified in Opicinus's Christian astrological imagination as the goat-devil, is at the heart of the schizophrenic splitting of the Italian priest's psyche, and it is a "prelude," Jung suggests, "of what today we are the shaken witness of." (p. 109) It is a dualism that we ourselves must reckon with if we are to meet the spiritual challenge of our time.

The central content of *The Solar Myths* thus provides us with an illuminating example of the symbolized psychological process of an individual in the wake of a spiritual revelation, failing to come to terms with the deep-rooted transformation impinging on the Christianized psyche. And the book's main theoretical contribution to Jungian psychology is its concise discussion of Jung's view of the collective development of consciousness in the context of solar myths. The inclusion of a wide selection of photographs, mostly from Eranos, including many of Jung himself, and biographical accounts of the two sources of Jung's lecture, Rivkah Schärf Kluger and Alwine von Keller, completes the truly fascinating and eclectic collection of materials within this volume. The publication is successful in bringing to life the spirit and personalities of the Eranos gatherings at that time, giving what feels like intimate access to the seminar, including a rare glimpse of Jung as a lecturer. For all these reasons, we owe Bernardini, Quaglino, and Romano a large debt of gratitude for making this material available to us.

Notes

[1] These descriptions are from two sources: (1) the words of Swiss artist Hedy Alma Wyss, from a short summary of the seminar written on August 28–29, 1943 some two weeks after the event; and (2) Olga Fröbe-Kapteyn's letter to Hans Conrad Bänziger on August 13, 1943, written after Jung's seminar on the preceding days: "From 9:30 until noon Jung spoke to about twenty-seven people in the best of moods and they had the feeling that the old days of the seminar had come back to life." (p. 25)

[2] C. G. Jung, "Psychology and Literature" (1950) in *The Collected Works of C. G. Jung*, vol. 15, ed. and trans. R. F. C. Hull (Princeton, NJ: Princeton University Press, 1966), § 141.

[3] See Mircea Eliade, "The World Sexualized," in *The Forge and the Crucible* (Chicago, IL: The University of Chicago Press, 1978).

[4] The position Jung advances in this lecture is broadly consistent with perspectives in recent work such as Charles Taylor, *A Secular Age* (Cambridge,

MA: The Belnap Press of Harvard University Press, 2007) and Richard Tarnas, *Cosmos and Psyche: Intimations of a New World View* (New York: Viking, 2006).

IX

Neptune through the Ages:
The Evolution of Religious Consciousness

In a Platonic sense, archetypes are transcendent principles existing outside of the sphere of human history, beyond the limits of time and space. Yet these transcendent universal factors find concrete expression in particular moments, manifesting in specific historical periods and geographical locations. The forms of expression of the archetypes are therefore not eternal and unchanging, but mutate and evolve over time, inflected by the environment in which they manifest. Thus, the experience of the Neptune principle, as it is understood in astrology, would be considerably different for a person in an ancient civilization or a traditional society than for a person in the early Christian world or in the Middle Ages.

The changing forms of expression of the Neptune archetype through history underlie the development or evolution of what the eminent scholar of Jewish mysticism Gershom Scholem termed "religious consciousness," with each stage revealing different dimensions of the archetype.[1] An early form of the expression of Neptune was the preconscious unity of the condition of *participation mystique*. This condition was described by Claude Levy-Bruhl in his study of premodern peoples, and it bears clear resemblances to the structures of archaic and magic consciousness described by integral theorist Jean Gebser. Neptune was manifest here in the undifferentiated unity of experience in which there was no clearly differentiated self sense—that is, no self separate from and fortified against the world, as the modern ego is, but rather a porous self (to borrow a term used by Charles Taylor), with a only a hazy sense of identity. In such a state it is hard to say where one's emotions end and the external world begins—the spirits of the forest and mountains seem to be the source of fear and awe. In the condition of *participation mystique* we might place the experience of a young child in whom the rational ego and acute self-reflective consciousness have yet to emerge. Neptune here can be recalled and invoked as recollections of the magic of childhood, in which the world has an enchanted glow. Although located in our collective and individual past, this form of expression of Neptune remains available to us in fleeting moments of reverie of our childhood past or in the breaking through of the revelation of the spiritual unity of all things. Problematically, we fall under the sway of Neptune in this form in our proclivity to unconscious projection onto the environment or when we become blinded or intoxicated by unrecognized fantasies or abandon reason in favor of magical and wishful thinking.

The historical phase of this primal unity was superseded by three further phases—the mythic, religious, and mystical—which are the focus of Scholem's study in his *Major Trends in Jewish Mysticism*. From the magical state of enchantment, human consciousness passes progressively, almost imperceptibly, to the age of myth, which Scholem sees as the first stage of a developing religious consciousness. "The first stage," of religious consciousness, he observes, is mythic, for it "represents the world as being full of gods whom man encounters at every step and whose presence can be experienced without recourse to ecstatic meditation."[2] We might think here of the era of the Olympian pantheon in ancient Greek myth, where the deeds and fates of men and gods were intimately entwined. In this mythical age of history, overlapping somewhat with the magical condition described above, there was an "immediate consciousness of the interrelation and interdependence of things, their essential unity which precedes duality." Here, Scholem concludes, "Nature is the scene of man's relation to God."[3] In this state of being, we feel a natural kinship with all of nature—a mood powerfully evoked by romantic poets such as Wordsworth and Hölderlin.

In the second phase, myth gives way to religion, and duality is born from the rupturing of the primal unity. "Religion's supreme function," Scholem claims, "is to destroy the dream-harmony of Man, Universe and God, to isolate man from the other elements of the dream stage of his mythical and primitive consciousness."[4] Depending on one's viewpoint, the exile from the dreamlike reality of the mythic era might be imagined either as the deliverance from a world of primitive superstition into the truth or as the fall into alienation in a existential separation from the divine (as in the exile from Eden). Either way, the result is the same: "Man becomes aware of a fundamental duality, of a vast gulf that can be crossed by nothing but . . . the voice of God, directing and law-giving in His revelation, and the voice of man in prayer."[5] The division between God and human beings, Scholem notes, is the root assumption of the major monotheistic religions, for whom "the scene of religion is no longer Nature, but the moral and religious action of man and the community of men, whose interplay brings about history as . . . the stage on which the drama of man's relation to God unfolds."[6] Jung describes this movement in vivid terms: "The gods first lived in superhuman power and beauty on the top of snow-clad mountains or in the darkness of caves, woods and seas. Later on they drew together into one god, and then that god became man."[7]

From the immediate field of participation in the mythic reality of gods and goddesses, the Neptune principle thereafter primarily takes the form of religious faith, worship, and devotion—the hallmarks of the expression of the Neptunian religious impulses in Judeo-Christian era. In Scholem's view, the emergence of religions opened up an "abyss" between man and God, which mysticism, as an expression of "the romantic period of religion," then tries to bridge or heal in an attempt to recover the lost unity at a higher level of consciousness.[8]

> It [mysticism] strives to piece together the fragments broken by the religious cataclysm, to bring back the old unity which religion had destroyed, but on a new plane, where the world of mythology and that of revelation meet in the soul of man. Thus the soul becomes its scene and the soul's path through the abysmal multiplicity of things to the experience of the Divine Reality, now conceived as the primordial unity of all things, becomes its main preoccupation.[9]

In this third phase of the development of religious consciousness, mysticism arises as a romantic countercurrent to religious orthodoxy and later to the rationalism of the Enlightenment and scientific materialism of the modern era.

Scholem notes that mysticism often promotes a renewal and reformulation of existing religions. The dogmatic orthodoxy of religion is followed by a creative, individualistic religious consciousness in which "new religious impulses"[10] challenge existing religious values and give rise to new interpretations of established dogma, much in the way that Jung attempted to recover and amplify Christianity, and in accord, too, with Joseph Campbell's view, set out in *The Masks of God,* of the transition in the modern era from the "grand unitary stages" of the orthodox religions to a period of creative mythology. In this later phase of the expression of the religious and mythic impulse associated with Neptune, the "mythogenetic zone" (to use Campbell's term), the place where myths arise, has now been transferred from specific holy sites in the world to the inner realm of the individual's psyche. The creative artist, in Campbell's view, has become mythmaker, and the individual in the quest for authentic spiritual experience has embarked on a variant of a mystical path. The individual path of realization, and with it the quest for direct experience of the divine, becomes increasingly necessary in an age when religious dogma loses its numinosum and becomes divorced from the experienced reality of people's lives, as it has for many in our own time. With no direct religious outlet, the Neptunian religious urge finds surrogate forms of expression—through alcohol, drugs, television, cinema, glamor, the idealization of celebrity figures, and the pursuit of paradise in material form. Equally, however, the unsatisfied spiritual longings associated with Neptune can inspire the individual quest for truth and an authentic way through life, providing the inspiration for a commitment to individuation, as described by Jung.

Jean Gebser sees the possibility of the recovery of magical and mythic modes or structures of consciousness in the emergence of what he calls "integral consciousness."[11] In this vein, I believe we might thus entertain an integral understanding of the experience of Neptune, drawing on each of these phases:

(1) a *participation mystique* with the environment, characteristic of early human consciousness, moving into a magical *animism*, defined by a spiritual feeling for and sense of connection with the Earth, with nature, with matter;

(2) the *polytheism* of mythic consciousness with its vivid drama of the interventions of the gods and goddesses in the sphere of human lives, immortalized by the Homeric epics;

(3) the *monotheism* of orthodox forms of religious piety and practice, as in Judaism and Christianity, informed by dogma, imbuing and inspiring a sense of sacrifice and service to the will of God and to the love of one's neighbor;

(4) the *atheism* of the modern secular world, for which "God is dead," has its Neptunian dimension, for with no God, the human potentially becomes divinized or idealized and the material world carries our religious projections, for better or worse;

(5) and, not least, the *mystical revelation* of the divine, both transcendent and immanent, fulfilling the yearning to experience

oneself as an expression of an encompassing divine source and manifestation. This yearning might inspire the creative individual pursuit of spiritual experience and the inner transformative journey of individuation.

As religious consciousness evolves from one era to the next, our conception of God and the gods changes, interpreted anew in accord with the spirit of the age. Astrology, as we will consider in the next chapter, can help us understand the timings of these transitions.

Notes

[1] Scholem, *Major Trends in Jewish Mysticism*, 7.

[2] Scholem, *Major Trends in Jewish Mysticism*, 7.

[3] Scholem, *Major Trends in Jewish Mysticism*, 7.

[4] Scholem, *Major Trends in Jewish Mysticism*, 7.

[5] Scholem, *Major Trends in Jewish Mysticism*, 7–8.

[6] Scholem, *Major Trends in Jewish Mysticism*, 7–8.

[7] Jung, *Psychology and Religion*, 102.

[8] Scholem, *Major Trends in Jewish Mysticism*, 8.

[9] Scholem, *Major Trends in Jewish Mysticism*, 8.

[10] Scholem, *Major Trends in Jewish Mysticism*, 8.

[11] See Gebser, *The Ever-present Origin*.

X

The Metamorphosis of the Gods:
Archetypal Astrology and the Transformation of the God-image in Jung's Red Book

A broader consideration of the significance of Jung's *Red Book* must take into account the historical moment in which it was created. If it is relevant not only to Jung himself, as the articulation of a personal mythology, but also to Western civilization at large, then we must turn our focus to the evolution of the modern West as revealed in its major historical and religious transitions. One way this might be done, in keeping with the tenets of analytical psychology, is to consider the archetypal factors impinging upon the Western psyche and the cultural Zeitgeist in the late nineteenth and early twentieth centuries, from the time of Jung's birth to the creation of *Liber Novus*. In so doing, we might gain some perspective on the significance of our own time and our evolving conceptions of the spiritual dimension of experience.

Taking an archetypal view can draw attention to a background order or formal cause in which the chains of historical events unfold and enable us to "see through" the events of history to their mythic background and archetypal reasons. James Hillman describes this perspective well: "Outer historical facts are archetypally colored, so as to disclose essential psychological meanings. Historical facts disclose the eternally recurring mythemes of history and of our individual souls. History is but the stage on which we enact mythemes of the soul."[1] To this end, an astrological analysis can help to illuminate the archetypal patterns underlying the events of any given era, in order to make known the universal principles as they find expression the concrete details of human experience at that time.

The Neptune-Pluto Cycle

By 1875, the year of Jung's birth, the slow-moving outer planets Neptune and Pluto, with orbital periods of 165 and 248 years respectively, entered the beginning of a rare conjunction in which they occupied the same section of space within the great circle of the Zodiac, a symbolic band inscribed around the Earth comprising the twelve well-known signs from Aries through Pisces. The Zodiac is the primary frame of reference used in astrology to map the movements of the planets. As seen from Earth, the planets were positioned within approximately twenty degrees of each other (the operative range for a conjunction between the outer planets) in the sign of Taurus for a period of just over thirty years, from roughly 1875–1908. A conjunction of these planets only occurs once every 500 years. Even more unusual, in this case the Neptune-Pluto conjunction also coincided with an opposition (a 180-degree alignment) with Uranus, first between Uranus and Pluto (1896–1907) and then Uranus and Neptune (1899–1918). Periods of history in which these three planets form major "axial alignments" (that is, conjunctions and oppositions) with each other are rare indeed. For instance, as Richard Tarnas has observed, one must look back to the heart of the Axial Age to find a conjunction of all three planets, when they were positioned within twenty degrees of each other (from 594 to 560 BCE)—the only such conjunction in recorded history.[2] This period, extending from 800 to 200 BCE, but centered on the sixth century, was like no other in human history, witnessing the emergence of Buddhism, Jainism, Confucianism, Taoism, Zoroastrianism, and Platonism, as well as major developments in Judaism and Hinduism. More recently, to give two further examples discussed by Tarnas, the three planets formed another highly significant alignment known as a T-square—with Uranus opposite Neptune, and both planets in 90-degree square alignments to Pluto—in the years around the birth of Shakespeare in 1564.[3] And in 1769–1770, the three planets entered 120-degree "trine" alignments with each other—a so-called Grand Trine—which, again, is an astronomical occurrence seldom witnessed. Remarkably, Tarnas observes, the period of this alignment saw the unique coincidence of the births of several towering creative geniuses, world-historic figures in every sense—Beethoven, Hegel, Napoleon, Wordsworth, and Hölderlin—who were to exert such an immense influence on the Western world in philosophy, religion, the arts, and socio-political history.[4]

Given the rarity of such alignments, and given the nature of the archetypes associated with Uranus, Neptune, and Pluto, any historical period accompanying major geometric configurations of these three planets is marked out as extremely significant, bringing forth deep-rooted and immensely consequential changes in human experience and witnessing the birth of individuals who effect such changes—a reflection, in both cases, of the combined archetypal qualities and themes associated with these planets. Uranus is specifically associated with awakening, freedom, liberation, revolt, trickster-like disruptions, and the urge to go one's own way in life, to realize one's uniqueness. It manifests in the spark of creative genius and the Promethean urge to birth the new, to pioneer, to invent, and to push beyond established limits and boundaries. Neptune is the principle associated with the realm of myth, dream, image, and fantasy. It is evident in spiritual experience and religious consciousness, in the aspiration toward the ideal and the longing for paradise, or simply in the urge to escape from or transcend the pressures and limitations of material existence and separate individual consciousness. It is connected with magic and enchantment, but also delusion, dissolution, and self-loss. Pluto finds expression as instinctual compulsion and power drives—in this respect it is reflected in Freud's concept of the id and in the Nietzschean will-to-power. As a Shiva-like principle of transformative creative-destructive force and elemental energy, Pluto is manifest in the power that impels evolution, purging and destroying old forms, driving the ongoing cycles of death-rebirth in nature. It is the principle of depth and symbolized as the mythic underworld.

In his 2006 publication, *Cosmos and Psyche*, Tarnas documented and interpreted the significance of periods of major alignments between the pairings of Uranus-Neptune, Uranus-Pluto, and Neptune-Pluto, identifying a number of themes that are manifest in cultural history at these times. He provides examples of the correlation between Uranus-Neptune alignments and the "birth of new philosophies," "spiritual awakenings and the birth of new religions," the "creative emergence of esoteric traditions," "revelations of the numinous," and the "birth of new forms of artistic expression."[5] In each case, the Uranus principle acts to awaken and catalyze a range of Neptunian experiences—often connected to the spiritual dimension of life. All of these themes were prominent in Jung's creation of the *Red Book*, principally between 1913 and 1918, during the Uranus-Neptune opposition of 1899–1918. By contrast, the Uranus-Pluto combination is associated in Tarnas's historical survey with themes such as the awakening of the Dionysian instincts, the eruption of powerful elemental forces, revolutions and the empowerment of mass protests, political extremism and the instinctually driven desire to make the world new in a radical overthrow and destruction of the ruling order, as exemplified by the period of the French Revolution and the revolutionary decade of the 1960s.[6] In these cases Uranus serves to stir and liberate the instincts—sexual, aggressive, and power drives—and to bring to the surface the contents of the Plutonic underworld: the base and barbaric, the primitive and the evil, but also the passion and power that might fuel one's individuation and vocational calling. Simultaneously, Pluto empowers and intensifies the creative impulses, innovations, and drive for freedom associated with Uranus, manifesting as periods of accelerated technological and socio-cultural change. These themes and others associated with the Uranus-Pluto archetypal complex are plainly manifest at the current time in coincidence with the Uranus-Pluto square of 2007–2020.

Both of these alignments fall within the more encompassing orbit of the Neptune-Pluto cycle, which is our primary focus. As Tarnas has described, this archetypal combination is associated with "especially profound transformations of cultural vision and the collective experience of reality, which often took place deep below the surface of collective consciousness."[7] Powerful undercurrents of change tend to coincide, during major Neptune-Pluto conjunctions and oppositions, with critical phases in the rise and fall of civilizations, marking the "beginnings and endings of immense cultural epochs of great historical magnitude."[8] To give one example, the fall of the Roman Empire in the 100-year period between 376 and 476 CE was centered on the Neptune-Pluto conjunction of 399–424 CE, with the exact alignment closely coinciding with the sack of Rome in 410 CE. This was the milieu in which Augustine lived and wrote, encountering a remarkably similar situation to the modern West since the late nineteenth century. "In the time of Augustine," Jung remarked, "the old gods were dying or dead, the old religions and the old temples were going fast. There was a great confusion, the world was neurotic, and it became necessary to have a new therapeutic system."[9]

In both periods the world was embroiled in a tumultuous transition between historical eras: The era of the Roman Empire gave way to the Middle Ages just as, in the early part of the twentieth century, the Age of Empire, driven by the colonization of the world by European powers, came to a bloody and violent end with the mass devastation of the First World War. It could be said that the Neptune-Pluto conjunction of this time signaled the beginning of the complex and chaotic struggle to establish a planetary civilization—a critical challenge facing us in the current 500-year cycle. In both periods, too, religious understandings were transformed by the influx of ideas from the East, which has also inspired, perhaps more than anything else, the spiritual diversity and global interpenetration of myths and religions in the present time.

From one era to the next, as Jung recognized, civilizations are shaped and sustained by certain ruling ideas or dominants, often taking form through a particular religious revelation or mythic vision that thereafter provides the spiritual and moral foundation for the entire civilization. When the religious forms and guiding myths lose their compelling numinous power, as has happened in the modern West, the culture might be plunged into crisis, lacking orientation and social cohesion and thus entering a phase of terminal decline and decay. In response, however, shaped by the needs of the historical moment and the *telos* of evolution, new myths and metaphysical visions arise from the creative matrix of the unconscious, bringing renewal and birthing new historical epochs. For religions and mythologies—and the images of the gods and goddesses that populate them—are not exempt from the cycles of nature and the universe; they too are born, flourish, decay, and die.

The religious revelation documented by Jung in his *Red Book* might be taken, I believe, as a transformation of just this kind, offering a new mythic vision that reflects or anticipates an evolution of our religious consciousness—a development entirely consistent with the meaning of the combined Neptune-Pluto conjunction and Uranus-Neptune opposition at that time. Especially relevant for understanding the archetypal factors shaping the *Red Book* are the Neptune-Pluto themes of the empowerment of the mythic imagination and what Tarnas characterizes as the "transformation in the experience of the numinous."[10] An example of particular relevance to the West and to Jung's own religious background was the writing of the Second Isaiah (circa 545 BCE) during the Axial Age, which brought forth, Tarnas notes, a "powerful declaration of a loving God sovereign over all history and all humanity" and a "metamorphosis of the prophetic imagination" exemplifying "the quintessential Uranus-Neptune theme of a radical transformation of the God-image and a revolutionary new understanding of the divine will acting in history—the latter especially appropriate to the presence of Pluto in the configuration with its archetypal association with both evolution and universal will."[11]

The Death and Rebirth of God
It was the same potent combination of planetary archetypes that was

activated during the Neptune-Pluto conjunction of the late nineteenth century, described by Tarnas as the "great crucible of metaphysical destruction and regeneration" of Western culture, that saw the discovery of the unconscious and the birth of depth psychology.[12] Friedrich Nietzsche and Jung were two of the central figures in this great transformation, which continues to unfold in our own time—indeed its implications are only just beginning to be worked out.

"God is dead . . . *we have killed him*—you and I"—Nietzsche's epochal proclamation, first made in *The Gay Science*, heralded the West's entrance into the post-Christian era.[13] His philosophy also anticipated the postmodern in its radical questioning of truth and exposure of hidden power drives underlying human motivations, especially in the spheres of politics and knowledge. Departing from the pious Christian environment of his youth, Nietzsche espoused a fervent atheism and nihilism, arguing that the Christian notion of God—a man-made image, in his view—was no longer relevant to human experience; indeed, it was an impediment to our further evolution. Christianity had made Western culture "decadent," promulgating values and ways of being that were injurious to the human spirit, keeping human beings in a state of servile and docile mediocrity subject to the oppressive and inverted values of the herd. "Man," as the "sick animal," had grown distant from the vitality of the instincts and forsaken the aspiration to excellence, caught in the embrace of the Christian conceptions of selflessness, purity, meekness, pity, and so forth—qualities that Nietzsche believed often masked an unconscious power drive or an avoidance of the necessary challenge of courageously living and affirming one's own life.[14] "Your love of your neighbour is your bad love of yourselves," he remarked, with characteristic insight.[15] Thus Nietzsche sought to "wipe away the horizon" of past metaphysical suppositions in a re-evaluation of all values, a repudiation of Christianity, and an affirmation of the Dionysian energy largely excluded from the Christian vision of the world.[16]

Nietzsche's influence on Jung can hardly be overstated. Sonu Shamdasani notes that Jung returned to carefully study *Thus Spoke Zarathustra* in 1914 in the midst of the influx of fantasies during his confrontation with the unconscious, which form the body of the *Red Book*.[17] Nietzsche's influence is apparent not only in the epic narrative style of the *Red Book*, which resembles that of *Zarathustra*, but also in its content—addressing, as if in response to Nietzsche, the death and transformation of God. Through the dramatic dialogues with his spirit guides, Philemon and Elijah, Jung responded in several distinct though overlapping ways, all of which illuminate the particular form of expression of the Neptune-Pluto themes working through him. Exploring these responses can yield insights into how we ourselves might relate to these archetypal principles today.

God as Creative Power

In a first response to Nietzsche's claim that "God is dead," Philemon issues a refutation and associates God with the power of creation: "God is not dead. He is alive as ever. God is creation, for he is something definite."[18] Later God is identified in the form of Abraxas, as "creative drive" and the "creative and created."[19]

The emphasis on creative power is also present in Nietzsche. He rejects the existence of God, describing God as merely a temporary supposition, but he then transfers the focus to the creative power of human will: "And you yourself should create what you have hitherto called the World: the World shall be formed in your image by your reason, your will, and your love!"[20] Thus the human being, rather than God, becomes a kind of world creator. Although in places Nietzsche presents this creative power as something other than his conscious willing, often he appears to appropriate the power as his own. Those familiar with a Jungian understanding of archetypal possession might judge the failure to recognize such power as originating outside of the personal human will as potentially dangerous, and perhaps therefore a contributory factor in Nietzsche's grandiose inflation, especially evident in his later writing.

The understanding of God as something like creative energy is also close to the view of Pierre Teilhard de Chardin, the Jesuit priest and paleontologist whose brilliant synthesis of Christianity and evolution inspired many in the 1950s and thereafter, and whose ideas later informed "new cosmology" theorists, including Thomas Berry, Mary Evelyn Tucker, and Brian Swimme. Jung's prophetic revelation in the *Red Book* was of the God "yet to come," a God of a wholly different character to the loving transcendent Father that had ruled for the 2000 years of the Christian era.[21] In a related shift, Teilhard described a transition from worship of the "God of the Above" to the recognition of the "God of the Ahead," manifest through continual creative acts, who is to be realized as the culminating goal of evolution.[22] Like Jung, Teilhard was born during the Neptune-Pluto conjunction of the late nineteenth century.

We find a similar emphasis in Indian philosopher Sri Aurobindo's "integral yoga," shaped by a vision of "involution" of the "Supermind" into matter and its subsequent evolution, gradually bringing about the "spiritualization" of matter and all existence.[23] Also born during the Neptune-Pluto conjunction, Aurobindo, like Jung and Teilhard, brought the Plutonic emphasis on evolution and transformation into relationship with Neptunian conceptions of the eternal spiritual ground and transcendent godhead—a prominent theme of this Neptune-Pluto conjunction. The focus on the creative power of evolution, now manifest through the individual, gives a decidedly Plutonic inflection to the experience of God, for the Pluto archetype finds expression as the motive evolutionary force in the universe, experienced as an inexorable life will or will-to-power.

God as an Aspect of the Pleroma

In a second response to the decay and destruction of the god-image announced by Nietzsche, Jung's revelation looks beyond the Christian conception of God in the recognition of the spiritual background of existence. In this view, God is not the ultimate frame of reference but is only one aspect or quality of the Pleroma, which is to be understood as the non-differentiated source in which opposites co-exist and cancel each other out. The Pleroma is the "empty fullness of the whole," imagined as "the maternal womb of the incomprehensible God."[24] The phrase *maternal womb* naturally puts us in mind of the Great Mother Goddess, a mythic personification of the originating and annihilating ground of all things, including all the gods and goddesses.

Therefore, if "God is dead," as Nietzsche claims, this might be taken only as the death of a particular conception of the divine. It implies not the end of religion and the acceptance of nihilism but the recognition that the dominant image of God, the particular form in which God has been imagined for the last two millennia and more, has died as part of a process of spiritual metamorphosis in which a new god-image might emerge from the Pleroma. We appear to be living, Jung proclaimed, "in what the Greeks call the Kairos—the right time—for a 'metamorphosis of the gods,' that is, of the fundamental principles and symbols" through which we order and make sense of our lives.[25] Elsewhere in the *Red Book* Jung restates a similar insight, arguing that God is an image and only one portrayal or aspect of the "supreme meaning," which ever renews itself in different forms as new images of the divine spring forth in response to the evolutionary needs of the time.[26] As Jung puts it: "The other gods died of their temporality, yet the supreme meaning never dies, it turns into meaning and then into absurdity, and out of the fire and blood of their collision the supreme meaning rises up rejuvenated anew."[27] Ultimately, all the gods and goddesses might be construed, to borrow an expression from Aurobindo, as "Personalities and Powers of the dynamic Divine."[28]

The Revelation of Abraxas

In a third response, Philemon advances the view that alongside and encompassing the "One God" of Christianity there is another unknown God, long forgotten and unrecognized, whom he refers to as Abraxas: "This is God you knew nothing about, because mankind forgot him."[29] Abraxas is the God of effectiveness—that is, the God of effective power. Elsewhere, as Shamdasani points out, Jung likens Abraxas to the Gnostic demiurge, Henri Bergson's *la durée créatrice,* and to Purusha and Shiva of the Hindu tradition.[30] To a large degree, like these other deities and principles Abraxas is a God with the qualities and attributes of Pluto: effective evolutionary force, creative-destructive power, instinctual and relentless, working through compulsion and possession, and manifest as the ceaseless motive force of life, at once empowering and terrible. Like the archetypal Pluto, Abraxas is "beyond good and evil" (to use Nietzsche's expression), subsuming all opposites. The qualities of Abraxas are recognizable in the Nietzschean ideas of the will-to-power, the *amor fati,* and the drive to self-overcoming—all of which pertain to the archetype of Pluto as the power that must overcome itself again and again in a Dionysian affirmation of life and an act of transformation that is essential for individuation and the further evolution of human consciousness.

Whereas the Christian understanding of the divine introduced a radical separation of good from evil, and spirit from nature, with the Devil coming to personify the instinctual dynamism excluded from the image of the all-loving purity of God and Jesus, in Jung's revelation good and evil, Christ and Devil, are seen as inextricably connected opposites. The "One God" of Christianity (which Jung also describes as the "Sun God") and the Devil represent mutually implicated aspects of the Pleroma. In the Pleroma the God of light and love is juxtaposed with the Devil, with Abraxas standing behind both. "Everything that you create with the Sun God," Philemon explains, "gives effective power to the devil. That is terrible Abraxas."[31]

We do not recognize this power because "Abraxas is the God who is difficult to grasp."[32] Jung's wording here is remarkably similar to the opening lines of Friedrich Hölderlin's poem "Patmos," quoted elsewhere by Jung:

The god is near and
Hard to grasp but
Where there is danger some
Salvation grows there too.[33]

Of Abraxas, Philemon declares: "His power is greatest because man does not see it."[34] Because Abraxas cannot be defined as either good or evil but embodies both poles and the "cruel contradictoriness of nature," this god cannot be intellectually comprehended.[35] Uniting and subsuming the opposites in a similar manner to Mercurius in alchemy, Abraxas is something like the primordial energy "that is at once life and death."[36] One might say that Abraxas represents unconscious compulsion, drive, and power that are so "near" to us we tend not to see them as anything other than our own desiring, feeling, and willing; we do not see them as manifestations of a deity or transpersonal archetypal power distinct from our own conscious identity. We are possessed and consumed by Abraxas, for we unconsciously identify with the flow of desiring, or else, denying the instincts, we eschew the overwhelming power of Abraxas and suffer from this renunciation.

Although unrecognized today, Abraxas was known to and named by the Gnostics in the early centuries of the Christian era and can, I believe, be recognized as the subject of Jesus's teaching in the Gnostic text the *Gospel of Thomas*, which was unearthed in the sands of Egypt in 1945 and dates from the first centuries of the Christian era. Several *logia* in this text appear to be concerned with a God quite unlike the God of Love in the New Testament, for they describe strategies for reckoning with a terrible power that might consume or destroy us if we are not able to come to terms with it and express it. *Logion* 70, for instance, reads as follows: "If you bring forth what is within you, what you bring forth will save you. If you do not bring forth what is within you, what you do not bring forth will destroy you."[37]

Abraxas, we discover in the *Red Book*, represents the world of becoming and passing, just as Pluto is associated with the inexorable will that ever destroys, transforms, and rebirths. As such, it might well be this particular God who inspires the instruction in the *Gospel of Thomas* to "become yourselves, passing away."[38] Could Jesus's Gnostic teaching be a strategy for navigating the power of Abraxas? Could it be that the Christ pattern, as the incarnate Holy Spirit within each of us, is the advocate for the human in our confrontation with the frightful power of the demonic Abraxas? Jung opens the *Red Book* with the memorable passage from the First Isaiah, immortalized in Händel's *Messiah*, celebrating the coming of Christ: "Wonderful. Counsellor. The mighty God. The everlasting Father. The Prince of Peace" (Isaiah: 1:6).[39] He ends the *Red Book* with Elijah reminding Christ (the "blue shade") of his identity with the serpent, thus bringing the Christ principle into relationship with the dark, chthonic side of Abraxas.[40] A transformation in the relationship between spirit (Neptune) and the instinctual power of nature (Pluto) appears to be central to the unfolding of the current Neptune-Pluto cycle. Pluto, like Mercurius in the alchemical tradition, represents the uroboric serpent power that ever consumes itself.

Recalling here, too, the Uranus-Neptune theme of the creative emergence of esoteric traditions, Jungian psychology might be construed as just this kind of emergence, falling in the lineage of a mystical Gnosticism, with the particular character of the revelation to do with the challenge of integrating the realm of experience associated with the archetypal Pluto—that is, the long-repressed abyss-like instinctual power of the unconscious.

The Many from the One

In a fourth response to Nietzsche, Jung contends that while the One God is indeed dead, as Nietzsche declared, the Divine has actually changed form, disintegrating into a multiplicity such that "the Old Gods have become new." "The One God is dead—yes, truly, he died. He disintegrated into the many, and thus the world became rich overnight."[41] The world in its substantive material reality henceforth became the sole focus of our concern—witness Nietzsche's decrial of the "Afterworldsmen" who are preoccupied with a heavenly afterlife at the expense of the here and now, and his exaltation of the earth and the body over the soul.[42] Witness too the cultural shift from religious piety to materialism and consumerism during the course of the Christian era. The aspiration towards the re-enchantment of nature and the emergence of ecological consciousness in the conception of the Earth as Gaia, which have become for many people the primary sources of religiosity, is an expression of this shift, with a spirituality of the immanent rather than the transcendent now impressing itself on the modern psyche.

The world became rich in a second way, in that we have entered a period of spiritual eclecticism and pluralism. No longer is Christianity the sole religious authority in the West, for it is now but one of a rich multiplicity of spiritual-mythic perspectives shaping the modern psyche.

One thinks of the plethora of spiritual paths pursued by individuals today, from yoga, healing, and paganism to Buddhism, rebirthing, and shamanic journeying. Philosopher Charles Taylor has noted that the liberty to find and follow one's own way in spiritual matters is a defining characteristic of the rise of the modern ego-self in our secular age.[43] As Joseph Campbell remarked, there is a veritable "galaxy of mythologies" in existence today.[44]

The theme of religious pluralism and individualism is associated with the archetypal combination of Uranus-Neptune—Uranus as the principle of individual freedom and creativity that, in relationship to Neptune, inspires us to pursue our own individual way through life, beyond the bounds of religious tradition, and brings forth new forms of myth, religious insights, and new spiritual paths. We see these themes in Jung's pioneering of individuation and the realization of the self as a spiritual path for the modern era—reflecting the Uranus-square-Neptune alignment in Jung's birth chart. We see it too in the life and work of Joseph Campbell, also born with these two planets in major alignment. It is especially evident in Campbell's emphasis on the individualism of the hero myth as a mythic model of the individual's unique life path, and in his recognition of the emergence of the era of creative mythology superseding the great epochs and stages of the established religious traditions.

The Human as Mediator of the Gods Within

Fifth, in a related move, Jung explains to Elijah that the multiplicity of renewed old gods is reborn in the individual soul: "And something also happened to the individual soul—who would come to describe it! But therefore men too became rich overnight."[45] We read in another passage that the Spirit of the Depths put Jung back in touch with his soul, "a living and self-existing being," and it was in the inner depths of the soul that the old gods were to be discovered.[46] The One God died and became a plurality of deities in the human psyche, which Jung conceptualizes in his formal writing as archetypes, describing them as "gods," "dominant laws and principles," and "ruling powers."[47] What was formerly imagined in metaphysical terms was henceforth conceived in psychological terms. The starry empyrean and Olympian host, and even the One God of Christianity, Jung suggests, "fell" from Heaven or the celestial sphere into the darkness of the unconscious, where they were rediscovered.[48] In astrological terms, then, we notice the impact of the Pluto archetype on Neptune: first destroying the old metaphysical conceptions, then initiating a fall of the old gods and dominants into the underworld of the unconscious, and finally empowering the mythic imagination to bring forth a new revelation of the gods and a new conceptual understanding of them as psychological factors—that is, archetypes.

What is more, in conceiving of the gods as psychological factors human beings now assumed a critical role in bringing the gods to consciousness, making them known, and thus rescuing them from the oblivion of unconsciousness and existential forgetfulness. "The Gods need a human mediator and rescuer," Jung's soul reveals to him. "With this man paves the way to crossing over and to divinity."[49] In a similar vein, Jung describes the "supreme meaning" as the "bridge of going across and fulfillment" leading to the God.[50] There are striking parallels here with Nietzsche's view of man as something that should be overcome, as a "dangerous going-across" to the superman.[51] The human, in this view, is not the endpoint of evolution but an uncertain transition or bridge to a higher form of being. For Nietzsche, "man is a rope between animal and superman—a rope fastened over an abyss."[52] Thus, as in the Second Isaiah, we meet again the Plutonic emphasis on evolution and will in relationship to Neptunian conceptions of spirit and God, except here the evolutionary drama has been transferred from God to the human, unfolding in the depths of the inner world of the psyche.

In Nietzschean fashion, Philemon propounds a similar idea: "Men have changed. They are no longer the slaves and no longer the swindlers of the Gods and no longer mourn in your name."[53] Rather, "man is a gateway through which crowds the train of the Gods and the coming and passing of all times."[54] However, whereas Nietzsche's *Übermensch* takes the godlike powers as his own and thus becomes susceptible to manic inflation, the role of the human being, in Jung's view, is as a participant or mediator granting "hospitality to the Gods."[55] Out of this insight grew Jung's approach to coming to terms with the depths of the psyche during individuation by carefully differentiating the conscious ego from the archetypes and thus coming to realize the Self.

The Dark Spirit in Nature

Sixth, the returning and rediscovered God, Abraxas, has a pagan, chthonic quality. Nietzsche had proclaimed the *Übermensch* as "the meaning of the earth" and championed the re-emergence of Dionysus, the ancient god of the vine and personification of intoxicated frenzy in which the *principium individuationis* is obliterated.[56] The Neptune-Pluto conjunction heralded the resurrection of a repressed and forgotten dark, chthonic "natural spirit," as Jung described it in *Mysterium Coniunctionis*, a spirit represented by figures such as Dionysus, Pan, Hades, the Devil, and the alchemical Mercurius.[57] In the *Red Book*, Elijah's vision portrays the pagan primeval quality of the unknown God: "The image that I saw was crimson, fiery colored, a gleaming gold. The voice that I heard was like distant thunder, like the wind roaring in the forest, like an earthquake. It was not the voice of my God, but it was a thunderous pagan roar, a call my ancestors knew but which I had never heard. It sounded prehistoric, as if from a forest on a distant coast. It rang with the voices of the wilderness. It was full of horror yet harmonic."[58]

We see here further evidence of the decidedly Plutonic quality of the Neptunian conceptions of spirit emerging from the turn of the twentieth century, for Pluto is associated with the primal, elemental power of nature and underworld of the instincts. J. R. R. Tolkien, born in 1882 during the Neptune-Pluto conjunction, gave exceptionally vivid expression to these themes in *The Lord of the Rings*.

Plutonic qualities were prominent too in the resurrection of the pagan deity Wotan irrupting into the collective consciousness of the German people during the 1930s, Jung believed, leading to the catastrophe of the Second World War. Nazism drew on the compelling hypnotic power of the Neptune-Pluto complex in propounding the warped ideology and mythos of Aryan supremacy. With this comes a warning. The combination of Neptunian fantasy and Plutonic instinct can pull us remorselessly under its sway, sometimes at the expense of morality, human feeling, and reasoned judgment. For better or worse, when it awakens and stirs, the long-repressed power of the unconscious can flood into human consciousness as an "avenging deluge," overwhelming us with a stream of captivating fantasies and gripping instinctual urges.[59] Thus the challenge for us today, as we move further into the 500-year Neptune-Pluto cycle, is to find a way to come to terms with the dark power of the reawakened chthonic god—the dark spirit in nature—without being devoured, consumed, possessed, or obliterated by it.

Archetypal Astrology as a Mythic Guide to Life

To explore the significance of Jung's *Red Book*, I have focused primarily on historical periods defined by the combined expression of the transpersonal archetypes associated with Uranus, Neptune, and Pluto, but astrology can also be used to gain insight into how these principles manifest in our own individual experiences. Our relationship to Pluto, as symbolized in astrological birth charts and transits, is particularly important in determining how the Abraxas-like instinctual power and creative-destructive energy associated with Pluto manifest in our lives. The Pluto archetype shows up in our passions, compulsions, drives, obsessions, and in the sense of being gripped and fatefully called. In relationship to other planets in birth charts and transits, Pluto indicates where we ourselves might encounter the power of the instinctual underworld of the psyche and can be transformed through it. Similarly, considering our relationship to Neptune can help us to become more conscious of how we engage with the spiritual dimension of life, how we seek oneness and unity and a more ideal and perfect life. It indicates too where we seek transcendence or escape from the pressures of life and look for a sense of enchantment and mystery, or find ourselves susceptible to projection and illusion. Jung's *Red Book* might serve as a guide as we seek to work out the relationship between the Neptune and Pluto principles in our lives, bringing the realm of the spirit as articulated in the religious traditions into dialectical engagement with the underworld of the instincts and the dark power impressing itself on our collective consciousness.

The various combinations of planetary archetypes are associated with sets of themes and complexes. We have seen several examples here of those pertaining to Neptune-Pluto and Uranus-Neptune. In each case, one can consider how the planets are related to each other in one's birth chart and in transits in order to determine themes prominent in one's own life and personality. If Saturn and Neptune come into a personal transit alignment, for instance, one would recognize in one's experience during this time any number of themes associated with this archetypal complex, such as religious skepticism and the denial of spiritual realities, loss of faith, dark visions and morbid fantasies, a poignant sense of life's sufferings and endings, and the puncturing of an illusion by the hard facts of one's reality.[60] As Tarnas points out, Nietzsche's revelation of the death of God in 1882 came out of this very archetypal pairing (during a conjunction of Saturn, Neptune, and Pluto), giving expression to many of these themes.[61] Or, to give another example, we might identify periods in life when Uranus and Neptune were in major geometric alignment and observe correlations with experiences of spiritual awakening or exciting, emancipatory, and perhaps destabilizing insights into the nature of reality, the nature of God, and the purpose of our existence.

In this way, archetypal astrology can be used to effectively map our personal relationships to the archetypes, the powers personified by the gods—the very powers engaged by Jung in the revelations that comprise his *Red Book*. In *The Archetypal Cosmos*, I describe archetypal astrology as a "meta-mythology" for it is not itself a myth, but it enables us to understand our individual relationship to the principles and themes expressed in myth and religion.[62] It offers a form of cosmological orientation that might help us to become more conscious of the forces shaping our psychological experience, as we try to navigate the uncertain transitions of our historical moment and play our part in the evolution of consciousness and the spirit.

Notes

[1] James Hillman, *Senex & Puer*, ed. Glen Slater (Putnam, CT: Spring, 2013), 29.

[2] See Richard Tarnas, *Cosmos and Psyche* (New York, NY: Viking, 2006), 409–410.

[3] See Tarnas, *Cosmos and Psyche*, 391–392.

[4] See Tarnas, *Cosmos and Psyche*, 456.

[5] Tarnas, *Cosmos and Psyche*, Part VII, 353–408.

[6] Tarnas, *Cosmos and Psyche*, Part IV, 139–205.

[7] Tarnas, *Cosmos and Psyche*, 417.

[8] Tarnas, *Cosmos and Psyche*, 417. Compare D. Stephenson Bond's theory of the lifecycle of myths in Bond, *Living Myth* (Boston, MA: Shambhala, 1993), 201–204.

[9] C. G. Jung, *Dream Analysis: Notes on the Seminar Given in 1928–1930 by C. G. Jung*, ed. William McGuire (Princeton, NJ: Princeton University Press, 1984), 419.

[10] Tarnas, *Cosmos and Psyche*, 415.

[11] Tarnas, *Cosmos and Psyche*, 414 & 411.

[12] Tarnas *Cosmos and Psyche*, 418.

[13] Friedrich Nietzsche, *The Gay Science*, trans. Walter Kaufmann (New York, NY: Vintage Books, 1974), 181, section 125.

[14] Friedrich Nietzsche, "The Genealogy of Morals," in *Basic Writings of Nietzsche*, trans. Walter Kaufmann (New York, Modern Library, 2000), section III:13, 557.

[15] Friedrich Nietzsche, *Thus Spoke Zarathustra*, trans. Richard J. Hollingdale (New York, NY: Penguin, 1968), 86.

[16] Nietzsche, "Genealogy of Morals," 181.

[17] Sonu Shamdasani, "Introduction," in C. G. Jung, *The Red Book: Liber Novus*, ed. Sonu Shamdasani, tr. John Peck, Mark Kyburz, and Sonu Shamdasani (New York, NY: W.W. Norton, 2009), 30.

[18] Jung, *Red Book*, 576.

[19] Jung, *Red Book*, 579.

[20] Nietzsche, *Thus Spoke Zarathustra*, 110.

[21] Jung, *Red Book*, 120.

[22] Pierre Teilhard de Chardin, *The Heart of Matter*, trans. René Hague (San Diego, CA: Harcourt Brace, 1978), 53–55.

[23] See Sri Aurobindo, *The Integral Yoga* (Pondicherry, India: Sri Aurobindo Ashram, 1993).

[24] Jung, *Red Book*, 523–524.

[25] C. G. Jung, "The Undiscovered Self (Present and Future)," in *CW*, vol. 10 (Princeton, NJ: Princeton University Press, 1964), par. 585.

[26] Jung, *Red Book*, 120.

[27] Jung, *Red Book*, 120.

[28] Aurobindo, *Integral Yoga*, 82–83.

[29] Jung, *Red Book*, 517.

[30] See note 93 in Jung, *Red Book*, 517.

[31] Jung, *Red Book*, 521.

[32] Jung, *Red Book*, 520.

[33] Friedrich Hölderlin, "Patmos," in *Selected Poems*, trans. David Constantine (Highgreen, UK: Bloodaxe Books, 1996), 54.

[34] Jung, *Red Book*, 520.

[35] Jung, *Red Book*, 523.

[36] Jung, *Red Book*, 521.

[37] Elaine Pagels, *The Gnostic Gospels* (New York: Vintage Books, 1989), xv.

[38] Hugh McGregor Ross, *The Gospel of Thomas*, second edition (London: Watkins Publishing, 2002), 33.

[39] See Jung *Red Book*, 117–118.

[40] Jung, *Red Book*, 553.

[41] Jung, *Red Book*, 546.

[42] Nietzsche, *Thus Spoke Zarathustra*, 42, 58–62.

[43] Charles Taylor, *A Secular Age* (Cambridge, MA: The Belnap Press of Harvard University Press, 2007).

[44] Joseph Campbell, *Creative Mythology: The Masks of God*, vol. IV (New York, NY: Arkana, 1991), 3.

[45] Jung, *Red Book*, 546.

[46] Jung, *Red Book*, 129.

[47] C. G. Jung, "On the Psychology of the Unconscious," in *CW*, vol. 7 (Princeton, NJ: Princeton University Press, 1966), par. 151.

[48] See C. G. Jung, Jung, "Archetypes of the Collective Unconscious," in *CW*, vol. 9/I (Princeton, NJ: Princeton University Press, 1968), par. 50.

[49] Jung, *Red Book*, 548.

[50] Jung, *Red Book*, 120.

[51] Nietzsche, *Thus Spoke Zarathustra*, 43.

[52] Nietzsche, *Thus Spoke Zarathustra*, 43.

[53] Jung, *Red Book*, 552–553.

[54] Jung, *Red Book*, 535–536.

[55] Jung, *Red Book*, 553.

[56] Nietzsche, *Thus Spoke Zarathustra*, 42.

[57] C. G. Jung, Jung, C. G. *Mysterium Coniunctionis*, in *CW*, vol. 14 (Princeton, NJ: Princeton University Press, 1963), par. 427.

[58] Jung, *Red Book*, 546.

[59] Jung, *Mysterium Coniunctionis*, *CW* 14, par. 364.

[60] See Tarnas, "The Ideal and the Real: Saturn-Neptune," in *The Birth of a New Discipline. Archai: The Journal of Archetypal Cosmology*, issue 1 (2009), second edition, edited by Keiron Le Grice and Rod O'Neal (San Francisco, CA: Archai Press, 2011), 175–199.

[61] Tarnas, *Cosmos and Psyche*, 344–345.

[62] Keiron Le Grice, *The Archetypal Cosmos* (Edinburgh: Floris Books, 2011), 61.

XI

The Dark Spirit in Nature:
C. G. Jung and the Spiritual Transformation
of Our Time

When Jung described "modern man" standing "upon a peak, or at the very edge of the world, the abyss of the future before him, above him the heavens, and below him the whole of mankind with a history that disappears in primeval mists," he was surely portraying something of himself and his own existential situation.[1] He was also characterizing the epochal nature of the time in which he lived—a time which, by all accounts, seems to have marked a critical juncture in human spiritual evolution, one that saw the emergence of a new relationship between spirit and nature, or the beginning of a new stage in the unfolding dialectic between them. In his contribution to this transformation, Jung can be justifiably seen as a world-historical figure, to use Hegel's term. The great person, as Jung himself points out, is one who is able to give expression to the universal constants in human experience within the unique requirements of the particular historical moment—and this is precisely what Jung did. To appreciate the significance of Jung's life, therefore, one must attempt to see it in broad historical context. Recognizing the importance of his own encounter with the unconscious psyche for the entire culture, Jung's life in many respects reflects the deepest level of expression of the archetypal conditions of his time, and this naturally makes him an especially apt figure for an archetypal astrological analysis of his life and work.

Jung was born on July 26, 1875 in Kesswil, Switzerland, at the beginning of the twenty-five-year conjunction between Neptune and Pluto, a planetary alignment heralding the onset of a new five-hundred-year cycle of radical transformation in our experience of and conception of the spiritual dimension of reality.[2] We have seen above that the Neptune archetypal principle is associated with spirituality, the divine, religion, the eternal, the transcendent, the collective unconscious, myth, fantasy, and dream, as well as problematic tendencies towards escapism, avoidance, illusion, and delusion. It is a principle that dissolves, synthesizes, spiritualizes, and sensitizes. The Pluto planetary archetype is associated with transformation, nature, instinct, biology, and evolution. It is a principle of elemental force, intensity, extremity, and power, and is related to the mythic themes of the underworld and hell, which symbolically portray the repressed instinctual dynamism within the "underworld" of the psyche— described by the Freudian Id and the Jungian shadow archetype. The combination of these two archetypal principles is therefore especially associated with the radical transformation (Pluto) of the expression of spirit (Neptune), and with the spiritualization (Neptune) of the instincts (Pluto). A Neptune-Pluto world transit brings forth deep underlying transformations of the cultural psyche and mythic-religious visions that powerfully shape human experience and our understanding of the nature of reality. In the late nineteenth century, for example, as Richard Tarnas observes in *Cosmos and Psyche*, the Neptune-Pluto conjunction marked

> the end of an age and a transformative threshold which was symbolized in the Nietzschean transvaluation of all values, the dying of the gods that had ruled the Western spirit for two millennia and more, the subterranean dissolution of conventional Christian belief and Enlightenment assumptions, the powerful upsurge of 'the unconscious'. . . and the emergence in Western culture of a range of long-suppressed and long-developing cultural phenomena and archetypal impulses.[3]

Jung was to become a seminal figure in the further unfolding of all these phenomena during the twentieth century. To understand the significance of his life within the context of what was occurring at this time, however, we first need to reflect for a moment on the dominant trends of the previous Neptune-Pluto cycle, which began with the conjunction of 1386 to 1411 (coinciding with the start of the Italian Renaissance) and which reached the midpoint of the cycle with the Neptune-Pluto opposition occurring between 1631 and 1660 (the start of the late modern era).[4]

The Neptune-Pluto Cycle

Focusing specifically on the spiritual dimension of experience, if one were to try to discern the major development of this period, one would, I believe, have to point to the growing conceptual and ethical separation between spirit and nature, especially as conceived within the Christian tradition. The course of human cultural and psychospiritual development during this 500-year cycle, particularly in the West, had effected a radical separation of spirit from matter, of the transcendent godhead from nature, and of human consciousness from instinct. In a number of ways, the dimensions of experience associated with Neptune and Pluto were thrust apart, even as the principles associated with these planets continued to mutually influence each other.

During this period, the element of human experience associated with Pluto was largely projected onto the figure of the Devil and excluded from the prevailing image of the divine. The Christian figure of the Devil, from the late Middle Ages (around the fourteenth century onwards, closely coincident with the start of the last but one Neptune-Pluto cycle), assumed a different character to the earlier biblical Satan, who was merely a consort of Yahweh rather than having the wholly evil and demonic character we now commonly associate with the Devil.[5] As Alan Watts observes, among the world religions "the Christian Devil is unique. No other demonic figure has ever been conceived to be so purely malicious, so sinister, and so totally opposed to the universal design."[6] Projected almost exclusively onto the figure of the Devil, Plutonic qualities—such as destruction, demonic power, ruthlessness, wrathfulness, vindictiveness, compulsion—although intrinsic to the Old Testament Yahweh, were not attributed to the person of Jesus or to the Father-God of the New Testament. Indeed, all forms of behavior and experiences connected to the instincts and nature (sex, aggression, power drives, and so forth) were concealed beneath an idealistic religious vision that excluded them from the prevailing conception of the divine. Such qualities and characteristics had nothing to do with God, it was supposed, who was conceived as all loving, all merciful, and wholly benevolent (even as His judgment cast unrepentant sinners into Hell), just as Jesus was pure and gentle, meek and mild, a celibate pacifist untainted with original sin. As Jung remarks, little reflection was given among Christians as to the significance of the New Testament accounts of Jesus stealing a mule, whipping money lenders, or his instruction to be "cunning as serpents" as well as "gentle as doves." Within Christian orthodoxy, sexuality, instinct, the bodily urges and passions (relating to Pluto) were seen as inherently sinful and evil, and thus excluded by the Christian moral separation of good (light, Christ, God, spirit) from evil (dark, Devil, nature, instinct). Good and evil,

God and nature, Christ and the Devil, were conceived as absolute opposites. People were taught to put themselves exclusively on the side on the good in the fight against evil. Accordingly, the Christian ethical distinction between good and evil meant that natural human instincts were often denied expression. As Friedrich Nietzsche realized, this brought a subsequent loss of life power and vital energy across a culture shaped by Christian morality. As Joseph Campbell points out, our usual understanding of the meaning of the word *demon* is illustrative of this point. Rather than signifying an evil power, the original meaning of this term, coming from the Greek *daemon*, is the dynamic of life. In the Christian tradition, the mythic and religious conceptions of the nature of reality in which the demonic is synonymous with evil put us in opposition to the life dynamic, such that Plutonic qualities of passion, desire, drive, and so forth were viewed in largely negative terms, and seen as antithetical to the spiritual life.

Simultaneously, however, the Pluto principle empowered and infused the Christian mythological imagination with its vivid portrayal of the grim fate of sinners facing an eternity in a fiery hell. Also apparent during this period was the unconscious empowerment (Pluto) of tendencies towards escapism, illusion, and avoidance (Neptune), which manifested as an excessive concern with an otherworldly afterlife in Heaven at the expense of the here-and-now, as well as the impassioned commitment to an increasingly rigid dogma espoused by Christian orthodoxy. In a sense, the Plutonic dimension of experience became cloaked behind a specious religious morality and lay simmering in the depths of the unconscious psyche, becoming increasingly charged until it was to erupt during the Neptune-Pluto conjunction and its subsequent unfolding through twentieth century.[7]

The full implications of this separation between spirit and nature were acutely realized and experienced in the life and person of Friedrich Nietzsche, as we considered in Chapter X. Under the Saturn-Neptune-Pluto triple conjunction of the early 1880s, a feverishly possessed and inspired Nietzsche called for the destruction of false religious ideals, the abandonment of Christianity (and all religions), and a return to the morality of the warrior caste of ancient Greece and Rome. Ruthlessly exposing what he saw as the deception and illusion fostered by the Christian image of the divine (a theme expressive of the Saturn-Neptune complex, driven by Plutonic intensity), Nietzsche effectively stood in judgment on a religious world conception based on the separation of spirit from nature, which had led to a repression of the instincts and the denigration of nature.[8] Stepping beyond the established religious and moral psychological boundaries of the modern West, Nietzsche experienced a volcanic eruption of the unconscious power of nature within his own psyche.

Freud and the early pioneers of depth psychology later assumed the urgent task of raising to conscious awareness the repressed instinctual basis of human experience through the more systematic approach of psychoanalysis. The repressed Plutonic dimension of experience was thus brought back into the foreground of human experience. Depth psychology confronted people with their unconscious desires, power drives, frustrated sexual impulses, and more—the lid was taken off the seething cauldron of the instincts. Much of what was considered evil, demonic, primitive, and uncivilized in human nature was to be faced immediately and directly as a personal psychological reality.

Jung was a key figure in this development, attempting to bring an awareness of the dark, "shadow" elements of human experience into the Christian conception of the godhead. Beyond this, by integrating the instinctual dynamism and evolutionary power of nature into modern psychology and spirituality, Jung's life and work were especially relevant to other major themes associated with the Neptune-Pluto archetypal combination. In its exploration of the shadow and the depths of human experience, and in its emphasis of radical psychological transformation, Jungian psychology is Plutonic; in its exploration of the numinous, myth, religion, dreams, and fantasies, it is Neptunian.

Planetary Alignments at Jung's Birth

Although in a wide orb at Jung's birth, the outer-planet alignment of Neptune and Pluto had a greater relevance to Jung's life than it might have had otherwise because of its relationship to the major aspects in his chart (see Figure 3). These aspects include the Sun square Neptune, which suggests the propensity to be particularly consciously attuned to and challenged by the spiritual dimension of experience; Saturn square Pluto, which, in Jung's case, relates to the Herculean labor of the transformation of the psyche through individuation; and Saturn and Pluto in a T-square configuration with Uranus, with this larger aspect pattern suggesting the sudden crisis of transformation Jung was to experience in his life—a topic we will consider shortly. Jung also had the Moon, in a conjunction with Pluto and close to exact square to Uranus, positioned approximately midway between the approaching Neptune-Pluto conjunction, suggesting a natural emotional attunement to themes associated with this world transit alignment. And his natal

Uranus square Neptune relates most especially to the sudden revelatory shifts of consciousness and insights that were to characterize Jung's life and work. Placed within the particular historical context of late-nineteenth century mainland Europe, it is this complex configuration of archetypal factors, finding expression through Jung's highly developed intellectual and spiritual sensibility, that, together with innumerable other factors—biographical, cultural, and more—has decisively shaped the contemporary understanding of and approach to spirituality and psychological transformation from the mid-twentieth century onwards, especially with the promulgation of Jung's ideas in recent decades. The expression of all these archetypal complexes in Jung's life was shaped at its deepest level by the archetypal dynamics associated with the Neptune-Pluto conjunction.

In the sections to follow, I will briefly examine three decisive biographical periods in Jung's life that are powerfully illustrative of some of the major archetypal complexes in his chart and expressive of the archetypal relationship between Neptune and Pluto, including Jung's childhood, the years of Jung's confrontation with the unconscious between 1912 and 1918, and the years of his major alchemical studies in the 1940s and 1950s. Considering these periods, it is possible to observe a diachronic sequencing of qualitatively similar archetypal themes, and also an evolutionary development in the expression of the archetypal complexes during the course of Jung's life as he worked through the various types of transformative experience associated with these complexes.[9] While focusing primarily on the relevance of Jung's life for the collective spiritual transformation associated with the Neptune-Pluto conjunction, this analysis will also examine how this archetypal complex finds specific expression in Jung's experience by considering the natal alignments in his chart and, to a lesser extent, his personal transits.

Jung's Childhood Dreams and Experiences

One is struck, reading Jung's autobiography, *Memories, Dreams, Reflections*, by the extent to which his life's work was prefigured and initiated in his early childhood dreams. The first dream, the earliest Jung could remember, occurred when he was between three and four years old:

> Suddenly I discovered a dark, rectangular, stone-lined hole in the ground. I had never seen it before. I ran curiously forward and peered down into it. Then I saw a stone stairway leading down.

Hesitantly and fearfully, I descended . . . I saw before me in the dim light a rectangular chamber about thirty feet long. The ceiling was arched and of hewn stone. The floor was laid with flagstones, and in the centre a red carpet ran from the entrance to a low platform. On this platform stood a wonderfully rich golden throne . . . a magnificent throne, a real king's throne in a fairy tale. Something was standing on it which I thought at first was a tree trunk twelve to fifteen feet high and about one and a half to two feet thick. It was a huge thing reaching almost to the ceiling. But it was of a curious composition: it was made of skin and naked flesh, and on top there was something like a rounded head with no face and no hair. On the very top of the head was a single eye, gazing motionlessly upwards.[10]

Jung recalled being "paralyzed with terror" when confronted by the enormous, worm-like "man-eater," as his mother described it within the dream. He realized, much later in his life, that the creature was a giant phallus, a "ritual phallus," which, in Jung's view, was a compensatory image produced by the unconscious, counterbalancing the prevailing conception of an all-loving, all-good "Lord Jesus." The phallus was a symbol of a "dark Lord Jesus," representing qualities many of his contemporaries were not willing to see in the Savior or in God; and the dream was also, Jung realized, a portrayal of the cannibalistic symbolism of the Christian Mass.

Here, then, at the very start of the Neptune-Pluto conjunction around 1880, came a vision that appeared to depict some kind of reactivation of a subterranean divinity, a powerful expression of the dark spirit of nature associated with Neptune-Pluto. This was the sexual, instinctual, chthonic, devouring principle associated with Pluto assuming imaginal form. Occurring around the same time as Nietzsche's *Thus Spoke Zarathustra,* which was addressing related themes, here was the repressed and ignored spiritual-instinctual power of nature graphically impressing itself on the mythic vision of the contemporary psyche.

Through this dream, Jung believed that he had been "initiated into the secrets of the earth," and entered "the realm of darkness." "What happened then," he explains, "was a kind of burial in the earth, and many years were to pass before I came out again."[11] The motifs of this dream, and its consequences, clearly reflect the particular combination of Moon-Saturn-Pluto in Jung's chart: the underground setting, the phallic monster, the descent, and the transformative initiation point to the archetypal Pluto; the stone chamber, the burial, and the entombment relate to Saturn; and the role of his mother and the fact the dream occurred in childhood are connected with the archetype of the Moon. The Saturn-Pluto combination also relates to the fateful quality of the dream and the experience of extreme fear, with the instinctual force of Pluto empowering the self-defensive, fearful responses associated with Saturn. The Saturn archetype is related to the ego-structure, and to the limitations, restrictions, and the often acute sense of separation that comes with ego-consciousness. Under the archetypal influence of Pluto, these characteristics are typically intensified and driven to an extreme. Unsurprisingly, then, the entire mood of Jung's life at the time was oppressive and foreboding. A fear of suffocation and an "unbreathable" atmosphere in the house gripped his waking hours; it was a time of dark, unspeakable secrets, and of overwhelming compulsions.[12]

The Moon-Saturn-Pluto alignment in Jung's birth chart gives us more precise information as to how he experienced the archetypal energies accompanying the Neptune-Pluto world transit, pointing in particular to the decidedly Saturnian nature of his experience of the Plutonic underworld of the psyche. The moral imperatives and boundaries (associated with Saturn) that had rendered the Plutonic dimension of experience taboo across the wider culture in the first place were instilled in Jung through his upbringing in the pious Protestant context in which he lived. Thus, to experience the dark power of nature through his childhood dreams and visions was to struggle against the morality of his time, against his own ingrained sense of good and evil, against the expectancy of divine punishment. To access experiences associated with the archetypal Pluto, Jung was to encounter great inner resistance and deep fear (Saturn). As he wrote later in his life:

> In order to grasp the fantasies that were stirring within me "underground," I knew that I had to let myself plummet down into them, as it were. I felt not only violent resistance to this, but a distinct fear.[13]

Yet the very extremity of the struggle was essential to Jung's realization. He had to hold both poles within him: the established morality of Western culture and his direct experience of the unrecognized subterranean divinity—a power which is "beyond good and evil" and which thus requires the moral discernment of a developed ego if one is to relate to it in a balanced and constructive manner.

A second experience from Jung's childhood further develops these themes. Again, contravening the moral conditioning of his childhood, Jung found himself compelled to entertain what seemed to him to be a blasphemous, sinful thought:

> I gathered all my courage, as though I were about to leap forthwith into hell-fire, and let the thought come. I saw before me the cathedral, the blue sky. God sits on His golden throne, high above the world—and from under the throne an enormous turd falls upon the sparkling new roof, shatters it, and breaks the walls of the cathedral asunder.[14]

The divine feces suggests something rejected, forced down into the bowels of the Earth or the underworld, some base elemental force crashing into the daylight "conscious" view of God's cathedral. Those aspects of the divine that had been overlooked were first to destroy and then to begin to regenerate the idealistic Christian spiritual vision and its metaphysical foundations. Just as for Nietzsche the Dionysian principle of impassioned frenzy and self-annihilation was the essential compensatory counterforce to the ordered beauty and control of the Apollonian sensibility and to Christian morality, here in Jung's vision was the dark, destructive power of God in nature, God in base, instinctual, unregenerate form, shattering the pristine Christian vision of the glory of the Almighty, seated on His throne in the sky—a theme that was still preoccupying Jung in his *Answer to Job* in the 1950s.[15] For the Pluto-Hades-Dionysus-Devil principle, largely excluded from the cultural imagination of the divine and therefore denied legitimate expression within personal experience during the previous centuries, was to unconsciously possess the culture and the psyche that denied its reality and that preferred to rest in the inadequate, childlike vision of a wholly benevolent deity, devoid of sin or moral ambiguity. The Plutonic dimension of experience—the biological, primitive, elemental, unconscious, instinctual, and sexual—was powerfully re-impressing itself on the Neptunian spiritual vision of late-nineteenth century and early twentieth century Western culture.[16] In the lineage of Goethe and Nietzsche, Jung was to be a pivotal figure in this reawakening.

The Confrontation with the Unconscious: 1912–1918
Jung's early visions anticipated the major themes and problems he was to work through in the future, but it was during his mid-to-late thirties that he was to dramatically revisit the underworld scenes of his early

years. The "confrontation with the unconscious," as he termed it, was triggered by the much-discussed break from Freud and the Psychoanalytic Association following the publication of his *Wandlungen und Symbole der Libido* in 1912 in which Jung presented his own interpretation of incest theory that emphasized the mythological, rather than the sexual, aetiology of incest fantasy. Cast adrift from his former intellectual and professional moorings following this break, Jung was thrown back onto himself and entered a state of deep introspection and existential turmoil—a psychospiritual crisis, as it might be called today.

Particularly relevant to understanding the archetypal dynamics of this crisis is the Saturn-Uranus-Pluto T-square in Jung's natal chart. Uranus is the archetypal principle associated with going one's own way in life, with expressing one's own individual genius. The Saturn principle is associated with the established order, protective and prohibitive boundaries, the status quo, authority, tradition, supporting structures, worldly roles, and responsibilities. It marks the threshold of what is known, accepted, and already established. In Jung's case, we can see that it was the impetus to advance his own theories rather than uphold the established psychoanalytic perspective that thrust him into his crisis period. Contravening the patriarchal authority of Freud, Jung chose to remain true to his own insights and experiences, and this meant professional and, to a certain extent, psychological isolation: "When I parted from Freud, I knew that I was plunging into the unknown. Beyond Freud . . . I knew nothing; but I had taken a step into darkness."[17]

In archetypal terms, Saturn-Uranus is particularly associated with the sudden crisis, when the problematic aspects of one's existence—one's fears, weaknesses, and any sense of inferiority—can be sharply and often suddenly accentuated, brought to a head in acute crises. This combination is associated with the experience of the "break"—whether breaking free, breaking through, or breaking down. Because Saturn and Uranus are in major aspect to Pluto in Jung's chart, this separation from the psychoanalytic movement was inextricably connected with the underworld descent and radical psychological transformation associated with Pluto, as well as instigating the ongoing power struggle with Freud.

By December 12th of 1913, Jung's crisis had reached a decisive moment:

I was sitting at my desk once more, thinking over my fears. Then I let myself drop. Suddenly it was as though the ground literally gave way beneath my feet, and I plunged down into dark depths.[18]

Both the sudden breakthrough against resistance and the unexpected fall into the depths are clearly related to the Saturn-Uranus-Pluto T-square. In Jung's case, this moment seems to have marked the sudden collapse of the ego-structure and its defenses, accompanied by the breaking through of unconscious contents into consciousness through an exceptionally vivid fantasy sequence. The Uranus archetypal principle, as Stephen Arroyo points out, relates to that which lies just below the surface of consciousness and is ready to emerge into awareness.[19] It is the principle that activates, emancipates, and releases; and in this case what was liberated in Jung was the Plutonic experience of the depths underlying normal ego-consciousness. The dark spirit of nature, the "spirit of the depths," as he called it in his own journals, irrupted into Jung's consciousness.

Following this descent, Jung faced an immense struggle to discipline and control the activated instincts, primitive drives, and undifferentiated emotions associated with Pluto. "I was frequently so wrought up," he explained, "that I had to do certain yoga exercises to hold my emotions in check."[20] However, Jung's concern was not principally to control and suppress his emotions, desires, and instincts, but rather to bring to consciousness the underlying motivations behind them in order that they might be transformed and integrated. "As soon as I had the feeling I was myself again, I abandoned this restraint on the emotions."[21] This interplay between restraint, control, and discipline on the one hand, and the abandonment of restraint, giving free reign to the instincts and emotions, on the other hand, again reflects the archetypal configuration in Jung's chart involving the Moon (emotions), Saturn (restraint, control), Uranus (freedom, liberation, breakthrough), and Pluto (the instincts, penetrating, depth, underlying motivations).[22]

Jung's journey through the underworld of the psyche pulled his attention away from the daylight realm of ordinary concerns into a world of visions, personified archetypal figures, dark oppressive moods, and fateful instructive dreams. Analyzing Jung's experiences during these years, one can again recognize the interconnection between the Neptune-Pluto world transit cycle under which he was born and the archetypal dynamics of his birth chart. During this time, Jung's consciousness was subject to an influx of streams of fantasy images infused with the dynamism and power of the instincts that had been repressed during the long course of ego-development, especially during the previous Neptune-Pluto cycle. Jung would later describe this experience, in the language of his own psychological theories, as a compensatory response by the unconscious to the one-sidedness of ego-consciousness, a response that was experienced as an "avenging deluge" in which the flow of instinctual power and imagery from the collective unconscious threatened to utterly overwhelm him.[23] With this deluge came the danger of self-loss, of dissolution in the collective psyche, or unconscious possession and psychosis—experiences that are directly expressive of the Neptune-Pluto complex, bringing together themes of flow, water, imagery, fantasy, dissolution, and unreality (relating to Neptune) with the power, instincts, unconscious compulsion, and states of possession (relating to Pluto). Together Neptune and Pluto can be experienced as ceaseless turmoil, as a maelstrom of emotions, images, visions, and drives.

To give more context, this was the same Neptune-Pluto conjunction present in the birth charts of a number of immensely influential figures whose lives and deeds have utterly transformed the modern world and world view. The Neptune-Pluto complex empowered the mythic imagination of J. R. R. Tolkien to bring forth *The Lord of the Rings* with its gripping vision of an enchanted world and its telling of the mythic adventures of Frodo Baggins, Gandalf, and their companions on the epic journey to destroy the Ring of Power. It was the same archetypal complex that forged the imaginative capacities of Walt Disney to create the fantastic adventures of Mickey Mouse and other inhabitants of the "Magic Kingdom," transmitted via his cartoon empire to generation after generation of children and adults alike. In physics, a similar empowerment of the imagination helped Albert Einstein re-envisage the nature of material reality with his Special and General Theories of Relativity, transforming his field much as Pablo Picasso, himself born during the Neptune-Pluto conjunction, had done in painting. As we have seen, the Neptune-Pluto combination also found expression in the evolutionary visions of Sri Aurobindo and Pierre Teilhard de Chardin (both also born during the conjunction) in which spirituality was recognized to be present within the natural world impelling human beings to evolve to ever greater levels of consciousness and self-realization. In shadow form, however, the same energies, present in the birth charts of Adolf Hitler and his contemporaries, were the driving archetypal factors behind the pathological ideology and mythos of Nazism and Arian supremacy (drawing in part on a warped interpretation of Nietzsche's ideal of the *Ubermensch*), which became fully manifest in the collective psychosis of the Second World War. This is the subject of Jung's essay on the Germanic god Wotan, a mythic personification of some of the characteristics associated with the archetypal Pluto. For better or for worse, then, in each of these examples, the human imagination became intensified and empowered to bring forth stirring new visions, fantasies, dreams, and creative works, which in some cases were populated with Plutonic themes such as extreme ordeals, fiery hells and underworlds, possession states, monsters of the depths, rebirth and renewal, destruction and creation, and transformation and evolution.

The following passage is an excellent account of Jung's own experience of the Neptune-Pluto complex at the time, mediated by the archetypal complex associated with the natal configuration of Moon-Saturn-Uranus-Pluto:

> An incessant stream of fantasies had been released, and I did my best not to lose my head but to find some way to understand these strange things. . . . I was living in a constant state of tension; often I felt as if gigantic blocks of stone were tumbling down upon me. One thunderstorm followed another. My enduring these storms was a question of brute strength. Others have been shattered by them—Nietzsche, and Hölderlin, and many others. But there was a demonic strength in me. . . . When I endured these assaults of the unconscious I had an unswerving conviction that I was obeying a higher will, and that feeling continued to uphold me until I had mastered the task.[24]

Jung's description of living under a "constant inner pressure" and being possessed of "a demonic strength" are themes associated with Saturn-Pluto. The Saturn-Pluto complex is typically associated with the struggle for self-control, the fortification of the will, the exercising of ego-strength, and the confrontation with or harnessing of demonic forces. Cultivating these qualities was imperative if Jung were to be able to contain the flow of drives and fantasies from the unconscious without being torn to pieces—a fate that, as Jung knew only too well, had befallen Nietzsche some thirty years earlier. Jung, however, was blessed with more favorable life circumstances than Nietzsche in that Jung had a wife and family and emotional commitments to his patients (Moon) that provided the necessary connection to consensus reality (Saturn) to anchor him during his descent into the underworld (Pluto). Simultaneously, Jung struggled to assert his own conscious identity and will (the Sun) against the disorienting deluge of images that threatened to overwhelm him (Neptune), repeating to himself his name, address, profession, and other details that would reinforce his personal identity against the threat of dissolution in the transpersonal psyche.[25]

With regard to personal transits, from an archetypal perspective the entire episode seems to have been triggered by transiting Uranus forming an opposition to Jung's natal Sun and square to his natal Neptune. True to its established meaning as a principle of awakening, liberation, creative change, and disruption, the Uranus principle seems to have been the catalyst for the influx of the stream of fantasy images (Neptune), and for the resultant pervasive sense of disorientation and identity confusion associated with the natal configuration of Sun-Neptune in Jung's chart. One could say that during the Uranus transit to the Sun-Neptune alignment the dam burst, as it were, leading to the sudden influx of the unconscious, calling forth Jung's creative genius for pioneering a new approach to interpreting the visions and fantasies produced by the unconscious. In his descriptions of this period of his life as a "state of disorientation," "inner uncertainty," and of being "suspended in mid-air," Jung captured the essence of a dominant theme of the Uranus-Neptune complex, which is associated with just this kind of pervasive uncertainty and disorientation arising from the jolting, disruptive effects of sudden glimpses into subtler dimensions of reality and the experience of non-ordinary states of consciousness.[26]

In the labyrinth of fantasy images and intoxicating states of consciousness Jung encountered, one can easily lose one's mind or one's grip on reality. To maintain a sense of control and a measure of detachment is therefore supremely challenging. "Only by extreme effort," Jung confessed, "was I finally able to escape from the labyrinth."[27] But emerge he did, and on later reflection Jung came to realize that his period of inner turmoil and struggle, for all its difficulties and dangers, had provided the *"prima materia* for a life's work."[28]

This period in Jung's life has been illuminated by the publication of the *Red Book* in 2009, containing records of Jung's fantasy sequences, active imaginations, and dialogues with the unconscious during these years. The book is a quite astonishing revelation of the dark mystery of the divine, among the finest recorded testimonies to the spiritual transformation associated with the Neptune-Pluto conjunction. In astrological terms, the "spirit of the depths," with which Jung interacts in the dialogues of the *Red Book*, perfectly expresses both Neptune (spirit) and Pluto (depth). Confounding the Christian image of a wholly benevolent deity, it is a revelation of the morally ambiguous nature of God, and of the gods (now conceived as archetypes), demonstrating the inextricable connection between good and evil, light and shadow, beatific divine love and terrible divine power. Fundamentally, the dimension of God that Jung is most engaged with throughout the *Red Book* is unmistakably Plutonic in nature. In the Appendix, for instance, Jung portrays the mysterious "God of the cosmos," the frightful Abraxas, who displays a litany of characteristics associated with Pluto, exemplified by the following passage:[29]

> He is the God of the cosmos, extremely powerful and fearful. He is the creative drive, he is form and formation, just as much matter and force. . . . He tears away souls and casts them into procreation. He is the creative and the created. He is the god who always renews himself, in days, in months, in years, in human life, in ages, in peoples, in the living, in heavenly bodies. He compels, he is unsparing. If you worship him, you increase his power over you. Thereby it becomes unbearable.[30]

We can recognize here, furthermore, that the particular inflection given to the character of the Plutonic god Abraxas is again Saturnian, no doubt reflecting the larger Moon–Saturn–Pluto complex in Jung's natal chart. Pluto relates specifically to the Shiva-like creative, destructive, and procreative power of Abraxas, to the god's capacity for inexorable renewal, and to his compelling ruthless power and extremity of expression. Saturn is connected to form, the measurements of time, and to fear, and also contributes to Abraxas' remorseless, unsparing character and inescapable influence, which are directed towards the soul (the Moon).

In another passage, Jung is led by the spirit of the depths to a radically new understanding of the nature of soul:

> The spirit of the depths considers the soul . . . as a living and self-existing being, and with this he contradicts the spirit of this time for whom the soul is a thing dependent on man, which lets herself be judged and arranged, and whose circumference we can grasp. I had to accept that what I had previously called my soul was not at all my soul but a dead system.[31]

"The spirit of the depths," he adds, "forced me to speak to my soul, to call upon her as a living and self-existing being."[32] In terms of the universal archetypal factors shaping Jung's experience, we can see in these passages the Saturnian "dead system" and "judgment" of the soul that was unexpectedly contradicted by the encounter with the spirit of the depths.

Awakening to the soullessness of modern life, it was impressed upon Jung that abstinence from the world, a turning within to face the depths of the psyche, and a firm control of the passions were unavoidable requirements if he were to rediscover his soul:

> He whose desire turns away from the outer things, reaches the place of the soul. If he does not find the soul, the horror of emptiness will overcome him, and fear will drive him with a whip lashing time and again in a desperate endeavor and a blind desire for the hollow things of the world. He becomes a fool through his endless desire, and forgets the way of his soul, never to find her again. . . . My friend, it is wise to nourish the soul, otherwise you will breed dragons and devils in your heart.[33]

Jung describes here some of the major challenges and dangers that are intrinsic to the experience of the Pluto archetype in association with Saturn: throwing oneself blindly into worldly commitments and hard work to which one is not suited, being ceaselessly driven by one's passion to the point of suffering, and being scorched by the fire of desire to the loss of one's humanity. With the Saturn-Pluto combination, the Plutonic instinctual drive and passion can feel inescapable, relentless, crushing, or painfully inhibited.

One could give example after example of the Plutonic nature of the spiritual revelation contained in the *Red Book*. Virtually every page reflects the mystery and power of the dark, chthonic side of the divine, pressing to make itself known to the consciousness of modern humans. Unsurprisingly, as we will now consider, the same themes were equally evident in Jung's central spiritual and professional concerns in the latter part of his life.

Alchemical Studies in the 1940s and 1950s

By the mid-1940s, when Jung's attention turned increasingly towards the study and interpretation of the arcane texts of alchemy, Neptune and Pluto had moved into the beginning of a long sextile (60-degree) alignment. This particular angular relationship, in keeping with its established meaning in astrology, brought with it an increasing sense of perspective on the geyser-like eruptions of the collective unconscious occurring during the previous conjunction.[34] If the conjunction had marked the bursting forth of new spiritual visions and powerful experiential manifestations of the dark spirit of nature, the sextile permitted an emerging insight, after the Second World War, into what had taken place during the conjunction—an open invitation, as it were, to explore and better understand in a more stable climate the relationship between these archetypal principles.

In this new archetypal context in the mid-twentieth century, Jung was able to work out the relationship in his own life between the Sun-Neptune and the Moon-Saturn-Pluto complexes in his chart. The symbolism of alchemy provided a language and a method to enable him to do this.[35] The relationship between the alchemical *Sol* and *Luna* was especially relevant as a symbol of the confrontation between ego-consciousness and its unconscious ground. As Jung explains:

> This confrontation is expressed, in the alchemical myth of the king, as the collision of the masculine, spiritual father-world ruled over by King *Sol* with the feminine, chthonic mother-world symbolized by the *aqua permanens* or by the chaos.[36]

The spiritual-father world of the alchemical king is a fitting symbol of Jung's natal Sun-Neptune combination, with the Sun as the father-king of the Neptunian spiritual dimension (one might recall here Jung's dream of the fairytale King's throne). The "chthonic mother-world," on the other hand, is a symbolic expression of the Moon-Pluto combination in Jung's chart, reflecting the Moon's association with the mother and the matrix of being and Pluto's association with the primitive, instinctual dynamism of the unconscious ground of existence. As Jung demonstrates, it is an essential element of the work of individuation to bring *Sol* and *Luna* into relationship, a process that is portrayed through the various transformative operations performed by the alchemists. "It is the moral task of alchemy," Jung proclaims, "to bring the feminine, maternal background of the masculine psyche, seething with passions, into harmony with the principle of the spirit— truly a labor of Hercules!"[37] The moral task is Saturnian in essence; the seething passions and maternal background to the psyche relates to Moon-Pluto; Neptune is the "principle of the spirit"; and the Herculean labor of transformation relates to Saturn-Pluto—the arduous work to be done in the underworld, containing and controlling the instincts and passions that they might then be transformed.

The goal of the alchemical process is to unite the transcendent spiritual principle with "the dark chthonic aspect of nature," which, Jung explains, "is not only the darkness of the animal sphere, but rather a spiritual nature or a natural spirit."[38] This insight relates directly to the Neptune-Pluto alignment as it was finding expression through Jung. In alchemy, the chthonic spirit is also known as the *anima mundi*—the world soul—that is thought to lie trapped within matter, caught up in the processes of nature, "imprisoned in the chains of *physis*."[39] The transcendent principle is the "counsel of the spirit" that calls the soul to awaken from her slumber in matter and imposes upon the conscious ego the task of actualizing the soul's release.[40]

Another mythic figure that reflects the new image of the divine, emerging at the turn of the twentieth century with the Neptune-Pluto conjunction, was the alchemical god-man *Mercurius* who, as a personification of the unconscious, is the central figure in the entire alchemical drama, both the subject and object of the alchemical work of transformation. In his extensive discussions of *Mercurius* scattered through his three volumes on alchemy, Jung provides a number of synonyms and associations that point to the fundamentally Plutonic character of the god, inflected as ever by the archetypal qualities pertaining to Saturn and the Moon: *Mercurius* is the *spiritus vegetavius*, the chthonic living spirit in matter and yet, paradoxically, the spirit which keeps the soul imprisoned therein[41]; he is the *unus mundus*—the original state of unconscious wholeness, the "undifferentiated unity of the world"; he is the king's instinctual animal side that is encountered in the descent into the realm of the unconscious and is the power that "darkens the sun"[42] and produces the *sol niger*—the black sun in the Earth[43]; *Mercurius* is also related to the anima, which, like the alchemical *Luna*, is to be transformed through its differentiation in the light of consciousness; he is also described as a "God Man," "the Son of God," and the "Anthropos,"[44]; finally, *Mercurius* is morally ambivalent, bright and dark, male and female, and is "beyond good and evil" as he represents the collective unconscious where such moral categories do not apply.[45] He is, as the aforementioned examples make clear, a symbol that embraces and reconciles all pairs of opposites.

In the alchemical transformation process, *Mercurius* is also represented by the serpent—a classic theriomorphic symbol of the Pluto principle. The alchemical work seeks to effect a transformation of the serpent into the *lapis philosophorum* (the philosopher's stone, which is the goal of the alchemical process) via a number of operations performed in the *vas alembic*. The alembic functions as a kind of uterus of spiritual rebirth: it is a vessel of transformation in which, through heating, poisonous impurities are eliminated. Jung elaborates:

Through the incubation [in the vessel] the snake-like content is vapourized, literally 'sublimated,' which amounts to saying that it is recognized and made an object of conscious discrimination.[46]

Poison is often represented by sulphur, which, according to Jung, is understood by the alchemists to constitute "the inner fire,"[47] which is to be found "in the depths of the nature of *Mercurius*."[48] Sulphur, we learn, is "evil smelling" and as a poisonous substance has the power to corrupt and to "blacken the sun."[49] As the fire of *Mercurius*, Jung therefore sees sulphur as corresponding to the "unconscious dynamism and compulsion" (Pluto) that thwarts the conscious will and thus forces the conscious ego to turn its attention to the unconscious.[50] In this way, sulphur is responsible for bringing about an expansion of consciousness, justifying its supposed identity with Lucifer, "the bringer of light."[51]

The serpent is one among many theriomorphic symbols of the transformation of *Mercurius* that occur during the alchemical opus. As Jung explains:

> the union of consciousness (Sol) with its feminine counterpart the unconscious (Luna) has undesirable results to begin with: it produces poisonous animals such as the dragon, serpent, scorpion, basilisk, and toad; then the lion, bear, wolf, dog, and finally the eagle and the raven. The first to appear are the cold-blooded animals, then the warm-blooded predators, and lastly birds of prey or ill-omened scavengers.[52]

The animal symbols represent the "dangerous preliminary stages" of the encounter with the unconscious, and the sequence of transformations into different animal forms reveals, in Jungian terminology, increasing degrees of conscious differentiation of the anima.[53] With each transformation, the primitive drives and instincts become progressively more tamed, more humanized.

As will be clear, this sequence of transformations, and the alchemical process in general, fits, with remarkable precision, archetypal themes associated with the Moon-Saturn-Pluto alignment in Jung's birth chart. Pluto is represented by the serpent *Mercurius* and the animal symbolism of the unconscious; it relates to unconscious compulsion and the challenge of overcoming such compulsion through the burning out of impurities. The archetypal Pluto finds expression as the purifying fire of transformation. Saturn is associated with the containing structure of the alchemical vessel, the labor and discipline of the process, and the base material that is transformed into spiritual gold. The Moon relates to the anima, the emotions, and the soul.

Ultimately, the aim of the alchemical opus is to liberate (Uranus) the soul (the Moon) from the chains of *physis* (Saturn). This goal may be achieved by the overcoming of desirousness, instinct, and compulsive grasping (relating to Pluto). When the soul is no longer subject to domination by the appetites, it may become a vehicle for the realization of the *anima mundi*, which is envisioned as the "slumbering spirit" of nature. The emancipation of the *anima mundi* from matter, and the separation of the soul from the appetites and desires of the body, is to be effected through a process known as *separatio* (or *distractio*).[54] By a withdrawal of projections, ascetic self-denial, and "the careful investigation of desires and their motives," it is possible to bring to an end the ego's "unconscious identity with the object" and grow free of "the turbulence of the emotions."[55] The natural state of *unio naturalis*, as the alchemists called it, in which the soul is inextricably bound up with the bodily sphere, is brought to an end by liberating the soul from the body, and then effecting a union of the rational-spiritual principle with the soul. This union is known the *unio mentalis*, the completion of the arduous first stage of the alchemical *coniunctio* of *Sol* and *Luna*, resulting in deep self-knowledge and producing "a realistic and more or less non-illusory view of the outside world."[56]

Again, in archetypal terms this process well describes the dynamics of Jung's Moon-Saturn-Uranus-Pluto complex: the unconscious identity of the soul and the bodily instincts refers to the initial expression of the Moon-Pluto complex, with Saturnian discipline and denial used to overcome emotional turbulence (Moon-Uranus-Pluto), and to bring to an end (Saturn) the initial state of unconscious identity with the instincts (Moon-Pluto). In these ways and more, this passage, and Jung's alchemical studies in general, describe the working out of the complexes in Jung's personality on a scale that was of significance not only to him personally, but to the cultural zeitgeist of the time and to the overarching evolutionary trajectory of the modern spirit. Through his alchemical investigations, Jung was actualizing one of the primary challenges of the unfolding Neptune-Pluto cycle, bringing together the Christian recognition of a transcendent divinity with the repressed and largely unrecognized dark spirit of nature.

The alchemical work and the process of individuation reach their fulfillment with the *coniunctio* of the conscious ego with its unconscious ground, personified as the union of *Sol* and *Luna* or *Rex* and *Regina*.

"Individuation," Jung explains, "is a 'mysterium coniunctionis,' the self being experienced as a nuptial union of opposite halves."[57] The Self as the new center of the psyche is realized, born into consciousness, from the "chymical marriage," of *Sol* and *Luna*.[58] Jung identifies three stages of this alchemical conjunction. The first, as mentioned, is the *unio mentalis*—the union of the rational-spiritual perspective (associated with ego-consciousness) with the soul, liberated from the unconscious world of matter and the body. The two further stages are the reunion of the separated *unio mentalis* with the body—a "reanimation" of the body[59]— and finally, the *mysterium coniunctionis* or *unio mystica*, which is tantamount, according to Jung, to a union of the individual with "the eternal Ground of all empirical being."[60] Here the alchemical work has reached its final end of triumphant rejuvenation and the union of nature (Pluto) and spirit (Neptune):

> It expresses, psychologically, the joys of life and the life urge which overcome and eliminate everything dark and inhibiting. Where spring-like joy and expectation reign, spirit can embrace nature and nature spirit.[61]

Jung's explorations of alchemy, then, drew to a conclusion the themes of his childhood experiences and the labor of transformation imposed upon him since the time of his "confrontation with the unconscious." Through his interpretation of the psychological significance of the alchemical texts, Jung helped to bring to consciousness and articulate for modern culture the deeper meaning of the Neptune-Pluto conjunction of the late-nineteenth century.

Looking back now, it seems to be the case that this world transit alignment marked the beginning of a new cycle of human psychospiritual evolution. This cycle is bringing forth, among other things, a spiritualization of the instincts—not through their repression, as before, but now through the integration of the instinctual power of the unconscious with consciousness, centered on the rational ego.[62] Through the dialectic between the ego and the unconscious during individuation, the modern human can participate in the process of the realization of the dark spirit of nature, helping to make this known in the light of human self-reflective consciousness, thereby contributing to the progressive evolution of the divine.

Notes

[1] Carl Gustav Jung, "The Spiritual Problem of Modern Man." In *Civilization in Transition*, 2nd edition, volume 10 of *The Collected Works of C. G. Jung*, translated by R. F. C. Hull (Princeton: Princeton University Press, 1989), 196–197.

[2] The Neptune-Pluto cycle is discussed by Richard Tarnas in *Cosmos and Psyche: Intimations of a New World View* (New York: Viking, 2006), 409–418. Following Tarnas, I am using an orb of twenty degrees for the conjunction in the Neptune-Pluto cycle, which is the longest of all the planetary cycles currently studied in astrology.

[3] Tarnas, *Cosmos and Psyche*, 418. I also discuss the correlations between the Neptune-Pluto conjunction and the evolution of consciousness in Keiron Le Grice, *The Archetypal Cosmos: Rediscovery the Gods in Myth, Science and Astrology* (Edinburgh: Floris Books, 2010).

[4] Tarnas, *Cosmos and Psyche*, 418.

[5] A point made by Alan Watts citing G. R. Taylor. See Alan Watts, *The Two Hands of God: The Myths of Polarity* (1963; Repr. London: Rider & Company, 1978), 39–40.

[6] Watts, *Two Hands of God*, 41.

[7] These themes are addressed by Nietzsche in *On the Genealogy of Morals, Beyond Good and Evil*, and elsewhere; and by Jung in *Answer to Job, Aion,* and in a number of other places throughout his collected works.

[8] See, for example, Friedrich Nietzsche, *Thus Spoke Zarathustra*, translated by R. J. Hollingdale. (London: Penguin, 1969).

[9] For a discussion of diachronic sequencing of archetypal patterns, see *Cosmos and Psyche*, 149–158.

[10] Carl Gustav Jung, *Memories, Dreams, Reflections*, edited by Aniele Jaffe, translated by Richard Wilson and Clara Wilson (1963; Repr. New York: Vintage Books, 1989), 26–27. The Moon is the archetypal principle most closely associated with childhood; Neptune is the principle associated with dreams and visions; and Uranus with awakening, revelations, sudden insights, and jolting experiences. Occurring in dynamic alignment in Jung's chart, these three principles together find expression as the sudden revelatory spiritual awakenings that defined Jung's childhood and anticipated the future direction of his life and work. Yet if the Moon-Uranus and Sun-Neptune combinations refer to the archetypal conditions behind the occurrence of such dreams, the actual content of the dreams unmistakably reflects themes associated with the Moon-Saturn-Pluto complex. In general terms, the Moon-Pluto-Saturn complex sometimes symbolizes childhood experiences of a dark, disturbing, traumatic, and fateful character. It was in keeping with the nature of the Sun-Neptune archetypal complex, that for Jung these experiences took place in the world of dream, vision, and fantasy, and not primarily as external events.

[11] Jung, *Memories, Dreams, Reflections*, 56.

[12] Jung, *Memories, Dreams, Reflections*, 21–39.

[13] Jung, *Memories, Dreams, Reflections*, 202.

[14] Jung, *Memories, Dreams, Reflections*, 56.

[15] For his discussion of Apollonian and Dionysian sensibilities in Greek tragedy, see Nietzsche's "The Birth of Tragedy" in *Basic Writings of Friedrich Nietzsche*, translated by Walter Kaufmann (New York: Modern Library, 2000).

[16] Plutonic themes in the human imagination are evident in the arts, especially in the Primitivist movement in painting, with its focus on a return to a primitive natural life, in Picasso's incorporation of African influences into his art (1907–1909), and in Fauvism (*les fauves* means "wild beasts") roughly between 1900 and 1910.

[17] Jung, *Memories, Dreams, Reflections*, 224.

[18] Jung, *Memories, Dreams, Reflections*, 203.

[19] Stephen Arroyo, *Astrology, Karma, and Transformation: The Inner Dimensions of the Birth Chart* (Sebastopol, CA: CRCS, 1978).

[20] Jung, *Memories, Dreams, Reflections*, 201.

[21] Jung, *Memories, Dreams, Reflections*, 201.

[22] For the contrast between Uranus-Pluto and Saturn-Pluto see *Cosmos and Psyche* chapters IV and V. The content of Jung's fantasy images not only reflected the Moon-Saturn-Pluto complex in his natal chart but also possessed a collective significance in that his fantasies conveyed themes associated with the Saturn-Pluto world transit of 1912–1916. This close attunement to collective events was a recurring pattern in Jung's experience. In particular, surveying Jung's life, one is struck by the influence on his psyche of both world wars, the first coinciding with his confrontation with the unconscious, the second marking the beginning of his comprehensive study of alchemy. See Deirdre Bair, *Jung: A Biography* (Boston, MA: Little, Brown and Company, 2003), chapter 30 "Rooted in Our Soil"). The Plutonic energy that had impressed itself on the culture through the imagination, myth, spirituality, and dream during the Neptune-Pluto conjunction became manifest more concretely during the two world wars, both beginning under hard aspects of Saturn and Pluto. Through his inner fantasies, Jung directly experienced the pressure and sense of dark foreboding manifesting across Europe. During his "confrontation with the unconscious" and again in the 1930s when he reflected on the Wotan possession occurring in Nazi Germany, Jung became particularly attuned to the darker undercurrents lurking beneath the facade of rational self-determination, morality, and civilized culture. "We know nothing of man," Jung bemoaned in an interview with the BBC's John Freeman. The greatest danger to the world, Jung realized, is our collective ignorance of the long-neglected powers of the unconscious.

[23] Carl Gustav Jung, *Mysterium Coniunctionis*, 2nd edition, volume 14 of *The Collected Works of C. G. Jung*. Translated by R. F. C. Hull (1955–1956, 1970; Repr. Princeton: Princeton University Press, 1989), 272.

[24] Jung, *Memories, Dreams, Reflections*, 200–201.

[25] Richard Tarnas has made this observation with respect to Jung's natal Sun-Neptune square alignment.

[26] Jung, *Memories, Dreams, Reflections*, 194. This episode in Jung's life, it is worth noting, took place under world transits between Uranus and Neptune (an opposition, from) and between Saturn and Pluto (a conjunction, between and which coincided with the outbreak of the First World War).

[27] Jung, *Memories, Dreams, Reflections*, 202.

[28] Jung, *Memories, Dreams, Reflections*, 225.

[29] Carl Gustav Jung, *The Red Book*, edited by Sonu Shamdasani, translated by Mark Kyburz, John Peck, and Sonu Shamdasani (New York: W. W. Norton & Co., 2009), 370.

[30] Jung, *Red Book*, 370.

[31] Jung, *Red Book*, 232.

[32] Jung, *Red Book*, 232.

[33] Jung, *Red Book*, 232.

[34] We can see examples of this increasing sense of perspective coinciding with the start of the Neptune-Pluto sextile in works such as Erich Neumann's *The Origins and History of Consciousness* (1954) and Joseph Campbell's *The Hero With a Thousand Faces* (1949), both of which apply the theories of Freud and especially Jung to illuminate mythology, spiritual transformation, and the evolution of consciousness. As Jung notes in his introduction to Neumann's book, developing a coherent vision of archetypal psychology was impossible in the early stages of the movement when ideas were initially bursting forth. By the time of the Neptune-Pluto sextile, however, the insights of depth psychology were more established, and could be viewed as a whole, interpreted, refined, and contextualized.

[35] Jung's discovery of alchemy through Richard Wilhelm's translation of *The Secret of the Golden Flower*, prompted Jung to abandon work on *The Red Book* from 1930 onwards. In alchemy, he felt he had discovered an objectively existing model of the transformative process he had been through. See Jung, *Red Book*, 360.

[36] Jung, *Mysterium Coniunctionis*, 359.

[37] Jung, *Mysterium Coniunctionis*, 41.

[38] Jung, *Mysterium Coniunctionis*, 310.

[39] Jung, *Mysterium Coniunctionis*, 472.

[40] Jung, *Mysterium Coniunctionis*, 472. For Jung's treatment of this topic, see his discussion of the stages of the conjunction, especially those passages relating to the attainment of the *unio mentalis*, in the final section of *Mysterium Coniunctionis*, 457–553.

[41] Jung, *Mysterium Coniunctionis*, 225.

[42] Jung, *Mysterium Coniunctionis*, 25.

[43] Jung, *Mysterium Coniunctionis*, 95.

[44] Jung, *Mysterium Coniunctionis*, 14.

[45] Jung, *Mysterium Coniunctionis*, 196.

[46] Jung, *Mysterium Coniunctionis*, 204.

[47] Jung, *Mysterium Coniunctionis*, 117.

[48] Jung, *Mysterium Coniunctionis*, 112.

[49] Jung, *Mysterium Coniunctionis*, 122, 114.

[50] Jung, *Mysterium Coniunctionis*, 128.

[51] Jung, *Mysterium Coniunctionis*, 114. For Edward Edinger's discussion of this topic, see *Ego and Archetype: Individuation and the Religious Function of the Psyche* (Boston, MA: Shambhala, 1972), 92–93. Edinger quotes Rivkah Scharf Kluger's description of Satan as "truly Lucifer, the bringer of light. He brings man the knowledge of God but through the suffering he inflicts on him, Satan is the misery of the world which alone drives man inward, into the 'other world'" (*Ego and Archetype*, 93).

[52] Jung, *Mysterium Coniunctionis*, 144–145.

[53] Jung, *Mysterium Coniunctionis*, 142.

[54] Jung, *Mysterium Coniunctionis*, 489. This process is also referred to as the *distractio* which, according to Jung, brings about the dissolution of the state in which "the affectivity of the body has a disturbing influence on the rationality of the mind" (*Mysterium Coniunctionis*, 471).

[55] Jung, *Mysterium Coniunctionis*, 473, 488–489.

[56] Jung, *Mysterium Coniunctionis*, 519–520.

[57] Carl Gustav Jung, *Aion: Researches into the Phenomenology of the* Self, volume 9, part I of *The Collected Works of C. G. Jung*, translated by R. F. C. Hull (London: Routledge, 1951), 64.

[58] Jung, *Mysterium Coniunctionis*, 89.

[59] Jung, *Mysterium Coniunctionis*, 521.

[60] Jung, *Mysterium Coniunctionis*, 534.

[61] Jung, *Mysterium Coniunctionis*, 490.

[62] For more on this topic, see Le Grice, *Archetypal Cosmos*, 44–54, 272–275, 282–287, 289–300.

BIBLIOGRAPHY

Addey, John. *Harmonic Anthology*. 1976. Reprint, Tempe, AZ: American Fedaration of Astrologers, 2004.

"Astrology and Science." http://www.rudolfhsmit.nl/hpage.htm Jung, Carl Gustav. Research results. http://www.rudolfhsmit.nl/d-rese2.htm (accessed August 3, 2009).

Arroyo, Stephen. *Astrology, Karma, and Transformation: The Inner Dimensions of the Birth Chart*. Sebastopol, CA: CRCS Publications, 1978.

————. *Astrology, Psychology, and the Four Elements*. Sebastopol, CA: CRCS Publications, 1975.

Assagioli, Roberto. *Transpersonal Development: The Dimension Beyond Psychosynthesis*. London, UK: The Aquarian Press, 1993.

Atmanspacher, Harald, "Quantum Approaches to Consciousness." In *The Stanford Encyclopedia of Philosophy*. Summer 2015 Edition. Edited by Edward N. Zalta. URL = <http://plato.stanford.edu/archives/sum2015/entries/qt-consciousness/> (accessed November 25, 2016).

Aurobindo, Sri. *The Integral Yoga: Sri Aurobindo's Teaching and Method of Practice. Selected Letters of Sri Aurobindo*. Pondicherry, India: Sri Aurobindo Ashram, 1993.

Bair, Deirdre. *Jung: A Biography*. Boston, MA: Little, Brown and Company, 2003.

Barton, Tamsyn. *Ancient Astrology*. London: Routledge, 1995.

Bobrick, Benson. *The Fated Sky: Astrology in History*. New York: Simon & Schuster, 2006.

Bohm, David. *Wholeness and the Implicate Order*. Repr. London: Routledge, 2002.

Bok, Bart J., and Lawrence E. Jerome. "Objections to Astrology." *The Humanist 35*, no. 5 (September/October 1975): 4–6.

Bond, D. Stephenson. *Living Myth: Personal Meaning as a Way of Life*. Boston: Shambhala Publications, 1993.

Campbell, Joseph. *Creative Mythology: The Masks of God, Volume IV*. 1968. Reprint, New York: Arkana, 1991.

———. *The Hero with a Thousand Faces*. 1949. Repr. London: Fontana, 1993.

———. "The Occult in Myth and Literature." In *The Mythic Dimension: Selected Essays 1959–1987* by Joseph Campbell. Edited by Antony Van Couvering. San Francisco, CA: HarperSanFrancisco, 1987.

Campbell, Joseph, and Bill Moyers. *Joseph Campbell and the Power of Myth with Bill Moyers*. New York: Mystic Fire Video, 1988.

Cambray, Joseph and Linda Carter, editors. *Analytical Psychology: Contemporary Perspectives in Jungian Analysis (Advancing Theory in Therapy)*. New York: Brunner-Routledge, 2004.

Campion, Nicholas. *The History of Western Astrology*. 2 vols. London: Continuum Books, 2009.

Capra, Fritjof. *The Tao of Physics: An Exploration of the Parallels Between Modern Physics and Eastern Mysticism*. 3rd edition. London: Flamingo, 1992.

———. *The Web of Life: A New Synthesis of Mind and Matter*. New York: Anchor Books, 1997.

Combs, Allan, and Mark Holland. *Synchronicity Through the Eyes of Science, Myth, and the Trickster*. 3rd edition. New York: Marlowe and Company, 2001.

Cornelius, Geoffrey. *The Moment of Astrology: Origins in Divination*. London: Arkana, 1994.

Cornelius, Geoffrey, Maggie Hyde, and Chris Webster. *Astrology for Beginners*. London: Icon Books, 1995.

Descartes, Rene. "Discourse on Method." In *Descartes: Selected Philosophical Writings*, translated by John Cottingham, Robert Stoothoff, and Dugald Murdoch, 20–56. Cambridge: Cambridge University Press, 1988.

———. *Meditations on First Philosophy with Selections from the Objections and Replies.* 1986. Edited by John Cottingham. Repr. Cambridge: Cambridge University Press, 2003.

Edinger, Edward. *Anatomy of the Psyche: Alchemical Symbolism in Psychotherapy.* Peru, IL: Open Court, 1994.

———. *Ego and Archetype: Individuation and the Religious Function of the Psyche* Boston, MA: Shambhala, 1972.

Eliade, Mircea. *The Forge and the Crucible: Origins and Structures of Alchemy.* New Edition. 1978. Repr. Chicago: University of Chicago Press, 1979.

Ferrer, J. *Revisioning Transpersonal Theory: A Participatory Vision of Human Spirituality.* Albany: State University of New York, 2002.

Freud, Sigmund. *Civilization and Its Discontents.* 1929–1930. The Standard Edition. Translated by James Strachey. New York: W. W. Norton & Company, 1989.

———. *New Introductory Lectures on Psychoanalysis.* 1933. Standard Edition. Translated by James Strachey. New York: Norton & Company, 1965.

Freud, Sigmund, and Carl Gustav Jung. *The Freud/Jung Letters: The Correspondence between Sigmund Freud and C. G. Jung.* Edited by William McGuire. Translated by Ralph Manheim and R. F. C. Hull. Princeton, NJ: Princeton University Press, 1974.

Frey-Rohn, Liliane. *From Freud to Jung: A Comparative Study of the Psychology of the Unconscious.* Translated by Fred Engreen and Evelyn Engreen. New York: Delta, 1974.

Gauquelin, Michael. *Neo-astrology: A Copernican Revolution.* London: Arkana, 1991.

Gebser, Jean. *The Ever-present Origin.* Translated by Noel Barstad with Algis Mickunas. Athens, OH: Ohio University Press, 1981.

Greene, Liz. *The Astrological World of Jung's Liber Novus: Daimons, Gods, and the Planetary Journey.* Abingdon, UK: Routledge, 2018.

———. *Jung's Studies in Astrology: Prophecy, Magic and the Qualities of Time.* Abingdon, UK: Routledge, 2018.

Griffin, David R., editor. *Archetypal Process: Self and Divine in Whitehead, Jung, and Hillman*. Evanston, IL: Northwestern University Press, 1990.

————. "Archetypal Psychology and Process Philosophy: Complementary Postmodern Movements." In *Archetypal Process: Self and Divine in Whitehead, Jung, and Hillman*, edited by David R. Griffin. Evanston, IL: Northwestern University Press, 1990.

Grof, Stanislav. *The Cosmic Game: Explorations of the Frontiers of Human Consciousness*. Albany, NY: State University of New York Press, 1998.

————. "Holotropic Research and Archetypal Astrology." *Archai: The Journal of Archetypal Cosmology*. Volume I. San Francisco, CA: Archai Press, 2009: 50–66, http://www.archaijournal.org/ 01_Archai_Journal_Issue01_v2.pdf (accessed August 3, 2009).

————. *Psychology of the Future: Lessons from Modern Consciousness Research*. Albany, NY: State University of New York Press, 2000.

Grof, Stanislav, and Hal Z. Bennett. *The Holotropic Mind*. San Francisco, CA: Harper Publications, 1992.

Harding, Michael, and Charles Harvey. *Working With Astrology: The Psychology of Harmonics, Midpoints, and Astro-Cartography*. London: Arkana, 1990.

Harvey, Charles. *Anima Mundi: The Astrology of the Individual and the Collective*. London: CPA Press, 2002.

Heron, J. "A commentary on Richard Tarnas' *Cosmos and Psyche.*" Network Review: Journal of the Scientific and Medical Network, No. 95, Winter 2007, 11–16.

Hillman, James. "Anima Mundi: The Return of the Soul to the World." 1982. In *The Thought of the Heart and the Soul of the World*. Dallas: Spring, 1992.

————. "Back to Beyond: On Cosmology." In *Archetypal Process: Self and Divine in Whitehead, Jung, and Hillman*, edited by D. R. Griffin. Evanston, IL: Northwestern University Press, 1990.

————. *Re-Visioning Psychology*. 1975. Reprint, New York: HarperPerennial, 1992.

————. *Senex & Puer*. Edited by Glen Slater. Putnam, CT: Spring Publications, 2013.

Hölderlin, Friedrich. *Selected Poems*. Second edition. Translated by David Constantine. Highgreen, UK: Bloodaxe Books, 1996.

Hone, Margaret. *The Modern Text-Book of Astrology*. Revised Edition. 1955. Repr. London, UK: L. N. Fowler & Co., 1972.

Howell, Alice O. *The Heavens Declare: Astrological Ages and the Evolution of Consciousness*. Second Edition. Wheaton, IL: Quest Books, 2006.

———. *Jungian Symbolism in Astrology*. Wheaton, IL: Quest Books, 1987.

Hyde, Maggie. *Jung and Astrology*. London: The Aquarian Press, 1992.

Jantsch, Erich. *The Self-organizing Universe*. New York: Pergamon, 1980.

Jones, Ernest. *The Life and Work of Sigmund Freud*. Edited and abridged in one volume by Lionel Trilling and Steven Marcus. New York: Basic Books, 1961.

Jung, Carl Gustav. *Aion: Researches into the Phenomenology of the Self*. Second edition. Volume 9, part II of *The Collected Works of C. G. Jung*. Translated by R. F. C. Hull. London: Routledge, 1951/1968.

———. *Answer to Job. The Problem of Evil: Its Psychological and Religious Origins*. 1960. Translated by R. F. C. Hull. Repr. Cleveland, OH: Meridian, 1970.

———. *The Archetypes and the Collective Unconscious*. Second edition. Volume 9, part I of *The Collected Works of C. G. Jung*. Translated by R. F. C. Hull. Princeton, NJ: Princeton University Press, 1968.

———. "Archetypes of the Collective Unconscious." 1954. In *The Archetypes and the Collective Unconscious*. Volume 9, part I of *The Collected Works of C. G. Jung*. Second edition. Translated by R. F. C. Hull. Princeton, NJ: Princeton University Press, 1968.

———. "An Astrological Experiment." 1958. In *The Symbolic Life*, 494–501. Volume 18 of *The Collected Works of C. G. Jung*. Translated by R. F. C. Hull. London: Routledge & Kegan Paul, 1977.

———. *C. G. Jung Letters I: 1906–1950*. Edited by Gerald Adler and Aniela Jaffé. Translated by R. F. C. Hull. London: Routledge & Kegan Paul, 1973.

————. *C. G. Jung Letters II: 1951–1961.* Edited by Gerald Adler and Aniela Jaffé. Translated by R. F. C. Hull. London: Routledge & Kegan Paul, 1973.

————. *The Collected Works of C. G. Jung.* 19 vols. Bollingen Series XX. Translated by R. F. C. Hull. Princeton, NJ: Princeton University Press and London: Routledge & Kegan Paul, 1953–1979.

————. "Commentary on the Secret of the Golden Flower." 1929. In *Alchemical Studies. Collected Works of C. G. Jung,* vol. 13. Translated by R. F. C. Hull. Princeton, NJ: Princeton University Press, 1968.

————. *Dream Analysis: Notes on the Seminar Given in 1928–1930 by C. G. Jung.* Edited by William McGuire. Princeton, NJ: Princeton University Press, 1984.

————. "Good and Evil in Analytical Psychology." 1959. In *Civilization in Transition.* Volume 10 of *The Collected Works of C. G. Jung.* Translated by R. F. C. Hull. Princeton, NJ: Princeton University Press

————. *Jung on Astrology.* Edited by Safron Rossi and Keiron Le Grice. Abindgon, UK: Routledge, 2017.

————. *Memories, Dreams, Reflections.* 1963. Edited by Aniele Jaffe. Translated by Richard Wilson and Clara Wilson. Repr. London: Flamingo, 1983; & New York: Vintage Books, 1989.

————. *Mysterium Coniunctionis.* Second Edition. 1955–1956. Volume 14 of *The Collected Works of C. G. Jung.* Translated by R. F. C. Hull. Princeton, NJ: Princeton University Press, 1989.

————. "On Synchronicity." 1951. In *The Structure and Dynamics of the Psyche.* Volume 8 of *The Collected Works of C. G. Jung.* Translated by R. F. C. Hull. London: Routledge & Kegan Paul, 1960.

————. "On the Nature of the Psyche." 1947/1954. In *The Structure and Dynamics of the Psyche.* Volume 8 of *The Collected Works of C. G. Jung.* Translated by R. F. C. Hull. London: Routledge & Kegan Paul, 1960.

————. *On the Nature of the Psyche.* 1947. Revised 1954. Translated by R. F. C. Hull. London: Routledge, 2004.

————. "On the Psychology of the Unconscious." 1917/1926/1943. In *Two Essays on Analytical Psychology.* Volume 7 of *The Collected Works of C. G.*

Jung. Second edition. Translated by R. F. C. Hull. London: Routledge, 1966.

———. *Psychology and Alchemy.* Second edition. Volume 12 of *The Collected Works of C. G. Jung.* Translated by R. F. C. Hull. Princeton, NJ: Princeton University Press, 1968.

———. "Psychotherapists or the Clergy." 1932. In *Psychology and Religion: West and East.* Volume 11 of *The Collected Works of C. G. Jung.* Translated by R. F. C. Hull. London: Routledge & Kegan Paul, 1958.

———. *The Red Book: Liber Novus.* Edited and Introduced by Sonu Shamdasani. Translated by Mark Kyburz, John Peck, and Sonu Shamdasani. New York: W. W. Norton & Co., 2009.

———. *The Red Book: Liber Novus.* A Reader's Edition. Edited by Sonu Shamdasani. Translated by Mark Kyburz, John Peck, and Sonu Shamdasani. New York: W. W. Norton & Co., 2009.

———. "The Relations between the Ego and the Unconscious." 1928. In *Two Essays on Analytical Psychology.* Second Edition. Volume 7 of *The Collected Works of C. G. Jung.* Translated by R. F. C. Hull. London: Routledge & Kegan Paul, 1966.

———. "Religious Ideas in Alchemy." 1937. In *Psychology and Alchemy.* Second edition. Volume 12 of *The Collected Works of C. G. Jung.* Translated by R. F. C. Hull. Princeton, NJ: Princeton University Press, 1968.

———. "Richard Wilhelm: In Memoriam." 1930. In *The Spirit in Man, Art, and Literature.* Volume 15 of *The Collected Works of C. G. Jung.* Translated by R. F. C. Hull. Reprint, Princeton, NJ: Princeton University Press, 1966/1971.

———. *The Solar Myths and Opicinus de Canistris.* Edited by Riccardo Bernardini, Gian Piero Quaglino, and Augusto Romano. Zurich: Daimon Verlag, 2016.

———. "The Spiritual Problem of Modern Man." 1928/1931. In *Civilization in Transition.* Second Edition. Volume 10 of *The Collected Works of C. G. Jung.* Translated by R. F. C. Hull. Princeton, NJ: Princeton University Press, 1989.

———. *Symbols of Transformation.* Second Edition. 1967. Vol. 5 of *The Collected Works of C. G. Jung.* Translated by. R. F. C. Hull. Reprint, Princeton, NJ:

Princeton University Press, 1976.

———. "Synchronicity: An Acausal Connecting Principle." 1952. In *The Structure and Dynamics of the Psyche,*. Volume 8 of *The Collected Works of C. G. Jung*. Translated by R. F. C. Hull. London: Routledge & Kegan Paul, 1960.

———. *Two Essays on Analytical Psychology*. Second edition. 1966. Volume 7 of *The Collected Works of C. G. Jung*. Trans. R. F. C. Hull. Repr. London: Routledge, 1990.

———. "The Undiscovered Self." 1957/1958. In *Civilization in Transition*. Second edition. Volume 10 of *The Collected Works of C. G. Jung*. Translated by R. F. C. Hull. Princeton, NJ: Princeton University Press, 1970.

Jung, Carl Gustav, and John Freeman. *Face to Face Interview: Professor Jung*. London: BBC Television, 1959.

Jung, Carl Gustav, and John Freeman. "The Face to Face Interview." 1959. In *C. G. Jung Speaking*. Edited by William McGuire and R. F .C. Hull. Princeton, NJ: Princeton University Press, 1977.

Kuhn, Thomas S. *The Structure of Scientific Revolutions*. 1962. Third edition. Chicago, IL: University of Chicago Press, 1996.

Le Grice, Keiron. *The Archetypal Cosmos: Rediscovering the Gods in Myth, Science and Astrology*. Edinburgh, UK: Floris Books, 2010.

———. "Astrology and the Modern Western World View." In *Beyond a Disenchanted Cosmology. Archai: The Journal of Archetypal Cosmology*. Issue 3. San Francisco: Archai Press, 2011.

———. 'The Birth of a New Discipline: Archetypal Cosmology in Historical Perspective.' In *The Birth of a New Discipline, Archai: The Journal of Archetypal Cosmology*, Issue 1, Summer 2009. Repr. San Francisco: Archai Press, 2011.

———. 'The Dark Spirit in Nature: C. G. Jung and the Spiritual Transformation of Our Time.' In *Beyond a Disenchanted Cosmology. Archai: The Journal of Archetypal Cosmology*. Issue 3. San Francisco: Archai Press, 2011.

———. *Discovering Eris: The Symbolism and Significance of a New Planetary Archetype*. Edinburgh: Floris Books, 2012.

————. "Land of Hope and Dreams: An Archetypal Analysis of Bruce Springsteen's Song Lyrics, Part Two." *Cultural Crisis and Transformation: Exploring Archetypal Patterns in World News and Culture. Archai: The Journal of Archetypal Cosmology*, Issue 2, edited by Keiron Le Grice, Rod O'Neal and Bill Streett. San Francisco, CA: Archai Press, 2010.

————. "A Last Chance Power-Drive: An Archetypal Analysis of Bruce Springsteen's Song Lyrics, Part 1." In *The Birth of a New Discipline. Archai: The Journal of Archetypal Cosmology*, Issue 1, Summer 2009. Repr. San Francisco: Archai Press, 2011.

Magee, Brian. *The Story of Philosophy.* London: Dorling Kindersley, 2001.

Mansfield, Victor. "An Astrophysicist's Sympathetic and Critical View of Astrology." 1997. http://www.lightlink.com/vic/astrol.html (accessed January 27, 2009).

Marx, Karl. *Selected Writings in Sociology and Social Philosophy.* 1963. Translated by T. B. Bottomore. Repr. London: Penguin, 1990.

Neumann, Erich. *The Origins and History of Consciousness.* 1954. Repr. Princeton, NJ: Princeton University Press, 1973.

Nietzsche, Friedrich. *Basic Writings of Nietzsche.* Translated by Walter Kaufmann. New York: Modern Library, 2000.

————. *The Gay Science, With a Prelude in Rhymes and Appendix of Songs.* 1887. Translated by Walter Kaufmann. New York: Random House, 1974.

————. "On the Genealogy of Morals." In *Basic Writings of Nietzsche.* Translated by Walter Kaufmann. New York: Modern Library, 2000.

————. *Thus Spoke Zarathustra.* 1885. Translated by R. J. Hollingdale. Repr. London: Penguin, 1968.

O'Neal, Rod. "Archetypal Historiography: A New Historical Approach." In *The Birth of a New Discipline, Archai: The Journal of Archetypal Cosmology*, Issue 1, Summer 2009. Repr. San Francisco: Archai Press, 2011.

————. *Seasons of Agony and Grace: An Archetypal History of New England Puritanism.* Doctoral dissertation. San Francisco: California Institute of Integral Studies (May 2008).

Pagels, Elaine. *The Gnostic Gospels*. New York: Vintage Books, 1989.

Phillipson, Gary. Review of *Cosmos and Psyche*. http://www.skyscript.co.uk/ rev_cosmos.html; accessed 25/03/2008.

Primack, Joel, and Nancy Abrams. *The View from the Center of the Universe: Discovering Our Extraordinary Place in the Cosmos*. New York: Riverhead Books, 2006.

Ross, Hugh McGregor. *The Gospel of Thomas*. Second edition. London: Watkins Publishing, 2002.

Rudhyar, Dane. *The Astrology of Personality*. Santa Fe, NM: Aurora Press, 1936.

———. *The Astrology of Transformation: A Multilevel Approach*. Wheaton, IL: Quest Books, 1984.

Sartre, Jean-Paul. *Being and Nothingness: An Essay on Ontology*. 1943. Translated by Hazel E. Barnes. Repr. Abingdon, Oxon: Routledge, 2005.

Scholem, Gershom. *Major Trends in Jewish Mysticism*. New York: Schocken Books, 1961.

Seymour, Percy. *Astrology: The Evidence of Science*. Revised Edition. London: Arkana, 1990.

Shamdasani, Sonu. *Jung and the Making of Modern Psychology: The Dream of a Science*. Cambridge: Cambridge University Press, 2003.

Skinner, B. F. *Beyond Freedom and Dignity*. 1971. Repr. Indianapolis: Hacket Publishing Company, 2002.

Spade, Paul Vincent. "William of Ockham," ed. Edward N. Zalta, in *The Stanford Encyclopedia of Philosophy*. 2006. http://plato.stanford.edu/entries/ ockham/(accessed September 23, 2009).

Sprigge, T. L. S. *Theories of Existence*. London: Penguin, 1985.

Stein, Murray. "Spiritual and Religious Aspects of Modern Analysis." In *Analytical Psychology: Contemporary Perspectives in Jungian Analysis (Advancing Theory in Therapy)*, edited by Joseph Cambray and Linda Carter. New York: Brunner-Routledge, 2004.

Stephenson, Leslie. *Seven Theories of Human Nature*. Oxford: Oxford University Press, 1974.

Stubenberg, Leopold. "Neutral Monism." In *The Stanford Encyclopedia of Philosophy*. Winter 2016 Edition. Edited by Edward N. Zalta. Forthcoming URL = http://plato.stanford.edu/archives/win2016/entries/neutral-monism/ (accessed 25 November, 2016).

Swimme, Brian. *The Hidden Heart of the Cosmos: Humanity and the New Story*. Maryknoll, NY: Orbis Books, 1996.

Tarnas, Richard. *Cosmos and Psyche: Intimations of a New World View*. New York: Viking, 2006.

———. "The Ideal and the Real: Saturn-Neptune." In *The Birth of a New Discipline. Archai: The Journal of Archetypal Cosmology*. Issue 1 (2009). Second Edition. Edited by Keiron Le Grice and Rod O'Neal. San Francisco: Archai Press, 2011, 175–199.

———. "An Introduction to Archetypal Astrology." www.cosmosandpsyche.com/pdf/IntroductiontoAstrology.pdf (accessed August 4, 2009).

———. *The Passion of the Western Mind: Understanding the Ideas That Have Shaped Our World View*. Repr. London: Pimlico, 1991.

———. *Prometheus the Awakener: An Essay on the Archetypal Meaning of the Planet Uranus*. Woodstock, CT: Spring Publications, 1995.

Taylor, Charles. *A Secular Age*. Cambridge, MA: The Belnap Press of Harvard University Press, 2007.

Teilhard de Chardin, Pierre. *The Heart of Matter*. Translated by René Hague. San Diego: Harcourt Brace, 1978.

Tester, Jim. *A History of Western Astrology*. Woodbridge, UK: Boydell Press, 1987.

von Franz, Marie-Louise. *Psyche and Matter*. 1988. Reprint, Boston, MA: Shambhala Publications, 1992.

Watts, Alan. *The Two Hands of God: The Myths of Polarity*. 1963. Repr. London: Rider & Company, 1978.

Whitehead, Alfred North. *Science and the Modern World*. 1925. Repr. New York: Free Press, 1970.

Whitfield, Peter. *Astrology: A History*. New York: Harry N. Abrams, 2001.

Yogananda, Paramahansa. *Autobiography of a Yogi*. London, UK: Rider, 1991.

ABOUT THE AUTHOR

Keiron Le Grice is a professor of depth psychology in the Jungian and Archetypal Studies specialization and the Engaged Humanities and Creative Life program at Pacifica Graduate Institute, California, where he teaches courses on archetypes, individuation, alchemy, synchronicity, astrology, and the history of depth psychology. He was educated at the University of Leeds, England (B.A. honors, Philosophy and Psychology) and the California Institute of Integral Studies in San Francisco (M.A., Ph.D., Philosophy and Religion). He is the author of several books including *The Way of the Archetypes, The Archetypal Cosmos, Discovering Eris, The Rebirth of the Hero, Archetypal Reflections*, and the forthcoming *The Lion Will Become Man*. He is also co-editor of *Jung on Astrology*, a compilation of Jung's writings on this topic.

Keiron's work has been central to the development of the field of archetypal cosmology. He is founder and former co-editor of *Archai: The Journal of Archetypal Cosmology*, now serving as senior editorial advisor, and in 2016 he co-founded the Institute of Transpersonal and Archetypal Studies (ITAS). He is an honorary lecturer in the Department of Psychosocial and Psychoanalytic Studies at the University of Essex, England, and he has also taught in the Philosophy, Cosmology, and Consciousness program at CIIS. He lives in Ojai, California, with his wife and son.

Cover image: detail from *Ojai Totem III* by Kathryn Le Grice.

Printed in Great Britain
by Amazon

32693711R00117